BILLY GRAHAM
Evangelistic Association
Always Good News.

Dear Friend,

I am pleased to send you the enclosed copy of my book, *Through My Father's Eyes*, about lessons I have learned from my father Billy Graham—a man wholly committed to God's call on his life to preach the Gospel of Jesus Christ.

My father has left behind a trail of victories and, yes, some regrets, but through it all he always fastened his eyes and focused his heart on Scripture and the lessons he learned *through his Father's eyes* in Heaven. I am pleased to share these stories with you.

For more than 65 years, the Billy Graham Evangelistic Association has worked to take the Good News of Jesus Christ throughout the world by every effective means available, and I am excited about what God will do in the years ahead. *"So our eyes look to the Lord our God"* (Psalm 123:2, NKJV).

We would appreciate knowing how our ministry has touched your life. May God richly bless you.

Sincerely,

Franklin Graham
President

If you would like to know more about our ministry, please contact us:

IN THE U.S.:
Billy Graham Evangelistic Association
1 Billy Graham Parkway
Charlotte, NC 28201-0001
BillyGraham.org
info@bgea.org
Toll-free: 1-877-247-2426

IN CANADA:
Billy Graham Evangelistic
Association of Canada
20 Hopewell Way NE
Calgary, AB T3J 5H5
BillyGraham.ca
Toll-free: 1-888-393-0003

IN AUSTRALIA:
Billy Graham Evangelistic
Association of Australia
P.O. Box 964
Kings Langley, NSW 2147
BillyGraham.org.au
Toll-free: +61 2 9241 1692

Through My Father's Eyes

Franklin Graham

with

Donna Lee Toney

W PUBLISHING GROUP

AN IMPRINT OF THOMAS NELSON

Published in Nashville, Tennessee, by W Publishing Group, an imprint of Thomas Nelson.

Published in association with Alive Literary Agency, Inc., 7680 Goddard Street, Suite 200, Colorado Springs, CO 80920. www.aliveliterary.com.

Cover portrait of Billy Graham by John Howard Sanden. Used by permission.

Page design: Walter Petrie

Thomas Nelson titles may be purchased in bulk for educational, business, fund-raising, or sales promotional use. For information, please e-mail SpecialMarkets@ThomasNelson.com.

Unless otherwise noted, Scripture quotations are taken from the New King James Version®. © 1982 by Thomas Nelson. Used by permission. All rights reserved.

Scripture quotations marked NASB are from the New American Standard Bible®. © 1960, 1962, 1963, 1968, 1971, 1972, 1973, 1975, 1977, 1995 by The Lockman Foundation. Used by permission.

Scripture quotations marked NIV are from the Holy Bible, New International Version®, NIV®. © 1973, 1978, 1984, 2011 by Biblica, Inc®. Used by permission of Zondervan. All rights reserved wordwide.

Scripture quotations marked KJV are from the King James Version of the Bible. Public domain.

Scripture quotations marked SPRL are from *A Translation of the Old Testament Scriptures from the Original Hebrew*, by Helen Spurrell (London: James Nisbet and Co., 1885).

Italics added to Scripture quotations are the author's own emphasis.

Any Internet addresses, phone numbers, or company or product information printed in this book are offered as a resource and are not intended in any way to be or to imply an endorsement by Thomas Nelson, nor does Thomas Nelson vouch for the existence, content, or services of these sites, phone numbers, companies, or products beyond the life of this book.

ISBN: 978-0-7180-1518-3 (eBook)
ISBN: 978-0-7180-2180-1 (IE)
ISBN: 978-1-4041-1039-7 (custom)

Library of Congress Control Number: 2018902988

ISBN 978-0-7852-2713-7 (HC)

Printed in the United States of America

18 19 20 21 22 LSC 5 4 3 2 1

Contents

Foreword
From the words of Billy Graham

Keep your soul diligently,
so that you do not forget the things which your eyes have seen
and . . . make them known to your sons.

—DEUTERONOMY 4:9 NASB

Someday I hope to write a book on the subject of "The End."[1] When we all reach the end of our earthly journey, we will have just begun.[2]

The word *departure* literally means "to pull up anchor and set sail." Everything that happens prior to death is a preparation for the final voyage. Death marks the beginning, not the end. It is our journey to God.[3]

For centuries mankind has been on an incredible journey taking him across every generation and through every conceivable experience in his search for God.[4]

Like every other journey, it has a starting point . . . and it has an end. . . . God meant for life to be filled with joy and purpose. He invites us to take the rest of our journey with Him.[5]

The entire world is in turmoil. We are living in a time of enormous conflict and cultural transformation. We have been stunned by shock-waves of change in nation after nation, all around the globe.[6]

We have seen the results of unrestrained greed, corruption, and manipulation on Wall Street, financial mismanagement in the halls of government, fraud and perversion at the highest levels of both church and state. Many people sense the possibility of an even greater un-raveling in the world. We are constantly confronted by the realities of new problems in this age of crisis.[7]

We have at our fingertips every pleasure that man is capable of enjoying, and man has abused every gift God ever gave him.[8]

The promoters of change offer a grand vision of world unity. While the globalists and international affairs specialists continue their chant for "peace, peace," we are reminded that the Bible says that there can be no lasting peace until Christ returns. So the world remains restless and uncertain.[9]

We are preoccupied with material things. Our supreme god is technology; our goddess is sex. Most of us are more interested in conquering space than conquering ourselves. We are more dedicated to material security than to inner purity. We give much more thought to what we wear, what we eat, what we drink, and what we can do to relax than we give to what we are. This preoccupation with peripheral things applies to every area of our lives.[10]

No matter how much you exercise, no matter how many vitamins or health foods you eat, no matter how low your cholesterol, you will still die—someday. If you knew the moment and manner of your death in advance, would you order your life differently?[11]

We read every day about the rich, the famous, and the talented who are disillusioned. Many of them are turning to the occult or Eastern religions. Some are turning to crime. The questions they thought were answered are left dangling: What is man? Where did he come from? What is his purpose on this planet? Where is he going? Is there a God who cares? If there is a God, has He revealed Himself to man?[12]

Our educational establishment has been brainwashed into thinking that its job is to educate the mind and build the body but to leave untouched the deeper questions that are essentially spiritual.[13]

The soul actually demands as much attention as the body. The soul was made for God, and without God it is restless and in secret torment.[14]

Truly, the world is in need of moral leadership that teaches the difference between right and wrong and teaches us to forgive one another even as we are forgiven by our Father in heaven. We do not need a new moral order; the world desperately needs the tried and tested moral order that God handed down.[15]

The good news is that we aren't alone. Not only did God carve out the path for us, but He wants to join us on the journey—to help us with challenges along the way, and eventually lead us home.[16]

The most important decision you will ever make is about eternity. Christ wants to give you hope for the future. He wants you to learn what it means to walk with Him every day. When you come to Christ, God gives you eternal life—which begins right now as you open your heart to Him.[17]

God requires something of us. We must confess our spiritual poverty, renounce our sins, and turn by faith to His Son, Jesus Christ. When we do that, we are born again. He gives us a new nature. He puts a little bit of heaven down in our souls.[18]

The central theme of the universe is the purpose and destiny of every individual. Every person is important in God's eyes.[19]

Man has two great spiritual needs. One is for forgiveness. The other is for goodness.[20]

I like announcing good news, but I cannot speak only of the good news.[21]

The world seems to be spinning faster and faster. Technology and time itself are racing past us at dizzying speeds. Who can keep up? Where will it end? We have to wonder if there are any answers for the crises of our time. But we must also ask if there is still hope for us—or is it as bad as we often fear?[22]

God undertook the most dramatic rescue operation in cosmic history. He determined to save the human race from self-destruction, and He sent His Son Jesus Christ to salvage and redeem it. The work of man's redemption was accomplished at the cross.[23]

When I picture Christ hanging on the cross, the spikes in His hands, the crown of thorns on His brow, the blood shed for our sins, I see the picture of God's grace toward men. Nothing can equal God's infinite love for sinful men.[24]

Ultimately, every human being must face this question: What do you think of Christ? Whose Son is He? We must answer this question with belief and action. We must not only *believe* something about Jesus; we must *do* something about Him. We must accept Him or reject Him.[25]

We must understand what this word *believe* implies. It means "commit" and "surrender." In every true conversion the will of man comes into line with the will of God.[26]

In my early teens I heard a prominent preacher say that after several thousand years of suffering the wicked would have a second opportunity for salvation. This sounded good to me. I could live as I liked here, and if I rejected salvation, I would still have another chance! But as I studied the Word of God carefully, I did not find one verse of Scripture that even hinted or indicated that there will be a second chance after death. Voltaire, the French atheist, said as he lay on his deathbed, "I am taking a fearful leap into the dark." But the Bible says, "Now is the accepted time; behold, now is the day of salvation" (2 Corinthians 6:2 KJV). What you do with Christ here and now decides where you shall spend eternity. Have you made preparation?[27]

The greatest, most exciting journey you could ever experience isn't always an easy journey, but even in the midst of our problems, temptations, and sorrows, life can be different. Most of all, it is a journey of hope, because it leads us to heaven.[28] The privilege of being in touch with heaven right now greatly enhances our time on earth. Knowing that heaven is real, and that we will be there someday, makes a great difference in the way we live. For one thing, heaven gives us hope—hope for today and hope for the future. No matter what we're facing, we know it is temporary, and ahead of us is heaven.[29]

Though cultures differ and times change, the Word of our God stands forever as an unchanging source of answers to all of life's problems. Every problem known to mankind has a spiritual origin. I have yet to discover a source of information, practical advice, and hope that compares to the wisdom found in the Bible.[30]

I am an evangelist, not a scholar.[31] The apostle Paul wrote, "I . . . did not come with excellence of speech or of wisdom declaring to you the testimony of God. For I determined not to know anything among you except Jesus Christ and Him crucified" (1 Corinthians 2:1–2).

If anything has been accomplished through my life, it has been solely God's doing, not mine, and He—not I—must get the credit.[32]

The same Gospel message God the Father gave to Jesus, He passed on to His disciples. This is the same message I have tried to proclaim and pass on to generations after me, just as the Bible has commanded.[33] Today the only bright spot on the horizon is the promise of the coming again of Christ. This is God's message. Do you think He is coming back? I don't think it; I know He's coming back— and soon. This is [the reason] for my hope.[34] Heaven is glorious. Heaven is perfect. Heaven is joyous, and heaven is active; but can we know—really know—that it is also certain? . . . The Bible says yes![35]

The most thrilling thing to me about heaven is that Jesus Christ will be there. I will see Him face to face. . . . He will meet me at the end of life's journey.[36] So when you read or hear that Billy Graham is dead, don't you believe a word of it! I shall be more alive then than I am now. I will just have changed my address. I will have gone into the presence of God.[37] This is the reason for my hope—salvation.

One of God's greatest gifts given to man on earth is the joy of family. My wife, Ruth, and I were blessed with five wonderful children. In 1952 we welcomed our first son into the world. His birth record certifies him as William Franklin Graham III, but we call him Franklin.

With four females in the house, Franklin especially may have craved my companionship. Ruth was right. I missed the children as they grew. But I have had the joy of working with all of them in some aspect of ministry since they became adults.

I watched Franklin run from Christ as a teenager, I challenged him to settle things with God as a young man in 1974, and I rejoiced to ordain him for the Gospel ministry in 1982. In the strange ways of providence, God led Franklin into worldwide ministry to those who suffer from diseases and disasters through his leadership of Samaritan's Purse and now, also, the Billy Graham Evangelistic Association (BGEA). Sensitivity to the needs of others is his consuming passion. He is driven not only by humanitarian generosity and disciplined business sense, but most of all he has a real yearning to see people come to know Christ.

Over the years I was thrilled to have him join me on many trips, to Eastern Europe, China, and the Middle East, places I never dreamed God would open doors for the Gospel to be preached. Now as an effective evangelist himself and president and CEO of the BGEA, his election to these roles not only ensures the continuity of our ministry but also signals a renewed commitment by the board of directors to the vision for world evangelism. We are grateful for our past and expectant for our future.

When Franklin was a boy and I was able to be home, I would take him up to a special spot on the mountain where we would spend time together. Years later when I became housebound, I looked forward to Franklin's visits on weekends when he was not traveling the world. We would take Sunday afternoon walks together and share the joys and challenges of family and ministry.

Franklin is now carrying on much of my own vision while expanding it to include what the Lord has put on his heart. Our visions of hope are included in these pages, and I say with the apostle Paul, "We fix our *eyes* not on what is seen, but on what is unseen" (2 Corinthians 4:18 NIV).

I invite you to go on a thrilling, adventuresome journey that testifies about the work of the Lord. I pray that you will see it through the eyes of our Father in heaven. To Him all hearts will turn and upon Him all eyes will rest.[38]

—BILLY GRAHAM
Montreat, North Carolina
June 2009

This foreword has been compiled from the writings of Billy Graham spanning seven decades (1947–2013). Whether he penned these nuggets of truth in the mid-twentieth century or the beginning of the new millennium, his words are as relevant to our nation and world as they were when he began proclaiming the Gospel in the 1940s. These are treasured excerpts that, mingled together, paint a picture of man's greatest need satisfied by his Savior's salvation freely offered through God's amazing grace.

Preface

Karl Rove, who served as deputy chief of staff for President George W. Bush, called my cell phone one evening and said, "Franklin, the president asked me to phone you. He wants to honor your father in some way. Doesn't he have a birthday soon?"

I had talked with Karl on occasion, but this call took me aback. Four weeks had passed since the terrorist attack and fatal collapse of the twin towers on 9/11. With all the president had on his mind, he was thinking of my father.

Arrangements were made, and on the eve of my father's eighty-third birthday, November 6, 2001, President and Mrs. Bush welcomed the Graham family to the White House for a small, private dinner. When the president clasped my father's hand and looked into his eyes, there was a connection between the two that spoke of the milestones shared between them.

President Bush welcomed us and encouraged us to enjoy "the People's House." He took us through adjoining rooms, graciously sharing historical anecdotes. As a prelude to dinner, the First Couple served punch and extended hospitality beyond description, making sure we were all comfortable and cared for.

I was particularly concerned for my mother because she had been in poor health. I had doubted whether she could even make the trip to Washington, DC. As I looked around the room to see where my parents were, I saw President Bush walking through the room holding my mother's hand, his other hand on my father's shoulder. He led them to wingback chairs and hovered over them, seeing to their comfort. When I observed the loving attention my parents received from President Bush, I decided their eldest son should remain in the shadows. My mind snapped a picture of this very tender moment. The leader of the free world had taken on the role of a son. Perhaps the president in some way felt as though he was a spiritual son, since he and my father had shared a very special moment years before, when they took a walk together along the Maine shore in 1985. According to President Bush, my father's words that day planted a mustard seed of faith in his soul.

There was no White House staff in view. The president had taken charge of the evening and gathered us into the dining room, where tables were beautifully set. The president hosted my mother at one table, and Laura Bush hosted my father at another.

"Franklin, please sit down," President Bush said with a grin. He had asked my father's secretary, Stephanie Wills, who might pray before the meal, and he liked her suggestion. "I'm looking around at all the preachers, wondering who might say grace, but I've decided to do it myself."

He asked us to bow our heads. He began to pray, not from a written prayer but from the heart. To recount the prayer word for word would be impossible, but it was memorable. With humility that was felt around the room, President Bush prayed for the citizens of our great country and thanked the Lord for seeing our nation through a critical time. Then he asked God to bless the evening and thanked "the Almighty" for the impact the heavenly Father had made in his own life through Billy Graham.

Following the meal, the first lady gave a signal and the White House chef entered the dining room with a beautifully decorated birthday cake. The president asked Cliff Barrows to lead everyone in singing "Happy Birthday to You."

After pictures were taken, President Bush reminded us that "all good people should be in bed soon." With handshakes and hugs, we departed 1600 Pennsylvania Avenue. A White House staffer told us as we left that the evening was a welcomed reprieve for the president, who had been carrying the heavy burden of that unforgettable September morning.

One month later, our family was invited once again to the nation's capital. Queen Elizabeth had written my father months before, wanting to bestow on him the title of Knight Commander in the Order of the British Empire. Because of my father's unstable health, he was not able to travel to England to receive the award at Buckingham Palace. Her Majesty the Queen requested that the ceremony be conducted by British ambassador Sir Christopher Meyer, at the British Embassy.

Upon receiving this high honor, my father said,

> With humility and unworthiness, I take [this high honor] as a symbol of the common historical ties that have bound our two nations together in war and in peace. I read a quote that appeared in *The Daily News* in 1903 about Queen Victoria. After hearing a sermon about Christ's return to earth, Queen Victoria said, "Oh how I wish that the Lord might come during my lifetime." When asked why, she replied, "I should like to lay my crown at His feet." And that's the way I feel tonight about any honor that may come to me. I'd like to lay it at His feet . . . and at my age, it won't be too long. Tonight I would like to say, God bless the United Kingdom, and may God bless Her Majesty the Queen.[1]

My father would be the first to say that his life should not be defined by honors, awards, and achievements. In his last years of life he told me many times, "An evangelist is called to do one thing: proclaim the Gospel. Anything else dilutes the evangelist's impact and compromises his message." It is one of the great lessons he taught me by example. I have learned a great deal from a man who has been many things to many people.

As I shared some of my reflections over lunch several years ago with my friend and publishing giant Sam Moore, he shoved back from the table and said, "Franklin, I encourage you to begin now writing down these lessons because others can benefit from what you have learned from your father." Sam's words seemed to take root in my thoughts, just as lessons learned from my father had taken root in my life.

This book reflects lessons not only from my earthly father; but as work progressed over the past several years, it became clear that the lessons were proven worthy because they were grounded in the truth of Scripture.

My father has left behind a trail of victories and, yes, some regrets. I suspect that I will continue to learn from my father even in his death and pray that the Lord will grant me the grace to finish as he did: strong in God's power and truth. In his autobiography he wrote, "More than anything else, I yearn for people to understand the message of Christ and accept it as their own."[2]

That very message is the theme of this book, written the way I have seen it—through my father's eyes.

—FRANKLIN GRAHAM
Boone, North Carolina

Introduction

I have covered you with the shadow of My hand.

—Isaiah 51:16

Billy Graham lived a remarkable life in the presence of his family and in view of the world. People will come to their own conclusions about him, but no one can speak more insightfully than a son who grew up in the shadow of his love.

Webster's Dictionary defines *shadow* as an "inseparable companion."[1] When my father was away, Mama was that shadow of influence of the man I have always referred to as Daddy. In my eyes, they were the true representation of what the Bible means for husband and wife to become one.

During my childhood, I watched my father come and go, pack again, and then rush through the front door to a waiting car as he kissed my mother and us children goodbye. Sometimes his absence was for two weeks, two months, and on occasion even longer. No matter the length of the journey, his goodbye was followed by a promise: "I'll be back." The assurance was tucked inside the pocket of his overcoat, next to his heart—a round-trip ticket.

My father visited nearly every continent on earth multiple times. But there was one trip he longed to make—a trip *out* of this world. When my father traveled to heaven, he did so with a one-way ticket, purchased more than two thousand years ago with the lifeblood of the Lord Jesus Christ. He completed a journey that required no baggage—no return ticket. His destiny was certain.

While my father looked forward to heaven, he dreaded the process of dying. For years he suffered from Parkinson's-like symptoms, caused by a buildup of fluid in the brain known as normal pressure hydrocephalus, along with various other ailments. However, with each passing birthday, the process became less burdensome, particularly after watching my mother leave their home for her eternal home on June 14, 2007. It seemed that part of my father went with her.

Though he had spent countless weeks away from her during his busy life, the sudden loneliness of her absence caused him a great deal of reflection. The realization that she wouldn't be coming back deepened his desire to leave their log home in Little Piney Cove and make his final journey to be with her in heaven forever.

While my father anticipated being reunited with my mother, the hope that anchored him was to look to his Savior and fix his eyes on the One he had preached about for seven decades. He spoke of it often, saying, "The most thrilling thing to me about heaven is that Jesus Christ will be there. I will see Him face-to-face."

Call from God

Billy Graham was focused—riveted to a call from God.

He was a man who realized his inability and grasped God's authority.

He was convicted by the message God put in his heart and comprehended its power.

He understood his calling and God's leading.

He set his hands to a heavenly task and firmly placed both feet on the narrow road, opposite the global highway, and followed the steps of the Lord wherever they led.

What God did through the life of Billy Graham is beyond a storehouse of words.

During his 1949 Los Angeles tent meeting, a clergyman lodged a complaint against my father, accusing him of setting the cause of religion back a hundred years. When my father heard this, he replied, "I did indeed want to set religion back—not just a hundred years but nineteen hundred years, to the Book of Acts, where first-century followers of Christ were accused of turning the Roman Empire upside down."[2]

No one thrives on criticism, but my father resolved not to let it distract him from his God-given task—to serve the Lord Jesus Christ with his life, and to "do what is right in the eyes of the LORD" (Deuteronomy 13:18).

The Big Leagues

Prior to his conversion as a teenager, my father set his sights on making his mark in the big leagues—baseball, that is. His dream was no different than that of many other boys his age: to play with the New York Yankees. His hero was Babe Ruth. In fact, my grandfather arranged for him to meet the "King of Swat" when he played an exhibition game in my father's hometown of Charlotte, North Carolina.

It's no wonder that when my grandparents took my dad to hear Billy Sunday preach in Charlotte a few years later, my father was captivated. When this athlete-turned-evangelist leaned over the edge of the platform, lifted his Bible dramatically, and proclaimed, "The Bible says," it made an impact in the heart of this young, impressionable country boy.

My grandmother, whom we always called Mother Graham, said, "It was Billy Sunday's preaching that kept Billy Frank on the edge of his seat. Life after that was never quite the same."[3]

The revival meeting, held in a gigantic frame tabernacle on the out-skirts of town, also had an impact on my grandfather and twenty-nine other men from Charlotte, including T. Walter Wilson Sr. (father of Daddy's friends, Grady and T. W. Wilson). In a book written by Mordecai Ham's nephew, Edward E. Ham, he told about this "band of men" who prayed that God would send revival to Charlotte and that "it might spread over the state, then out to the ends of the world!"[4] Little did my grandfather realize that God would answer this prayer by call-ing his eldest son into a worldwide ministry.

In 1934, evangelist Mordecai Ham held a revival in Charlotte. "A great giant of a man [preached] in such a way as I had never heard," my father recalled. "Halfway through his message he pointed right in my direction and said, 'Young man, you are a sinner.' I thought he was talk-ing to me, so I ducked behind the person in front of me and hid my face! 'Why, I'm as good as anybody,' I told myself. But then he began to quote Scripture, 'There is none righteous, no not one.' For the first time in my life I realized that I was a sinner, that my soul was bound for hell and that I needed a Savior."[5]

The next night my father walked down the aisle, repented of his sin, and received God's forgiveness and the Savior's love. It was in that meeting my father surrendered his life to Jesus Christ. What a legacy.

An Innovative Ministry

My father grew up during the Great Depression and understood the hardships created by World War II. Across the nation, home life suf-fered as men went to battle and women went to work. This shift in the workforce altered American culture and created problems that changed family life. When the war ended and the United States began to rebound, commercial air travel allowed people to move quickly and families began to scatter.

My father sensed the urgency of God's call in his life and utilized the latest technology to create a launching pad for mass evangelism, enabling him to communicate a never-changing message through ever-changing forms of technology. He was a pioneer in using the power of radio and television to spread the Good News.

Though man might take credit for modern technology, it was Creator God who opened the way. Still today, it is God who places innovative spirits in the minds and hearts of His creation. And it is God who placed in my father's heart a passion for souls.

I saw through my father's eyes what the Lord can do with a life surrendered to Him. He taught me how to live by example. The Bible says, "My son, . . . let your eyes observe my ways" (Proverbs 23:26).

My father left behind a testimony to God, a legacy not buried in a grave but still pointing people to a heaven-bound destiny. The Lord will say to my father, and to all who served Him obediently, "Well done, good and faithful servant" (Matthew 25:21).

Lift Up Your Eyes

Throughout his life my father enjoyed retreating to a rocker on the front porch—breathing the fresh mountain air, listening to the gentle summer wind, and watching the leaves turn gold in the fall.

Not long ago I visited my parents' home in Little Piney Cove. They loved that log house that sits at the side of a ridge thirty-two hundred feet above sea level, overlooking the Blue Ridge Mountains and a portion of Pisgah National Forest. Sitting there on the porch, I leafed through my Bible and read, "Go up to the top of Pisgah, and lift your eyes toward the west, the north, the south, and the east; *behold it with your eyes*" (Deuteronomy 3:27).

Though my father longed to spend more time with his family at home, when he lifted his eyes and looked to the north, south, east, and west, he realized the corners of the world were still in darkness. And after a little rest, he packed up and carried on.

My father didn't dwell on the past. He had an unusual ability to focus on what was in front of him. He drew strength from knowing that God would guide him along his journey to do his part in reaching a lost and dying world for Christ.

The Bible says, "The eyes of the LORD run to and fro throughout the whole earth, to show Himself strong on behalf of those whose heart is loyal to Him" (2 Chronicles 16:9).

Through the Father's Eyes

My father left behind a legacy that will be carried into future generations, and the Father in heaven is calling others to step into His pathway. "Ponder the path of your feet, and let all your ways be established" (Proverbs 4:26).

The Bible says, "Give attention to my words; incline your ear to my sayings. Do not let them depart from your eyes; keep them in the midst of your heart; for they are life to those who find them" (Proverbs 4:20–22).

The earliest memories of my parents are bound up in the unconditional love they demonstrated in our home, but it wasn't without their guidance and correction. My wife, Jane Austin, and I have tried to follow their example. As my father many times so wonderfully credited his wife for fulfilling the role of both mother and father because of his long absences, I, too, express my love to Jane for providing a loving home for our children and constantly being there for them.

While working on this book, I reflected on the relationship I enjoyed with my father for sixty-five years. Even though I dreaded the day my father would no longer be just a short journey away, I wanted to end the book with his journey to heaven because this was his greatest longing, to finally see life through the eyes of his Father in heaven.

I

My Father in Heaven

They desire . . . a heavenly country.
Therefore God . . . has prepared a city for them.

—HEBREWS 11:16

My home is in heaven. I'm just traveling through this world.

BILLY GRAHAM

"I will travel anywhere in the world to preach," my father once said, "if there are no strings on what I am to say." And travel he did: on ocean liners and in postwar automobiles before interstates rolled out across America. Then the jet age roared into the mid-twentieth century, and my father became known as a globe-trotter for God, but it wasn't without turbulence. He determined early in his journey that the Word of God was the only road map he needed to guide him along the highways of life, spattered with potholes.

"Ruth and I have said goodbye many times in our life together," my father wrote. "Sometimes we were separated by oceans and time differences. But the absences made the homecoming much sweeter."[1]

It may seem a little strange, then, to say that as a boy I lived many exciting moments through my father's eyes, since he was gone so much. My mother would share stories about what he was doing wherever he was in the world, grabbing our attention with the slightest detail. When he returned home, it felt in some ways as though we had been with him the whole time.

I can recall him describing a voyage on the SS *United States*, recounting the ship as it sliced its way through the Atlantic storms. His hand glided through the air, demonstrating how the vessel maneuvered into dock at Southampton, England. He was a great storyteller. Every scene he described I saw clearly through his penetrating eyes, as blue as the sky over North Carolina where we lived.

Through my father's eyes, I was introduced to six of the seven continents of the world: Asia, Africa, North and South America, Europe, and Australia. Learning about different cultures and exotic locations inspired my childhood imagination. My father and mother exposed me to the possibilities of serving God with my life, and their example molded and shaped me to follow in step where the Lord would lead. As I learned about the world through my earthly father's eyes, little did I realize that someday I would experience for myself the world's diversity through the eyes of my Father in heaven.

A Father's Forgiveness

The parable of the prodigal son in Luke 15 is a message my father and I both have preached many times. There is much in the story I could relate to in my late teens. Not that I rebelled against my father as the prodigal son did, but at that time in my life I certainly did not share my father's commitment to serving the Lord with all my heart, soul, and body. I respected everything he believed, preached, and lived, but I was not about to follow in my father's footsteps. I was not interested in seeing the world through his eyes anymore. I wanted to feast my eyes on what the world could offer me—and I did for a time.

I will never forget the day I drove home to North Carolina after being expelled from LeTourneau College in Texas. Dread swelled as I approached my parents' log home in the Blue Ridge Mountains. I imagined my father's look of disapproval when he would fix his eyes on his eldest son and namesake, who had failed to make him proud.

But when I rounded the last curve, my father's long legs stepped off the porch and he walked toward me with arms wide open. Following a gripping hug, I looked into my father's forgiving eyes.

I often think of that moment when I stand in the pulpit and watch as men, women, and children answer God's call to repentance. When they bow in prayer, confessing their sin to God, and receive His salvation, surely they look into the forgiving eyes of the Savior, who loves them unconditionally and provides all they need to begin a new walk in His steps.

Though I never had visions of following in my father's footsteps, his world travel sounded exciting to me. I recall hearing a friend of his talk about two missionary ladies who needed a four-wheel-drive Land Rover for their hospital work in northern Jordan. When my father agreed to buy one for them, I immediately devised a plan to pick it up in England and drive it across Europe and into the Middle East. When I shared the idea with my father, I thought I could fool him by using a spiritual-sounding excuse to not return to college. "If you'll buy the Land Rover, Daddy, I'll deliver it to Jordan and stay and help those missionaries finish building their hospital."

His eyes glared. Mine stared—waiting for his response. After my parents discussed the pros and cons, my father concluded that maybe an experience like that was just what God had in mind for my troubled soul. In his wisdom, my father understood that I was probably going to sow some wild oats. He was smart enough to realize that some seed just might fall on fertile desert sand, opening the door for the Holy Spirit to blow a seed of faith into my calloused heart.

My father was a true Southern gentleman. When he was not in the pulpit, he spoke softly. His words were tender, gracious, and kind. In contrast, when he preached, his eyes snapped with passion and were fixed on one thing—the proclamation of the Gospel of the Lord Jesus Christ. His heart was anchored to his calling to preach the Word of God.

My father was a friend to presidents, a counselor to world leaders, and a confidant to royalty. In his early interviews with the media, they ridiculed and acclaimed him. I have learned through my father's eyes that the all-important thing to hold on to in good times and bad is the Anchor—Jesus Christ. I believe my father's steadfastness found favor in the eyes of the heavenly Father because God granted him more than seventy years in service to the King of kings.

The foundational message my father preached became a banner for his meetings. In John 14:6, Jesus said,

I AM THE WAY, THE TRUTH, AND THE LIFE.

In bigger-than-life letters, this Bible verse was stretched across the platform, symbolizing the crux of what would be heard from the pulpit: "No one comes to the Father except through Me" (the Lord Jesus Christ). Billy Graham never wavered from this singular message. It wasn't, however, without criticism. His steely blue eyes stared beyond it and fastened with assurance to the Author, who penetrates men's hearts with this same message today.

Andraé Crouch wrote lyrics to a song that most Christians can identify with:

I thank God for the mountains,
And I thank Him for the valleys;
I thank Him for the storms He brought me through;
For if I'd never had a problem,
I wouldn't know that He could solve them,
I'd never know what faith in God could do.
Through it all,
Through it all,
Oh I've learned to trust in Jesus,
I've learned to trust in God.
Through it all,
Through it all,
Oh I've learned to depend upon His Word.[2]

This is certainly true of my father. There were many times that my father struggled to understand God's truth, but the outcome was always the same: he learned to depend upon God's Word. His worldwide travel proliferated a global awareness of the message he preached—the Gospel of the Lord Jesus Christ.

Until the day he died, my father held tight to the claims of Christ that confront the human race about the ultimate choice—where to spend eternity. He preached on heaven many times, warning listeners to prepare to meet Almighty God. Every soul will meet Him someday, either in heaven, where Christ reigns, or at the throne of judgment, where all those without Christ will be doomed.

To proclaim the truths of heaven is thrilling. The reality of hell is daunting, but it also must be preached. My friend Dr. John MacArthur has boldly stated, "The most loving message a preacher of the Gospel can proclaim is the reality of hell, because it sounds the alarm—warning sinners to repent and turn to the Savior—the hope of heaven."[3] The Bible says, "How shall we escape if we neglect so great a salvation?" (Hebrews 2:3).

The Snare

There are many things I have learned in my own ministry by observing my father through the years. I have drawn from his example and have learned important lessons on how to handle the good that comes and, even at times, the snares. Believers in Jesus Christ will face traps throughout life; this is Satan's clever method of stealing joy and victory in the life of a Christian.

One of the last print interviews my father did was with Jon Meacham, managing editor of *Newsweek*. In his cover story, Jon went right to the heart of evangelism when he asked my father if "heaven will be closed to good Jews, Muslims, Buddhists, Hindus or secular people." The printed reply from my father stated, "It would be foolish for me to speculate on who will be [in heaven] and who won't."[4]

WorldNetDaily dissected this interview with blasting judgment, stating, "Meacham describes Graham's embrace of universalism in glowing terms" and "calls Graham 'a resolute Christian who declines to render absolute verdicts about who will get into heaven and who will not' and as someone who 'refuses to be judgmental.'"[5]

My father was dismayed when he saw this statement in print. He was deeply discouraged that after a life of preaching God's truth, it *appeared* that he had failed to complete his answer.

Jon Meacham's evaluation, in part, is actually true. Billy Graham cannot render absolute verdicts about who will be in heaven and who will not, but he preached and wrote about the One who will make those judgments, based on the heart and soul of the Gospel: all who receive eternal life must repent of sin, accept Jesus Christ as Lord and Savior, and follow Him in obedience. If there were any other way, there would have been no need for the ultimate sacrifice of Christ on the cross and there would be no Gospel. This is what my father preached his entire life.

The Truth

Jesus said, "Not everyone who says to Me, 'Lord, Lord,' shall enter the kingdom of heaven, but he who does the will of My Father in heaven" (Matthew 7:21).

What is the will of the Father? "Jesus Christ . . . gave Himself for our sins, that He might deliver us from this present evil age, according to the will of our God and Father" (Galatians 1:3–4). "For God so loved the world that He gave His only begotten Son, that whoever believes in Him should not perish but have everlasting life" (John 3:16).

So will some perish? "The Lord . . . is longsuffering toward us, not willing that any should perish but that all should come to repentance" (2 Peter 3:9).

What about those who do not repent? "In accordance with your hardness and your impenitent heart you are treasuring up for yourself wrath in the day of wrath and revelation of the righteous judgment of God, who *will render to each one according to his deeds*" (Romans 2:5–6).

So, then, the answer is found in Scripture to the question, can those who reject Christ as Savior be saved? "This is the verdict: Light has come into the world" (John 3:19 NIV). "I am the light of the world. Whoever follows me will never walk in darkness, but will have the light of life" (John 8:12 NIV). "I am the way, the truth, and the life. No one comes to the Father except through Me" (John 14:6).

It is important to point out that religions do not reject Christ; people do. Religion is a belief system built upon man's ideas. Nowhere in the Bible do religious systems have a claim on heaven. Men's souls are bound for heaven or hell. Christians do not follow religion; they follow their Father in heaven by obedience and absolute faith in His Son Jesus Christ according to the Word of God—this is our road map to living life in His name.

These truths are contained in the body of work—in spoken and written form—compiled by my father that thoroughly answers these questions that pull at the heartstrings of all people. From the crusade pulpit to the press conference podium, my father clearly stated his position through the years. In his book *Facing Death—And the Life After*, he wrote,

> Some teach "universalism"—that eventually everybody will be saved and the God of love will never send anyone to hell. They believe the words "eternal" or "everlasting" do not actually mean forever. However, the same word that speaks of eternal banishment from God is also used for the eternity of heaven.
>
> The person being presented for entrance into heaven must be admitted on the basis of God's grace alone, not by any good works or noble deeds done on earth. Our only right for admission to heaven lies in the provision God made for our sins: His Son Jesus Christ.
>
> Will a loving God send a man to hell? The answer from Jesus and the teachings of the Bible is, clearly, "Yes!" He does not send man willingly, but man condemns himself to eternal hell because of his blindness, stubbornness, egotism, and love of sinful pleasure. He refuses God's way of salvation and the hope of eternal life with Him.
>
> Some believe God gives a second chance. But the Bible says, "Now is the day of salvation" (2 Corinthians 6:2). The Bible teaches there is hell for every person who rejects Christ as Lord and Savior. "The Son of Man will send out his angels, and they will weed out of his kingdom everything that causes sin and all who do evil. They will throw them into the fiery furnace, where there will be weeping and gnashing of teeth" (Matthew 13:41–42 NIV).[6]

The Blood-Stained Label

In answer to Jon Meacham's question, there will be no religions or sects in heaven—only the redeemed, those who are washed in the blood of the Lamb. "You were not redeemed with corruptible things . . . but with the precious blood of Christ, as of a lamb without blemish and without spot" (1 Peter 1:18–19).

Many have been steeped in philosophies instead of the truth, trapped by "another gospel," thinking they will go to heaven by believing half-truths. The apostle Paul told Timothy,

> Command certain men not to teach false doctrines any longer nor to devote themselves to myths. . . . These promote controversies rather than God's work—which is by faith. . . . Some have wandered away from these and turned to meaningless talk . . . and for whatever else is contrary to the sound doctrine that conforms to the glorious gospel of the blessed God, which he entrusted to me. (1 Timothy 1:3–4, 6, 10–11 NIV)

This was a continual theme in Paul's preaching, indicating the confusion caused by preaching "another gospel":

> See to it that no one takes you captive through hollow and deceptive philosophy, which depends on human tradition and the basic principles of this world rather than on Christ. For in Christ all the fullness of the Deity lives in bodily form, and you have been given fullness in Christ, who is the head over every power and authority. (Colossians 2:8–10 NIV)

When men and women are saved out of darkness, they no longer identify with their former belief systems. Receiving Christ means a complete turning away from heresy to the absolute truth.

In my father's book *Hope for the Troubled Heart*, he wrote, "I believe that if people paid more attention to death, eternity, and judgment, there would be more holy living on earth."[7] The Bible says, "Therefore, if anyone is in Christ, he is a new creation; old things have passed away; behold, all things have become new" (2 Corinthians 5:17).

My Father's Friend and Mine

A close and dear friend of my father, Roy Gustafson, became a father figure to me as a young man. My father encouraged me to travel and spend time with Roy.

Roy had a profound impact in my life. My wife and I named our second son after him. I was honored to preach his memorial service in 2002. I miss him still today.

Roy was well traveled. A gifted preacher in his own right, he became an ambassador to the land of the Bible for the Billy Graham Evangelistic Association (BGEA). Not only did he have an in-depth understanding of Jewish history, but he was also able to dissect the trappings of world religions and unravel their claims.

In a message Roy often preached, he said, "There are thousands of religions, but there is only one Gospel. You see, religions come as a product of the reasonings of the human mind. The Gospel is the revelation of God's mind. Religions originate on earth. The Gospel originated in heaven. Religions are man-made. The Gospel is the gift of God. Religions—all of them—are the story of what sinful people try to do for a holy God. The Gospel is the wonderful story of what a holy God has already done for sinful people. Religion is mankind's quest for God. The Gospel is the Savior-God seeking lost men and women. Religion is the opinions of sinful people—the Gospel is [God's] Good News."[8]

My father and Roy are now in heaven. No longer do they travel from city to city. They are now permanent residents in the city of God.

Heavenly Real Estate

One of the most important issues we face in life is where to live, work, and raise our families. We peruse the real estate market for the ideal location; we consider the cost of the best-built house and then push the limit to obtain a bank loan, all for the purpose of providing the most comfortable living environment for our families. Yet the most important choice people will ever make in life is where they will spend eternity.

My father said, "We are so caught up with the affairs of this life we give little attention to eternity."⁹ Few give thought to what happens after death. Such a monumental, eternity-altering decision seldom reaches priority level. God will not make that choice for us. He does not force anyone to choose heaven. Those who accept His forgiveness and mercy will deposit their riches in heaven, "the city which has foundations, whose builder and maker is God" (Hebrews 11:10).

The question is often asked, "How do you know you will be received into heaven?" I answer as my father did. I belong, body and soul, not to myself but to my faithful Savior, who paid for all my sins wholeheartedly. That makes me want to live for Him now and forevermore.

The picture in my mind of my earthly father worshipping at the feet of my Father in heaven puts a longing in my soul for that eternal home. True followers of Jesus Christ should never get too comfortable in this world because we do not belong here. Like my father, we are simply passing through.

The Bible says, "For we know that if our earthly house, this tent, is destroyed, we have a building from God, a house not made with hands, eternal in the heavens" (2 Corinthians 5:1). Someone said, "What we call life is a journey to death. What we call death is the gateway to life."

Billy Graham understood the dilemma that the apostle Paul wrote about in Philippians—whether to live life on earth or depart from the earth to live in the presence of God. Paul said, "Christ will be magnified in my body, whether by life or by death. For to me, to live is Christ, and to die is gain. But if I live on in the flesh, this will mean fruit from my labor; yet what I shall choose I cannot tell. For I am hard-pressed between the two, having a desire to depart and be with Christ, which is far better" (Philippians 1:20–23).

In his book *Facing Death—And the Life After*, my father stated, "I'm not afraid to die, for I know the joys of heaven are waiting. My greatest desire is to live today in anticipation of tomorrow and be ready to be welcomed into His home for all eternity. Will you be making the journey with me?"[10]

In other words, are you ready to stand before Almighty God? This was the question that underscored my father's preaching ministry. I came to understand his driving passion that profoundly affected my life in significant ways. My father was interested in the souls of mankind and longed to take the world with him on the never-ending journey of eternal life with Christ.

Author and educator Herbert Lockyer said, "Where is there a country without sin, crime, lawlessness, bloodshed, disease, death, sorrow and heartache? . . . In God's country there are . . . no undertakers because there are no graves. . . . Who would not yearn for this better and more desirable country in which there are no separations, no broken homes, no drunkards, no prisons, no hospitals, no beggars? . . . Are you not homesick for heaven?"[11]

I am now more homesick for heaven than ever. Why? Because the two people on earth that influenced my life most are together again in God's country.

While I have been entrusted with the mantle of leading the BGEA and am privileged to preach in crusade pulpits around the world, I have not stepped into Billy Graham's shoes. I do pray, however, that my eyes will always be fixed on my Father in heaven as I proclaim His great truths—just as my father pointed multitudes of people to the Savior who is waiting with open arms to forgive.

My father's soul is very much alive, and someday I will be joined again with him in heaven. Then I will clearly see all things through my Father's eyes.

2

Made in China

Who can find a virtuous woman? For her worth
is far beyond pearls.
The heart of her husband safely trusts her. . . .
She reaches out her hands to the needy.
Strength and honor are her clothing. . . .
Her children rise up and call her blessed. . . .
A woman who fears the Lord, she shall be praised.

—Proverbs 31:10–11, 20, 25, 28, 30 sprl

We were called by God as a team.
My work through the years would have been impossible
without Ruth's encouragement and support.

BILLY GRAHAM

I was taxiing down the runway with thoughts of my mother. I had just
finished preaching a crusade in New York and was back in North

Carolina on Sunday, June 10, 2007—my mother's eighty-seventh birthday. I had called earlier in the day to wish her a happy birthday and had grown accustomed to hearing her weak voice. Lingering in bad health for months, she had a few remaining days on this earth, but I did not realize at the time that this would be my last phone conversation with her.

"Franklin," my sister Gigi said when she called early the next morning, "Dr. Rice said you should come home to see Mama."

I had developed a bad cold and said, "Gigi, I don't think I should come right now. She might catch what I have."

Gigi responded, "Franklin, it won't matter. Mama won't last the week."

I hit the road.

The Lord was gracious to give my siblings and me time to be with her for four memorable days. We each took turns having private time with her. She was able to converse for short periods, but in-depth conversations were now past. As I sat and watched her feeble body break loose from life's chains, my mind wandered, much as it did when I was a boy. Her voice was real to me as I recalled so many things—my mother's practical jokes, her love of life, and her uncanny way of knowing all the trouble I got into even when out of sight. My mother's one-of-a-kind technique made her discipline adventuresome. Recounting story after story, my memory drifted to the 1950s, when I was a small boy.

I was fascinated by the workmen who were building our log house. They smoked one cigarette after another. My mother was scared to death that their smoking would influence me—and it did. I laughed, recalling the day she made me smoke a whole pack of cigarettes at one time and blow the smoke up the chimney. She thought it would prevent me from ever wanting to smoke again. It didn't, but it sure made me sick.

Her adventures of chasing a rattlesnake with the marshmallow fork and shoving firecrackers under my locked bedroom door to wake me added to my fun growing up.

I looked over at her frail body and recalled all the nights as a boy, when I crawled in bed next to her in that very room while she told stories about life in China as a young girl. We would talk of finding old moonshine stills when our property on the mountain was first purchased. Before she tucked me in for the night, she read Bible stories and explained them. Then we would get on our knees and pray.

And then there were all the nights as a teenager. No matter how late I stayed out, my mother did not go to bed until I got home. I can recall driving up in front of the house and seeing her bedroom light on. As soon as I would walk in the house and look down the hallway, the light would click off. Other times she would be sitting by the fire and say, "I'm glad you're okay," as she kissed me and turned in for the night.

My childhood memories are rich, but so are my memories as an adult. I found my thoughts drifting to the spring of 1992.

The Welcome Mat

I was sitting in my Boone office, stunned by unfounded accusations. As president and CEO of Samaritan's Purse, a Christian relief and evangelism organization that had been entrusted to me since 1979, I had worked hard to pattern the organization after the BGEA, which my father had started in 1950.

Samaritan's Purse had become a voluntary member in an accountability group, subscribing to its standards. The Samaritan's Purse board of directors encouraged me to ask the group to review our organization's policies and procedures and advise us about what could be strengthened. Since this was a service provided to all members, I did so with excitement, knowing that holding to the highest standard possible would give us continued credibility with our donors. I never dreamed that the standards would be opened to personal interpretation and others' personal agendas.

While I was on an overseas trip to assess our work in various countries, a reporter tracked me down. "Mr. Graham, do you want to comment on your membership being suspended?" I was stunned.

When I returned home several days later, a review council assembled at my office in Boone, consisting of members from the accountability group, Samaritan's Purse, and BGEA. Their reason for coming was to present a list of concerns they claimed violated their standards. Each proved to be a false accusation, and the underlying reason for this onslaught began to crystallize in my mind. These were men who sought to call into question my leadership so that my father and his board of directors would not consider entrusting BGEA to me when the time came to pass the responsibility of this worldwide evangelistic ministry to the next generation. Franklin Graham, in a sense, was intended as the sacrificial lamb.

This became apparent even to my mother. On the eve of the last review meeting, my mother appeared at my office, eyes snapping with mischief. She was prone to use amusing tactics to express herself. As she walked through the lobby door, she rolled out a doormat to welcome the accountability group the next morning. It said:

OH NO. NOT YOU AGAIN!

Simply signed, "Ruth."

It seemed to break the ice—at least for me. But when the review board arrived, the men did not chuckle when they saw the huge letters. More humorous was to watch as they sidestepped the doormat. I wondered if they had grasped my mother's unspoken message—that they were making her son their doormat. Or perhaps her intended message was for them to explore their motives.

My mother's fun-loving prank did not soften them. However, after the meeting concluded and weeks passed, the allegations proved to have no merit, and our membership was reinstated.

The firestorm that was created in the media brought my name into question and caused my ministry to be viewed as suspect. I couldn't help but think about the reproach it could bring on my parents' good names and, more important, the name of the Lord.

False allegations often find their way into headline news, but retractions are seldom acknowledged. While Samaritan's Purse was exonerated, it remained a dark period for me. I realized that there were forces lurking in the shadows that might not fade.

My father said only one thing to me during that difficult time. "Franklin, don't fight back. Smile and do what God has called you to do. Let the world know of the work being done in the name of the Lord."

My mother, on the other hand, kept a careful eye on the matter from afar. Hardly a day passed that she did not make contact with me. She reminded me of times when my father had experienced public ridicule and encouraged me to respond as he did in the face of tales that had no foundational truth.

A few weeks later, I was sitting in my office, leaning back in my chair with feet propped on the corner of the desk. Unable to concentrate on the work before me, I asked the Lord to give me strength to get victory over the negative perception and do it in such a way to bring honor to Him.

Earlier that morning, my mother had called and ended the short conversation with, "Dad and I are praying for you." I figured she was still at home, two hours away. Instead, she stood just outside my office, peering at her bewildered son. When she saw the look of shock on my face, she knew she had pulled off one of her best surprises.

I jumped up to greet her. "What are you doing here, Mama?"

She stayed long enough to say, "I just wanted to come and give you a hug, look into your eyes, and tell you that I love you." Then she got in the car and drove home.

The five-minute visit—seeing her smile and feeling her support—helped me move forward with renewed confidence derived from a mother's love. She encouraged me through Scripture and reminded me how my father dealt with criticism: "Concentrate on what God is doing, not on what man attempts to do."

With wise counsel from colleagues and God's direction, we turned our attention back to the work of Samaritan's Purse, and the Lord granted favor.

Media outlets began printing positive stories that highlighted our work at home and abroad. It was a powerful lesson for me in how God can take someone's wrong intention and turn it into something good.

Sometimes the hardest thing to do is be still. Yet the Bible instructs us to do just that in times of conflict, realizing that "He makes the plans of the peoples of no effect" (Psalm 33:10).

A few years later, the BGEA board of directors gave me their vote of confidence and elected me as president. This allowed me to strengthen my father's ministry as his health began to decline. It also gave a sense of renewal to the ongoing work he had begun years before.

It was not easy following my parents' counsel, but by their example they taught me how to view things through the eyes of my Father in heaven. The lesson I learned was that God will sometimes use Satan's fiery darts to bring glory to His name.

"And There Will I Be Buried"

Now standing at Mother's bedside, I missed the twinkle in her eyes that had always brought joy. Looking at her steady gaze, I wondered if she was recalling some of these same memories. Some brought laughter; others, tears.

Months before my mother passed away, a controversy hit the national news, implicating a storm of dissent within the family about where my parents would be buried. There was an attempt by some to cause a rift between my mother and me, to pit sibling against sibling, and to drive a wedge between my parents over a very personal decision regarding their burial site.

Years before, my mother had hoped to be buried at Little Piney Cove—the name she gave to the place she chose to build our family's log cabin. We had a small graveyard on the property where close friends and my mother's sister were buried.

Plans, however, developed for my parents to be buried at the Billy Graham Training Center at The Cove. My mother was not thrilled about the idea, but over time she had agreed to be laid to rest there, just a few short miles from their home. As the years passed, my father longed to return to his roots.

The Billy Graham Library in Charlotte was to officially open in June 2007. As my mother and father grew older and weaker, some of our board members and longtime friends of my father proposed that my folks consider being buried in the prayer garden behind the library, not far from where my father had been born and raised. As I walked the property's tree line along the Billy Graham Parkway and listened to the quiet breeze blowing through the pines, it seemed a tranquil resting place.

When this idea was presented to my father, he said to his colleagues and me, "You know, I've been praying about that. All of my ancestors—even my parents—are buried nearby. I'd like to go back to Charlotte when the time comes."

Knowing how much my mother loved her mountains, I said, "Daddy, you'll need to work this out with Mama. You know she's always wanted to be buried on the mountain."

My father asked me to explain to my mother the plan for the Billy Graham Library and how it would honor the work that had been done in the name of the Lord Jesus Christ. People would come from all over the world and would hear the Gospel.

My mother listened intently but still was unsure she wanted to be buried there. When the story broke that the family was divided on the issue of my parents' burial site, my father quickly stopped the flow of speculation and announced publicly that he and my mother would make the decision without influence from family or friends. My parents worked through this decision together.

Early in their marriage, my mother had always been grateful that my father let her choose where they would live since he would be traveling a great deal. It seemed only right that my father should choose where to be buried in death.

My mother had chosen to live in a little Presbyterian hamlet called Montreat, where her parents resided. For my mother, it was an ideal place to raise children and would allow her the privilege of being close to her mother and father, whom she needed with my father gone so much.

Before my mother became too weak to converse, I sat at her bedside and told her that I did not want a division in the family over this matter, nor did I want to come between her and my father. She always believed that children should honor and respect their father—and she never wavered.

"Mama, tell me, where do you want to be buried?" I asked.

With a satisfied resolve she answered, "Next to your father, of course!"

My parents arrived at their decision to be buried in Charlotte a few months before her death, but they had not announced it to anyone until two days before her death. Their decision had been put in writing and witnessed by their attorney, trusted associates, and their family physician, Dr. Rice.

All of us children considered Montreat home—that's where we grew up and where our parents remained—so it was only natural to think of them buried nearby. By the same token, my father had been raised in Charlotte and longed to return to his roots—even in death—with his wife by his side. I can understand why the decision upset some family members.

When my mother married my father and said "I do," nearly sixty-four years earlier, she aligned herself with the words from the book of

Ruth, for which she was named: "Wherever you go, I will go. . . .Where you die, I will die, and there will I be buried" (Ruth 1:16–17).

Several weeks later, she literally rested on that promise.

And When I Die

My mother thrived on having family and friends visit. In the last hours of her earthly life, I had hoped that Aunt Peggy's arrival from Dallas, Texas, would somehow revive her.

Aunt Peggy had lost her husband, my mother's only brother, Dr. Clayton Bell, a few years before, his life snuffed out by a massive heart attack. Uncle Clayton served as senior pastor of Highland Park Presbyterian Church in Dallas until his retirement. He, Aunt Peggy, and my mother had shared many wonderful times together.

My mother's older sister, Rosa Montgomery—a spry eighty-nine at the time—had come from Washington State months before to stay by my mother's side. She did Mother's errands and helped with her daily mail.

When Aunt Rosa was a young woman, she contracted tuberculosis and was sent to a sanatorium in Albuquerque, New Mexico, for treatment. My mother left college to be with her for months. Now Aunt Rosa was returning the favor and was invaluable to our family during this time. She was the only family member, other than my father, who was with my mother every day in her last six months of life.

Aunt Rosa sat at my mother's bedside and passed the days and nights reminiscing about their experiences in China, where she and Mama had solidified their foundational beliefs. Her presence, along with Aunt Peggy's, seemed to bring comfort to all of us as family stories were told.

From the time my mother was a young girl, she had a deep reverence for the Lord. Her great desire in life was to serve Jesus Christ so much that as a child of missionaries in China she prayed that she could become a martyr for the Lord, believing it would point people to the Savior. Her prayer was not answered in that way, but the Holy Spirit cultivated her servant heart to respond to others in need. Her anticipation in death was to see the Lord Jesus Christ in all of His glory. She wrote about this burning desire her whole life. This is the hope that all followers of Jesus Christ have in life—and in death.

My mother's bedroom was a wonderful place of reflection, sort of a walk-in curio filled with pictures, books, and an array of knickknacks. But the most memorable one hung from a rusty nail above her desk— a crown of thorns.

In the last days of life when Mama's pain intensified, she would ask to be turned toward the desk so that she could see the crown of thorns. Living a life of physical pain reminded her of the most excruciating pain endured by her Savior on the cross.

In the last hour of life on earth, my mother's eyes were alert—if not to all of us in the room, to something beyond our realm.

It was a particularly beautiful summer afternoon. The mountain breeze blew through the open windows, carrying inside the aroma from the flower boxes and the sound of chirping birds. My mother had always taken great pride in her flower gardens. I can still picture her down on hands and knees, working a root spade deep into the soil. From childhood she had a green thumb and enjoyed the fruits of her labor.

My father had gone to his room to rest and encouraged Aunt Rosa and Aunt Peggy to join Gigi, Anne, Bunny, Ned, and me as we circled my mother's bed. Holding her hands and stroking her brow, we wanted to believe she was looking into the faces of those who deeply loved her. I suspect, though, that her eyes were beyond the world she had known for years.

As her breathing became more labored, we called my father back into the room. Just as he walked to my mother's bed, their eyes met. She took her final breath as he squeezed her hand.

The day before, my father had heard Mama's last words when she looked at him and whispered, "I love you." He stroked her hand and whispered the same.

My mother began writing poetry as a child. Later in life, many of her poems were published. While my father heard the last words she spoke audibly, we will always treasure a poem she left for us, describing what she hoped death would be for her.

> And when I die
> I hope my soul ascends
> slowly, so that I
> may watch the earth receding
> out of sight,
> its vastness growing smaller as I rise,
> savoring its recession
> with delight.
> Anticipating joy
> is itself a joy.
> And joy unspeakable
> and full of glory
> needs more
> than "in the twinkling of an eye,"
> more than "in a moment,"*
> Lord, who am I to disagree?
> It's only we
> have much
> to leave behind;
> so much . . . Before,
> These moments
> of transition
> will, for me, be
> time to adore.[1]

---

* 1 Corinthians 15:52

I will always remember my mother's eyes filled with zest for life. But on this day her eyes were fixed with hope on something far greater—they were set on the Savior of her soul. Her spirit seemed to say that she was not missing one moment of her ascension from this world to occupy the joy of her heavenly home.

My mother did what most mothers do so masterfully: she comforted us even in death. On June 14, 2007, at 5:05 p.m., my mother closed her eyes on earth and opened them in heaven.

Mother of Pearl

The last ten years of my mother's life were physically challenging, but I have never watched anyone enjoy a challenge more than my mother. The radiance of her smile far outweighed the agony of pain.

When my schedule afforded me a weekend at home, I would make the ninety-mile drive on Sunday afternoons through the twisted mountain roads from my farmhouse in Boone, North Carolina, to Little Piney Cove. Nestled among the Carolina poplars and dogwood, it was a place of warmth and lighthearted fun for her children—even as adults—and a place of refuge for my father. Nothing warmed my mother's heart as much as gathering the family around her laughing fire.

Former first lady Barbara Bush, who was a close friend of my mother's, is remembered for wearing a string of pearls. Perhaps it is generational, but my mother loved pearls also. Even as her health faltered and she became bedridden, I could always tell when she anticipated my visit. Whether she was sitting in a wheelchair or propped up in bed, her engaging smile greeted me—and there she would be with pearls hanging from her neck. I think my heart would have slumped a little had I walked in and not seen what became a symbol of anticipation.

My mother's own sense of expectation was evident. In life she knew that the One who would someday call her home would never disappoint her. The Bible says, "Eye has not seen, nor ear heard . . . the things which God has prepared for those who love Him" (1 Corinthians 2:9).

I cannot help but envision my mother stepping onto the shores of heaven, placing her gnarled hand in the nail-pierced hand of her Savior, and hearing the long-awaited words: "Welcome home, My child."

China Pearl

When two thousand colleagues, friends, and neighbors joined our family to honor my mother's life, Aunt Rosa brought smiles and laughter into Anderson Auditorium in Montreat, where my mother's funeral service was held. She declared in her opening remarks, "Ruth and I were both made in China."

Something else made in China was discovered nearly four thousand years ago, according to ancient Chinese history. A delicate stone—appealing to the eye with its soft luster—was uncovered during a search for food on the ocean floor. This rare and precious jewel became known as the China pearl. The Chinese have been harvesting pearls ever since, boasting "the oldest pearl production tradition anywhere in the world" and also developing the first "cultured pearls, around AD 1082."[2]

When my father was a student at Wheaton College, he also discovered a China pearl. Her name was Ruth Bell. When they met, my father knew he had found a rare and precious jewel. Her unique childhood opened my father's eyes to a whole new world beyond the scope of his.

My mother passed on to me, as well as my siblings, her passion for harvesting something greater than China pearls. We shared her longing to see a great harvest of souls won to Christ's kingdom in the vast country of China and regions beyond.

Born to medical missionary parents in China 150 miles north of Shanghai, my mother remained thankful for her missionary roots, which added a splash of adventure to her childhood. Decades before,

Christianity had made very little impact in China, one of the world's oldest civilizations. But through the Lord's obedient servants, the truth of God's Word began to break down barriers, and the hearts of many Chinese men, women, and children were turned to the Lord.

In time, the church in China began to be persecuted, and missionaries like my grandparents, Dr. and Mrs. L. Nelson Bell, were forced to leave China before the United States entered World War II. They left behind a remnant that many believe today is fifty million to one hundred million strong. But with a swelling population of 1.3 billion, there is still a great spiritual darkness that envelops this mysterious culture.

As a young woman, my mother dreamed of serving the Lord in Tibet as a missionary. Though her life took a different turn after she met my father, her love for China never grew cold. After my parents married, my mother prayed that my father would have the opportunity to preach in what she considered her homeland. Some fifty years after leaving, the Lord answered that prayer. She returned to her beloved China alongside my father.

In 1988, I experienced the trip of a lifetime as I joined my parents on a visit to my mother's childhood home in Tsingkiangpu and Love and Mercy Hospital. I had grown up hearing all of the stories my mother and grandparents told. They seemed more like fantasy to me. To walk where my mother had played and where my grandfather had served as a medical doctor from 1916 until the beginning of the war was a dream come true for me.

While the Communist government would not allow my father to preach in stadiums or outdoor plazas, my mother's prayer had been answered when officials granted permission for my father to "lecture" in universities and preach within the walls of church buildings. In seventeen days, he covered two thousand miles across mainland China, sharing the Gospel.

My mother saw much of my father's ministry through his eyes, but on this memorable trip, he saw ministry through the eyes of my mother and comprehended much more the impact that China had made in her heart.

China is a fascinating land—its history rich in culture but sterile in true faith. I often wonder what pearls are yet to be cultivated in this land where faith in God is discouraged and, at times, the faithful are persecuted.

The Pearl of Great Price

My mother's pearls will always remind me of the parable our Lord told when he compared heaven to the pearl of great price (Matthew 13:45–46). So it seemed appropriate when Richard Bewes, retired rector of All Souls in London, England, and a dear friend to my parents, read the following passage from Malachi (the last book of the Old Testament) at my mother's graveside:

> Then those who feared the LORD spoke to one another,
> And the LORD listened and heard them;
> So a book of remembrance was written before Him
> For those who fear the LORD
> And who meditate on His name.
>
> "They shall be Mine," says the LORD of hosts,
> "On the day that *I make them My jewels.*" (Malachi 3:16–17)

I couldn't help but think of how my mother would have been comforted to hear Reverend Bewes's eloquent prayer:

Dear Lord, another of Your precious saints has been added to Your treasury of glory. On this Father's Day, all here are witnesses to this momentous event with holy angels of heaven as unseen witnesses around us.

In days to come, our Father, perhaps a hundred years from now, men, women, girls, and boys will come to this place where we are now gathered, speaking to one another in gratitude of things concerning Christ. Some perhaps seeking comfort, some seeking solace, others searching for meaning and inspiration. Some as pilgrims, some as wayfarers, buffeted by life's storms and perhaps representative of those many to whom Ruth, Your servant, ministered all of her life.

May it be that all who come will pause beside this graveside and hear Your voice speaking from the victorious testimony and life of Ruth Bell Graham, whose mortal remains we are about to commit to the ground. May many who visit this place have the joy of having their names added to Your book of remembrance so they themselves become a saved jewel purchased at Calvary of whom You can truly say, "They shall be Mine."

O God, we cannot tell You how much we are looking forward to that day when the stars shall fall from heaven, when the sun turns black as night, when the skies recede and vanish—and the Son of Man as the bright morning star returns to collect the lot of us. Fortify us for that day. Prepare us for that moment when we see the Lord in glory. We pray all these things for Your holy name's sake, amen.[3]

My father stood in silent reflection at the foot of my mother's casket. A cascade of cherished memories filled his thoughts. In a sentimental hush, he said his last goodbye to the woman who had loyally stood by his side, providing joy, comfort, and love.

Kissing a red rose, he feebly placed it on top of the lily blanket covering the pine chest that held his earthly treasure. My mother was laid to rest at the foot of a cross-shaped walkway in the prayer garden behind the Billy Graham Library. As my father concluded his brief comments, he said, "Perhaps the next time I'm here, I'll be reunited with Ruth in death."

While he was able to visit several times after, my father was eventually laid to rest in that beautiful setting—Mother at his side.

From Prison Bars to the Gates of Pearl

While visiting with my mother one day, I told about preaching at the Louisiana State Penitentiary known as "the Farm" in Angola. Many friends have shared with me how difficult it is to talk with parents about funeral plans, but since my mother leaned a bit unorthodox, I knew she would appreciate it when I said, "Mama, I bought you something."

She was in bed but managed to raise her head from the pillow.

"Oh, goody," she said. "What is it?"

"I bought you a casket made by murderers—men who have given their lives to Christ at Angola. I got one for Daddy too. It's made from simple pine plywood with a cross on top . . . you will love it!"

Mama grinned.

She wanted to know all about my visit to Angola. This eighteen-thousand-acre prison farm was named after the African country from which former slaves had come. I had been invited to preach to the inmates at this notorious site. In the late 1960s, Angola became known as "the bloodiest prison in the South" due to the number of inmate assaults.

My mother was particularly interested in this opportunity for the Gospel. She had always been drawn to those who were defeated in life by bad choices they had made. She knew that in Christ they could find true freedom beyond the iron bars that held them captive, if only they could hear the salvation message proclaimed.

Then I told about touring the prison with Burl Cain, the warden at the time, who had been responsible for a transformation among the Angola population. New Orleans Baptist Theological Seminary had placed an educational extension at the prison, providing a way for inmates who had been saved to earn a Bible degree during their incarceration. These men would then become chaplains behind "the wire."

My mother keenly listened. She had visited with prisoners throughout her life. In fact, during my father's 1977 crusade in Asheville, North Carolina, my mother persuaded me to go with her to prisons throughout western North Carolina and bring my close friend Dennis Agajanian—the fastest flat-pick guitarist, according to Johnny Cash. The county jail allowed us to go from cell to cell. The prisoners applauded as Dennis played. Then my mother would pray for each of them. Oftentimes she followed up on her visits with letters and books. Most of all, she loved hearing their stories of redemption.

In her poem titled "Prayer for the Murderer," she wrote,

I leave him in Your hands, O God, Who are both merciful and just.
Numb with the horror of this deed,
Its hideous stench, one surely must know how to pray.[4]

Warden Cain told me of one such man. Richard "Grasshopper" Liggett had been convicted for second-degree murder. He repented in prison, found salvation in Jesus Christ, and lived his last days as a resident of Angola.

The warden took me through Angola's museum, which held memorabilia telling the history of the famous prison camp. I asked him about a plywood casket sitting against the wall.

Warden Cain told me that when men entered the prison system with a life sentence, their wives would often visit the first few months, but within a year's time, they never returned. Mothers, on the other hand, were faithful visitors—until they became incapacitated or died. He said that it was not unusual for men to live in prison twenty years or longer without one visitor. Consequently, when prisoners died, their bodies would not be claimed; they would be buried on the prison farm in cardboard coffins—no dignity, no remembrance.

The warden told me how burdened he became about this situation. So he instructed the cabinet shop to begin making coffins. I followed him to a black hearse on display as he described a prison funeral.

"Franklin," he said, "one of the inmates nicknamed 'Bones' puts on a black top hat with a black New Orleans–style tuxedo with tails.

He and other inmates follow behind this black horse-drawn hearse, singing hymns in a slow, solemn march all the way to the graveyard. Scripture is read, and the deceased prisoner is buried with dignity."

My mother hung on to every word as I repeated the story. Then I told her what I had requested of the warden. If she had been with me that day, she would have beaten me to the punch.

"Warden, could your men build two of these caskets for my parents?"

He was speechless. When he realized that I was serious, he said, "Absolutely."

And the inmates wasted no time. Their work was done with precision—the finish impeccably tasteful with plain brass hinges, and a simple wooden cross nailed to the top. The names of the men who built the caskets were burned into the wood.

Less than two years later, Grasshopper was placed in one of the last coffins made by his own hands after losing a battle with cancer, thirty-one years into his life sentence.

My mother's eyes filled with tears. She had prayed for so many behind bars. She was deeply moved to know that her earthly vessel would be buried in a coffin made by the hands of prisoners whose hearts had been forgiven and guilt-ridden souls freed.

Mark Twain once said of his mother, "She had a slender, small body but a large heart—a heart so large that everybody's grief and everybody's joys found welcome in it and hospitable accommodation."[5]

That describes my mother as well. She was obedient to the scriptural instruction, "Remember the prisoners as if chained with them" (Hebrews 13:3).

Visiting with prisoners caused my mother to reflect on the Savior, who died on an old rugged cross between two thieves. He reached out to them as His hands were violently nailed to the cross. His love extended beyond their sin. In death, He offered them forgiveness. They represented the world for which He was about to die. One thief accepted His redemption, and the other rejected His sacrifice.

This is a picture of our world today: those who accept and those who reject.

In a sense, we are all thieves. We rob God of His glory when we reject His ultimate sacrifice—forgiveness, redemption, and salvation—wrapped in the greatest expression of His love: His outstretched arms drained of His life-giving blood.

My mother rejoiced to know that the prisoners at Angola had heard the Gospel truth and that many had come to know Him as their personal Savior.

The day of her funeral, I thought about all those who welcomed my mother in heaven: her parents, a sister, a brother, many in-laws, friends, Chinese converts through her father's own ministry, and "Grasshopper" Liggett. My mother would be the first to say that they were all prisoners set free by God's mercy and grace. In heaven, the Lord will see them all as His jewels, welcoming them, along with my mother and now my father, inside the gates of pearl.

"Now I saw a new heaven and a new earth. . . . The twelve gates were twelve pearls: each individual gate was of one pearl" (Revelation 21:1, 21).

Cultured Pearls

Everyone who experiences a mother's love and devotion eventually senses the void of her absence in death. I do, and I suppose I always will. Until the day my father died, he missed his own mother and longed to sit and talk with the woman we all called Mother Graham.

I could not fully comprehend this until weeks turned into months. The realization hit me: I will never again walk into my childhood home and see my mother sitting there with pearls of expectation. She masterfully lived out her role to her children and was always ready with a word of encouragement, a word of caution, and a thought from the Bible. Many times she spoke as a mother and a father (in his absence), representing my father's most heartfelt sentiments. We never doubted her words were from his heart.

A string of cultured memories brings my mother close in thought. Her devotion to my father was rare, particularly in today's society. Her goal was to be his helpmate, but my father called her his soul mate. And there is no doubt that she spent her life teaching her children to look at life through the eyes of our Father in heaven.

When the leadership of the BGEA was placed in my hands, my number one goal was to help my father finish well, and I could not have done that without my mother's wise counsel.

Finally Home

Sunrays glistened through the lush greenery that canopied my mother's final resting place on June 17, 2007. The earthly vessel she occupied now lies in the same rich soil that holds the spiritual roots of the man with whom she spent her life. Their souls rest in His presence.

The apostle Paul spoke of death with victorious hope:

Flesh and blood cannot inherit the kingdom of God. . . . We shall not all sleep, but we shall all be changed—in a moment, in the twinkling of an eye, at the last trumpet. For the trumpet will sound, and the dead will be raised incorruptible, and we shall be changed. . . .

"Death is swallowed up in victory." . . . Therefore, . . . be steadfast, immovable, always abounding in the work of the Lord, knowing that your labor is not in vain in the Lord. (1 Corinthians 15:50–52, 54, 58)

My mother slipped out of my reach, but her soul sailed into Glory. Heaven seems a bit closer to me now, and each rich memory is more precious than a China pearl.

3

The Bible Says . . .

Keep the words of this book.

—REVELATION 22:9

God "designed" the Bible to meet the needs of all people of all ages.
Discover the Bible for yourself.

BILLY GRAHAM

Google the phrase "the Bible says," and it will take you to places you probably don't want to go. Does that surprise you? It did me. It would take hours to go through the more than ten million entries. In just the first 150 entries, "the Bible says" something on issues from A to Z—according to just one of the mega search engines. The inexhaustible pop-ups reference everything from reality to the unimaginable. Catch an abbreviated glimpse about:

- What the Bible says about angels and demons
- What the Bible says about marriage and homosexuality
- What the Bible says about parenting and abortion
- What the Bible says about money and greed
- What the Bible says about software and blogging
- What the Bible says about midterms and illiteracy
- What the Bible says about meteors and zoology

An interesting observation is that the majority of entries focus on issue-oriented topics instead of what the Bible actually says. Few entries mention God, whose very Word *is* the Bible. The Bible is the inspired, spoken, and unchangeable Word of the living God. Yet if a person took time to search through the A to Z accounts, they would come up empty on truth. Why? Because these entries document people's viewpoints about what they think the Bible says, not what the Bible actually says.

Anyone who has ever listened to my father's sermons or interviews has heard him say with assurance, "The Bible says . . ." He was well known for preaching sermons that were filled with Scripture passages and verses spoken directly from the Word of God.

In the last years of his ministry, my father often spoke about the information explosion, yet there are many today who know less about God's Word than ever before. The Bible says that in the last days, men who have a "form of godliness" but deny the power of God's Word will be "always learning and never able to come to the knowledge of the truth" (2 Timothy 3:5, 7).

This is where we get into trouble—listening to what others say instead of what God says. Even more appalling about an Internet search of "the Bible says" is the lack of entries as to what the Bible says about Jesus Christ, what the Bible says about sin, or what the Bible says about living our lives in obedience to Him.

My father encouraged people to explore the Bible's authenticity. To do that, we must go to the Source—what God says about Himself in the Bible. Without understanding this basic truth, we have no foundation. What does God say about Himself, and what does God say about His Word—the Bible?

Man's opinion, at best, wavers. The Word of God is authentic, bona fide, and genuine. My father once said, "God's spoken Word [the Bible] has survived every scratch of the human pen."[1]

Let your fingers walk through the Internet, and you can see what bloggers are saying to whoever wants to read, listen, or respond in the blogosphere. Some bloggers ask, "How do we know what the Bible says?" Others key in what the Bible doesn't say. That will link you to the skeptic blogger who exclaims, "I don't care what the Bible says!" If you scroll down another page or two, you'll find the one who protests, "Who cares what the Bible says?"

A friend of mine went online and typed in the response: "God cares." It was a way of introducing into the thought process the One who speaks from the pages of the Bible, "So shall My word be that goes forth from My mouth; it shall not return to Me void, but it shall accomplish what I please, and it shall prosper in the thing for which I sent it" (Isaiah 55:11).

God's Word did go forth when He sent His only Son two thousand years ago into a darkened world to save mere man from his miserable sin. And His Word did not return void. After Christ's death on the cross and His resurrection from the dead, He ascended to His Father, and the Savior of the world presented to His Father in heaven the redeemed (Revelation 5:9).

Today, His Word is still going forth and snatching men from the clutches of the "sinnersphere." God did not speak forgiveness and redemption into cyberspace. He dipped His finger into the shed blood from His precious Son and wrote on the hearts of His creation: *I love you.*

The apostle Paul told Christ's followers that their lives reflect the power of His Word in their transformed hearts.

The Bible doesn't just *contain* God's Word—the Bible *is* God's Word. His mercy, grace, and love were demonstrated to mankind when He sent His Son from heaven to communicate the infallible Word of the living God through the ultimate sacrifice on the cross.

During a CNN interview, my father said, "This is the book of the ages. The Old Testament looks forward to [Christ]. The New Testament looks back to [Christ], but the center of the scriptures is Christ."[2]

God's Word enlightens the minds and hearts of those who follow Him. From the Old Testament to the New Testament, from Genesis (which means "beginning") to Revelation (which means "divine disclosure"), the Bible says:

- "In the beginning God created the heavens and the earth" (Genesis 1:1).

- "In the beginning was the Word, and the Word was with God, and the Word was God. He was in the beginning with God" (John 1:1–2).

- "And the Word became flesh and dwelt among us, and we beheld His glory, the glory as of the only begotten of the Father, full of grace and truth" (John 1:14).

- "Blessed is he who keeps the words of the prophecy of this book" (Revelation 22:7).

The Conclusion: The Bible Is the Word of God.

Webster's Dictionary defines the Bible as "the sacred scriptures of Christians comprising the Old Testament and the New Testament . . . a publication that is preeminent especially in authoritativeness."[3]

But God does not define the Bible as a publication or as being for only the Christian. Jesus said, "These are the Scriptures that testify about me" (John 5:39 NIV). The Bible was intended to convict the unrepentant heart as much as it was written to instruct those who have repented.

The Word of God is intended for the whole world, as we see in the writings of the apostle Paul, who said the Scriptures are "made known through the prophetic writings by the command of the eternal God, so that all nations might believe and obey him . . . through Jesus Christ" (Romans 16:26–27 NIV).

Notice what God says about His Word: "This Book of the Law shall not depart from your mouth, but you shall meditate in it day and night, that you may observe to do according to all that is written in it" (Joshua 1:8).

The apostle James, the leader of the church in Jerusalem, said, "Be doers of the word, and not hearers only" (James 1:22).

God's Word existed before the beginning of time and will live forever. As the psalmist declared, "Forever, O LORD, Your word is settled in heaven" (Psalm 119:89).

It's Not What I Think

As a young preacher in the 1940s, my father was challenged by Charles Templeton, a popular Christian evangelist-turned-agnostic and close friend at the time, to question the reliability of God's Word. My father has told the story many times. He was at Forest Home Conference Grounds in the San Bernardino Mountains of California and took a walk one moonlit night in the woods, Bible in hand. He placed the Bible on a tree stump and said, "O God! There are many things in this Book I do not understand. I can't answer some of the philosophical and psychological questions Chuck and others are raising, but Father,

I am going to accept this as Thy Word—by faith! I'm going to allow faith to go beyond my intellectual questions and doubts, and I will believe this to be Your inspired Word."[4]

The Bible says, "All Scripture is given by inspiration of God, and is profitable for doctrine, for reproof, for correction, for instruction in righteousness, that the man of God may be complete, thoroughly equipped for every good work" (2 Timothy 3:16–17).

My father settled it that day. He would stand firm, by faith, on what the Bible says.

Over seven decades, my father was interviewed by radio, television, and newspaper personalities. He always felt that it was God who opened the doors to communicate the truth of the Gospel across the airwaves—the highest forms of communication technology at the time. While the media had no intention of giving him a platform for the Gospel, he knew that the Lord would put the words in his mouth to draw the public's attention to the person of Jesus Christ.

Inquiring minds wanted to know what Billy Graham thought about political issues, problems of the human race, and anything else that made headlines. Early in his ministry, my father made it clear that it mattered not what he thought but rather what God thinks. In time, Billy Graham's name became synonymous with the phrase "The Bible says . . ." because as he preached, he always quoted from God's Word.

The Bible Says . . . to All Generations

"When we preach or teach the Scriptures," my father often said, "we open the door for the Holy Spirit to do His work. God has not promised to bless oratory or clever preaching. He has promised to bless His Word, regardless of the culture."

My father learned this throughout his ministry. The decade of the sixties ushered in perhaps the most turbulent period on American soil in the twentieth century. Racial tension rocked US cities. Vietnam

War protestors burned draft cards and Old Glory (the American flag). Civil unrest permeated the country from north to south, east to west. Parents who had been children during the Great Depression now parented the baby boomer generation.

University campuses housed youthful rebels defying parental and government establishments. The hippie culture emerged to flaunt its free love theory in rebellious festivals from Frisco Bay to Woodstock. Society was marked with troubled disorder that today is credited for bringing a shift in the fabric of our foundational beliefs in the political arena, the home front, and the church. Its effects are still seen today.

In the seventies, we sighed with a bit of relief as the sixties' revolt ebbed—or so we thought. Years of rebellious behavior reared its head as the boomers carried into their adult world outspoken immorality and defiance to anything conventional. This seemed to shake the bedrock of our culture.

The morality and ethics of young America had been shaped by biblical standards. Yet the political correctness that emerged hurled our nation into a different realm than what previous generations would have thought possible. Freedom of speech became the highest priority of our society.

Higher technology had sprinted onto the scene and taken root. American living rooms were bombarded with sordid pictures that displayed the gruesome reality of sin blinking like neon through television. What shocked most Americans then now pales, as around-the-clock news flashes every form of debasement known to man.

Amid this cultural and moral turmoil, my father was invited to appear on numerous talk shows. One such popular program was *The Woody Allen Special*. The interview took place in front of a live studio audience. This forum blazed new trails as "anything goes" came into our homes—the YouTube of the day.

Woody Allen, the famed Hollywood actor and comedian known for his lack of scruples, introduced my father to the viewers: "Whether you agree with his point of view or not on things, he's always extremely interesting to talk to. I don't agree with him on a great many subjects— there are a few we do agree on."

My father responded with a smile: "It's very nice to be with you, Woody, and I would like to say that there are some things I don't agree with you on."

Woody seemed surprised at my father's candidness as the audience reacted. After sparring with my father a moment or two, Woody continued, "The question is, which one of us will be converted? I hope I can convert you to agnosticism by the time the show is over."

"Well," my father said with a cordial resolve, "I have had a lot of people try, and the more they try, the firmer I get in my conviction."

With head cocked, Woody suggested they take a question from the audience, while he contemplated my father's response.

"Mr. Graham," the young man asked, "I read that you don't believe in premarital sexual relations. Is that true?" The audience snickered, thinking the question would make my father uncomfortable.

With compassion in his eyes, my father responded, "It's not a matter of what I believe; it's what the Bible says."

The audience grew quiet. Perhaps they had never heard what the Bible said on the subject. Perhaps they had only heard what a preacher, or teacher, or parent said on the matter. My father introduced the young audience to God's Word as he continued. "The Bible teaches that premarital sexual relations are wrong. . . . God has laid down certain rules . . . for our own good, to protect our bodies and our minds from harm. . . . He expects [us] to live up to a standard that He has made, and if you don't live up to it, then the Bible says that you are falling short and that's when you need God's help for redemption."[5]

The Bible says, "Flee sexual immorality. Every sin that a man does is outside the body, but he who commits sexual immorality sins against his own body" (1 Corinthians 6:18).

My father often said, "I have found that most young people really want us to spell out a moral code. They may not accept it or believe it, but they want to hear it, clearly and without compromise."

God Speaks Through the Bible

When the Bible speaks, God speaks. When my father declared, "The Bible says," no one argued.

Whenever my father was asked why the Bible was so important to him, he would often say, "God speaks from heaven through the Bible. This is why I use the phrase 'the Bible says.' I would not have the authority to say what I do in sermons unless it was based upon the Word of God. He has spoken in such a way that men and women are without excuse if they do not hear and understand."

Through the years, I have learned from my father to take every opportunity to make this same proclamation because I have observed the power that the Bible has—even to those who may not believe. I also learned that when my father failed to answer a question based on God's Word, he lived in regret until he could repair the damage done. Like him, I regret the times when I have attempted to answer questions apart from God's Word.

What I have learned through my heavenly Father is this: if people rebel against God's Word, God will deal with them. If we as Christians fail to speak God's Word, He will take it up with us. May every Christian be able to say with Jesus, "I have given them Your word" (John 17:14).

Jesus said, "Whatever I speak, just as the Father has told Me, so I speak" (John 12:50). The Bible says that God's Word is not to be compromised.

The more culturally sensitive we become, the easier it is to make concessions. And we see it happening as technology is overtaking society. Go into a restaurant or airport, and you'll see travelers checking e-mail, working on their laptops, or walking in rhythm to whatever is blasting through their iPods and smartphones. The information age may be filled with boundless high-tech possibilities, but it will never reach the height or depth or breadth of God's wisdom and salvation that He is willing to impart to an imperfect people.

We may hit the Escape button and think our sin will disappear into eternity, never to confront us again—but eternity belongs to God, and His Word is eternal. One day we will stand before Him and recall His words: "Heaven and earth will pass away, but My words will by no means pass away" (Matthew 24:35).

My prayer is that you will hit the Pause button and contemplate just what the Bible says. "For the word of God is living and powerful, and sharper than any two-edged sword, piercing even to the division of soul and spirit . . . and is a discerner of the thoughts and intents of the heart" (Hebrews 4:12).

The Bible Reveals . . .

A friend of mine, the late David Lee Hill, inscribed the following words in a Bible he gave me as a teenager:

The Bible reveals the mind of God,
the state of man, the way of salvation, the doom of sinners,
the happiness of believers.
Its doctrines are holy, its precepts binding, its histories are true,
its decisions are immutable.
Read it to be wise, believe it to be safe, and practice it to be holy.
It contains light to direct you, food to support you, and comfort to
cheer you.
It is the traveler's map, the pilgrim's staff, the pilot's compass,
the soldier's sword, and the Christian's character.
Here paradise is restored, heaven opened, and the gates of hell
disclosed.

Christ is its grand object, our good is its design, the glory of God
    its end.

It should fill your memory, rule the heart and guide the feet.

Read it slowly, frequently, and prayerfully.

It is given in life, will be opened in the judgment,

and will be remembered forever.

It involves the highest responsibility, will reward the greatest labor,

and will condemn all those who trifle with its sacred contents.[6]

The sacred Word of God has been trifled with throughout history.
You only have to read the first three chapters of the Bible to see how
Satan added to God's Word:

And the LORD God commanded the man [Adam], saying, "Of every
tree of the garden you may freely eat; but of the tree of the knowledge
of good and evil you shall not eat, for in the day that you eat of it you
shall surely die." . . .

Now the serpent was more cunning than any beast of the field
which the LORD God had made. And he said to the woman, "Has God
indeed said, 'You shall not eat of every tree of the garden'?"

And the woman said to the serpent, "We may eat the fruit of the
trees of the garden; but of the fruit of the tree which is in the midst of
the garden, God has said, 'You shall not eat it, nor shall you touch it,
lest you die.'"

Then the serpent said to the woman, "You will not surely die. For
God knows that in the day you eat of it your eyes will be opened, and
you will be like God, knowing good and evil." (Genesis 2:16–17; 3:1–5)

This is the account of man's disastrous fall. The apostle John iden-
tifies the serpent as Satan: "The great dragon was cast out, that serpent
of old, called the Devil and Satan, who deceives the whole world"
(Revelation 12:9).

Satan slithers onto the first pages of the Bible, coiled in masterful deception. His cunning temptations continue to pull mankind into the depths of degradation.

Eve slipped into a slimy trench when she spoke to the serpent. Satan knows how to twist and corrupt the Word of God in our minds. When we turn our listening ear to Satan's hiss, we stroke his massive ego, and the devil wins the battle. We join in this corruption by entertaining his viewpoint.

The Bible says, "He who sows to his flesh will of the flesh reap corruption, but he who sows to the Spirit will of the Spirit reap everlasting life" (Galatians 6:8). So Satan gripped Eve's heart with his enticing interpretation of God's message. She did not stop to consider his lie—she listened, and then she believed. Satan added to God's Word by implying that if she ate of the fruit, she would be like God. In essence he was saying to her, what's so bad about that?

Many ask, how could Eve have disobeyed God? The answer is obvious. She did what we have all done at times—grabbed hold of Satan's lie instead of clinging to God's truth. So Eve ate, the serpent struck, and mankind fell.

Thousands of years later, Satan is still up to his devious sport. His playbook is cloaked in allurement hard to resist. "To do evil is like sport to a fool" (Proverbs 10:23). "Satan himself transforms himself into an angel of light" (2 Corinthians 11:14). That's what the Bible says.

- Satan dangles some "angel dust" (cocaine) or alcohol in front of a teenager and tells him he'll forget all his troubles.
- The devil whispers to a young girl that she can turn the boys' heads if she flaunts her body.
- The great deceiver convinces parents to refrain from correcting their children to win favor with them.
- Kids want to be popular with their friends, so they go along with the crowd.

- Adults want to be seen as tolerant, so they excuse the ills of society, blaming bad behavior on circumstances.

The spiral downward may start with Satan's temptation, but the result depends on our response. If we look and listen, we'll follow and fall.

My father once said, "Man cannot control himself, and if he will not be controlled by Jesus Christ, then he will be controlled by Satan. Temptation is not a sin; it is the yielding that is sin."

The Bible says, "Each one is tempted when he is drawn away by his own desires and enticed. Then, when desire has conceived, it gives birth to sin; and sin, when it is full-grown, brings forth death. Do not be deceived" (James 1:14–16).

Satan's objective is to convince us to go against what God says. And oh, is he convincing. After all, he persuaded a third of the angelic host to join his rebellion against God (Revelation 12:4). When Satan convinces our minds that God is prohibiting our pleasure, our wills often rebel and submit to the wrong message. God will empower us to put Satan on notice and turn our hearts to the One who saves. "Submit to God. Resist the devil and he will flee from you" (James 4:7).

Remember, Satan believes that the name of Jesus carries greater power than he and his demon band together will ever possess—he just doesn't want us to know it.

The work of Satan is somewhat of a mystery. But God has given men free will to choose good or evil. We can accept or reject God's salvation, but the Bible says that it is God's desire that all men be saved.

What Do You Believe In?

Believing is crucial to the faith in Jesus Christ that brings repentance and salvation to all who accept Him. Satan certainly believes in God's glory. He lived in it, but he wanted it for his very own (Isaiah 14:13).

Satan also believes in Jesus' power and tried to persuade Him to lay it down. In the Gospel of Matthew we read, "The devil took Him up on an exceedingly high mountain, and showed Him all the kingdoms of the world and their glory. And he said to Him, 'All these things I will give You if You will fall down and worship me.' Then Jesus said to him, 'Away with you, Satan! For it is written, "You shall worship the Lord your God, and Him only you shall serve"'" (4:8–10).

Believing in the existence of someone is different from believing *in* someone. Voltaire, the French author and philosopher born in 1694, said that he disbelieved in God yet tried all his life to find Him.[7] When speaking of faith in God, my father often said, "I can believe that a simple chair can hold my weight, but it is not until I commit myself to that chair by sitting down in it that I show by faith that it can hold me up." This is what we do when we say we believe in God. We are willing to commit ourselves to Him.

Have you ever looked up the little two-letter word *in*? The dictionary says it is "a function word to indicate inclusion or position; to enter a destination or to incorporate; to be in one's presence, possession, power or control; from a condition of indistinguishability to one of clarity."[8]

To say that we believe in Christ is to say that we are in Christ—that is our position. We are in His presence, possession, power, and control.

To believe *in* Jesus is to accept Him as genuine, to acknowledge His ability to do what He says He will do. A commitment to Jesus Christ, then, is made on the basis of the evidence of His Word firmly planted in faith. With no reservations, we immerse ourselves in Him and let Him live *in* and through us. We hand ourselves over to the only One who saves, the only One who forgives sin, the only One who transforms lives, and the only One who will judge righteously. It also means that believing in the righteousness of God will make man holy—to become more like Him in our thinking and in our living because we are clothed in His righteousness.

When Satan was cast out of heaven, he set his sights on taking multitudes with him to hell. Do you believe in Jesus Christ as Satan does? Or do you believe in Christ to the point of obeying His Word—to walk as Jesus walked? The proper belief will effect change in the human heart. The Bible says, "Let everyone who names the name of Christ depart from iniquity" (2 Timothy 2:19).

The Way

Not only is Satan's handiwork powerful in destroying our personal lives, but it is potently destructive when it comes to the most precious relationship Christ has with His church.

The Bible says that there is only one true church, and it is the very body of Christ. It does not embody a collection of belief systems, a conglomerate of denominations, or buildings scattered among the nations. The church of Jesus Christ is made up of people who believe in Him, put their sole trust in only Him, and follow Him according to His Word alone.

I have learned from my father's own example how important it is to identify and work with local Bible-believing churches. Our crusades would not be possible without their partnership. It is the greatest strength of our ministry because God empowers His people. These are the saints in Christ, collectively known as the bride of Christ—His beloved church.

It is important to keep in mind that while we may hold membership within a particular denomination, that does not make us part of Christ's church. There are many church members who say they believe the Bible but do not do what it says. There are many church members worshipping statues and praying to the dead. There are those in church who observe the writings of men, thinking they can work their way to heaven.

Those living in Christ will not do these things. Why? Jesus preached against unbelief (Mark 6:6). Jesus preached that we must worship only

Him (John 4:24) and pray only to our Father in heaven (Matthew 6:9). Jesus preached that we are to abide only in His Word (John 15:7).

These were the teachings of the early church preached by the apostles. Appropriately, the church was called "the Way" (Acts 19:9, 23), and this is the church to which all true followers of Jesus Christ belong to this day (unrelated to the denomination by this name).

Actions can reveal someone as a genuine follower of Christ or a fraud. The Bible says, "You will know them by their fruits" (Matthew 7:16). My father said often, "Many Christians who profess Christ do not live as though they possess Him."

In the apostle Paul's day, people saw the transformation that had taken place in his life after the encounter with the Lord on the road to Damascus. His powerful testimony of what Christ had done in his life was riveting. During his trial before Governor Felix, Paul said, "I admit that I worship the God of our fathers as a follower of the Way" (Acts 24:14 NIV).

God sent His Son to point the way to His creation—lost and headed down all kinds of religious paths except the right one. Notice that Paul said he was a follower of "the Way." We can be members of a civic club and never attend; we are members in name only. We can be members of a church and fill a pew, but we are members in name only. What makes us true members of Christ's church is repenting of sin, receiving Jesus Christ as Savior, and following Him as Lord.

Before I was born, my father was in South Korea, preaching to the troops during the Korean War. Like him, I have had the opportunity to visit military bases and naval ships and preach the Gospel. Men and women who serve in the United States military take the oath, wear the uniform, follow orders, are deployed on command, and are committed to giving their lives, if necessary, to protect their country. Why should those who belong to the body of Christ do less?

There is much confusion today about which organized religious institution accurately represents the first church. Many claim that the church was stifled after the days of the apostles and emerged in 1517 at the time of the Reformation. But Christ would never have allowed His church to lie dormant for centuries.

God said His truth endures to all generations (Psalm 100:5). Jesus said that His church would prevail (Matthew 16:18). Paul admonished the church to remain alert and sanctified until the day it is snatched out of this world (1 Thessalonians 5:6).

The apostles warned against the vicious attempts many would make to disorient "the Way," causing others to question the true church of the living God. Belief in what the Bible says is vital to foundational truth about the church—those who follow Christ.

There are many Bible verses that speak of believing. For example, "You believe that there is one God. You do well. Even the demons believe—and tremble!" (James 2:19).

In a world that flirts with tolerance, various denominations have begun leaning to the way of the world so that the world will accept the church. Satan has turned the tables. The true church is to be separate from the world, not indistinguishable. This is Satan's tactic: to confuse the minds of men, especially when it comes to God's most precious relationship—His church.

Sin Is the Common Thread

We are living in the age where ecumenicalism (another word for liberalism or the emerging church) has gained strength in evangelical circles. Matters of faith in Jesus Christ must align with what the Bible says, not with what the world says.

Mankind never tires of searching for answers. From the beginning, man's desire to know God has prevailed. We ask questions, but we must be open to the only Voice that deserves our listening ear. Men are bound by one common thread, and it is found in what the Bible says: "For *all* have sinned and fall short of the glory of God"

(Romans 3:23). But "God our Savior . . . desires all men to be saved and to come to the knowledge of the truth. For there is one God and one Mediator between God and men, the Man Christ Jesus, who gave Himself a ransom for all" (1 Timothy 2:3–6).

Jesus Christ is the only One in all of history who sacrificed His blood for our redemption. He is the only One with the power to die in our place and to raise Himself from the dead to offer eternal life.

Satan knows God is real, yet it hasn't changed his efforts to alter God's Word. Others down through the ages have tried to stamp it out. Voltaire, who died in 1778, famously claimed, "One hundred years from now, there will be no Bibles. I have gone through the forests and I have cut down all the trees of revelation."[9]

History records that the very room in which he spoke those words now serves as a center from which Bibles are distributed all over the world. In 1932, all of Voltaire's works were gathered and sold for eleven cents. In the same year, one manuscript of the Word of God sold for $500,000.[10]

"O God . . . Your enemies roar in the midst. . . . They seem like men who lift up axes among the thick trees" (Psalm 74:1, 4–5).

Agnostic Robert Ingersoll, a nineteenth-century American political speechwriter who became known as the American Voltaire, vowed, "I am going to put the Bible out of business."[11] The Internet Public Library some years ago roughly estimated six billion copies of the Bible had been printed in more than two thousand languages and dialects, saying, "It is by far the best-selling book of all time."[12]

The Bible says, "He who despises the word will be destroyed" (Proverbs 13:13). And "at the name of Jesus every knee should bow . . . and that every tongue should confess that Jesus Christ is Lord" (Philippians 2:10–11).

My father confessed around the world that Jesus Christ is Lord and looked forward to the day he would bow before Him.

In the last years of life, my father suffered macular degeneration, as did my mother, and Bible reading became difficult. But they never stopped praising the Lord with their lips and often reflected on how grateful they were that they had committed multiple Scripture passages to memory.

My father once said, "The Word of God hidden in the heart is a stubborn voice to suppress."

We all will be held responsible for what we do with God's Word. He speaks today from ages past. At times, He speaks through His Word with a still, small voice to guide and comfort. In unsuspecting moments He pours forth His love through discipline in order to keep His church strong and effective. This is a vital component in winning souls for Christ.

Through the course of life, I have attended flight schools to learn how to pilot various aircraft, each having its own pilot operating manual. A pilot cannot fly a jet by following the manual for a single-engine airplane. My father illustrated this point by saying, "God has given us an operation manual—the Bible—that instructs us how to live in obedience to Jesus Christ."

The Word of God is the all-knowing authority, the standard-bearer, and the all-sufficient guidance counselor. In His Word we have the fullness of Christ Jesus, who said, "You are mistaken, not knowing the Scriptures nor the power of God" (Matthew 22:29).

My father often stated that he regretted not spending more time studying Scripture. I would say that every follower of Jesus Christ would feel the same. But hearing this from a preacher who faithfully preached God's Word should compel all who follow to thirst for a deeper understanding of Jesus Christ.

As I look back over my life, I am thankful to God for parents who believed the Bible, taught the Bible, preached the Bible, and lived the Bible. I have comfort in knowing that my feet are planted in the foundational truths of God's Word.

God has given us this speakable treasure. It is possible to read God's

Word with understanding about His love, His forgiveness, and how He wants us to live. All we have to do is blow the dust off the cover, open the Bible, and let the Holy Spirit sweep into our hearts the words that speak of Him.

The apostles and saints have lived these truths, and many died for them so that the preaching of God's Word would go on, just as the Bible says.

4

For Those Watching by Television

Be glad and rejoice forever in what I create.

—Isaiah 65:18

I am greatly helped in reaching the audience by radio and television.

BILLY GRAHAM

What a vision: A living room with wall-to-wall people. Some sitting on chairs, way too many squeezed onto the sofa, children sitting on Grandma and Grandpa's laps, and teenagers cross-legged on the floor. The room is filled with anticipation and dozens of eyes fixed to a screen filled with static, while someone fiddles with the wire rabbit ears sitting on top of the highly polished cabinet. The year was 1948.

This was the only television in the neighborhood, and the proud owners had invited their friends to join them for an evening with "Mr. Television," Milton Berle. For one hour every week, this new form of entertainment gave people reason to laugh and lose touch with life's problems and responsibilities.

Berle's sway with the audience was so commanding that young parents made sure their children heard his sign-off, when he would say to the little ones, "Listen to your Uncle Miltie and go to bed." And they would! His power was not only with the young. Milton Berle was credited with the spike in TV sets sold—two million in 1949.[1]

Television's influence enhanced society's appetite for leisure and amusement, forming a union that became the center of nearly every household. It eventually became a babysitter for children and a companion to adults.

Billy Graham watched with interest the power of television's golden age, never realizing that this scene would be repeated throughout his seventy-year ministry and continue when a twentieth-century invention would carry God's message into the twenty-first century, transforming souls of men, women, and children.

A farm boy named Philo T. Farnsworth conceived the basic operating principles of electronic television. He is credited with effecting change so profound and far-reaching that we're still incapable of knowing the half of it.[2] The term *television* is a hybrid word first coined in the early twentieth century by Russian Constantin Perskyi at the International World's Fair in Paris.[3] *Tele*, meaning "far" (in Greek), and *vision*, meaning "sight" (in Latin), seemed to be the best identifier for transmitting moving and talking images into the privacy of homes around the world.

Today we no longer have to sit in our living rooms to watch the "talking box." Family automobiles are equipped with DVD players, and we can transform our phones into video players by a stroke on the keypad. This entertainment icon has been a far-reaching medium for the past seventy years. In fact, *USA Today* reported in 2006 that "the average American home now has more television sets than people."[4]

Televising, Evangelizing

While television has monopolized the entertainment market since the mid-1950s, it has also revolutionized the outreach of the church.

Prior to radio and television, fulfilling the Great Commission depended on footsteps—missionaries and itinerant preachers who would go to the darkest corners of the earth. These efforts found aid through this invention called television, a wonderful new communication tool.

It was the dawn of a new day for preaching the Gospel. God had been moving deep in the heart of a young man known at the time as Billy Frank.

My father's source of entertainment as a boy was on the ball field. He had grand visions of slamming a home-run ball into the stands at New York's Yankee Stadium. But God had a *far* different *vision* for him. You might say that God's vision is both nearsighted and farsighted: near enough to plant a longing for God in man's heart and far enough to stretch a ministry around the world.

God has precision vision. He knows exactly what man needs, and He stands ready to meet that need. With the coming population explosion, God was harrowing out a method for His people to spread His Word to the masses.

Less than ten years after television became the focal point in living rooms, it also became a means for evangelism. Television is to entertainment what the pulpit is to preachers—a platform for communication.

The Hour of Decision

My father discovered how television could enhance his vision to preach to the nations. He had already been effectively using radio as a means for broadcasting the Gospel when he launched *Hour of Decision*, a program that Walter Bennett and Fred Dienert had persuaded him to try. With the program's popularity, my father and his friend and colleague Cliff Barrows launched a television program in 1951, but they found taping a weekly program draining and unrealistic for their ministry schedule.

However, in 1957, a dear friend of my father's, Charles Crutchfield from Charlotte, encouraged my father to televise the crusade at Madison Square Garden. The idea intrigued him. Would people watch a religious program in prime time? The competition was highly charged. After all, television was designed for the purpose of entertainment—and the news.

The news? That was the answer. Of course! Why not use television to spread some Good News? It was a huge and risky step, but my father was compelled to investigate the possibilities.

Struggling with the pros and the cons, my father and his team petitioned the Lord for direction. The pros were obvious—the potential of the Gospel being heard by millions; the cons were a contrary hurdle—$50,000 a week for airtime in 1957.

My father had been a teenager during the Great Depression. He knew what a hard-earned dollar meant to most. He also had to consider how his supporters, donors to the ministry, would feel about such expenditure. Television was still rather new to the public, and few realized the enormous cost of airtime. But people persisted, urging, "Billy, you've got to go on television."

Leonard Goldenson of American Broadcasting Corporation (ABC) had been instrumental in helping the *Hour of Decision* hit the airwaves through radio. He indicated an interest in televising the crusade over four weeks, every Saturday night.

After consulting with a multitude of people—team members, donors, and television executives—my father felt in his heart that God was moving him forward.

Lights, Camera, Action

Walking through the door of faith on June 1, 1957, my father stepped onto the platform at Madison Square Garden, and ABC aired the *Hour of Decision with Billy Graham* live from New York.

To everyone's astonishment, when the ratings came in, an ABC executive stated that "approximately 6.5 million viewers watched Dr. Graham, enough to fill Madison Square Garden to capacity every day for a whole year."[5]

Interest grew, and excitement surged as Americans looked forward to tuning into the telecast each week. It was especially surprising to ABC. They had not enjoyed strong ratings because the prime-time slot was up against the two most popular weekend variety shows: *The Perry Como Show* and *The Jackie Gleason Show*. The crusade was extended seven weeks and culminated with a huge crowd gathered at Yankee Stadium on July 20.

In 1930, when a farm boy won a patent for his electronic TV and was hailed a "boy genius,"[6] God was preparing another farm boy to preach to the nations twenty-seven years later using that very invention.

My father was not accustomed to the bright lights. He took every precaution to prevent getting caught up in the thrill of what television could do to those who appeared on screen. Stepping to the podium at the Garden, he said, "We've not come to put on a show or entertainment. We believe that there are many people who have hungry hearts. You can find everything you have been searching for in Jesus Christ."

What I have learned from watching my father on television is that he had a way of connecting with hearts beyond the stark lights and probing cameras. No matter how intense the spotlight, he zeroed in on God's message. Like a laser beam, he pointed others to the cross.

When it came time for the invitation to accept Jesus Christ as Lord, it was not only to those inside the stadium. As hundreds streamed down to the platform, my father turned his piercing eyes to a camera stage right and said, "For those watching by television . . . if you feel a tug at your heart, if you hear a small voice calling to you, don't ignore it. That is the voice of God calling your name to come to Him."

He peered into the camera as though sending through the airwaves a plea to aching souls he could not see, nevertheless bidding them to the foot of the cross.

The result? Souls won for Christ. Not just in New York City, and not just in New York State, but all over the country. It was the precursor to what would become the cornerstone of my father's evangelistic ministry—crusade telecasts that would someday reach beyond the shores of North America.

Following the meetings, the *Wall Street Journal* reported that Bible sales were up dramatically in New York during the crusade.[7] Pastors reported that they were seeing new members come into their churches as a result of salvation decisions made during the telecast. My father's heart overflowed, and he thanked God for multiplying the vision and the donor dollar to strengthen Bible-believing churches with new converts to Jesus Christ.

Bat or Bible?

Through television, my father began to understand the power of the airwaves. But he and his team never realized that this avenue would lead the way in evangelizing those who may never darken the door of any church or perhaps reach others who would never consider sitting in a sports complex to listen to a preacher.

My father never fulfilled his dream to play baseball at Yankee Stadium. He exchanged a baseball bat for the Word of God, and his childhood fantasy for God's vision. God did what no one could have ever imagined—He sent a farm boy to a baseball stadium in New York

City to preach God's Word to thousands in the stands and those watching by television. This is the true work of God in one's life, exchanging our desire for His.

Clicking to Jesus

Who doesn't love the handy little companion to the television called the remote control? My children do not remember the days of hassling with the TV antenna or having to get up to turn the channel. Instead, they just sit back in their easy chairs and click from channel to channel.

I am always amazed to see how God uses the smallest of inventions in the hands of unlikely souls searching for something new. It doesn't matter where I go in the world, the testimonies I hear are innumerable. It is not unusual for people to start off by saying, "I was clicking around on the TV and saw your dad preaching."

This happened when I was preaching a crusade in Panama. I was introduced to a man who was part of our musical platform that week. I learned that Luis Conte, a Cuban refugee to the United States, had become a famous percussionist playing with artists like Santana, Ray Charles, and Eric Clapton, to name a few. When he told me how he had been saved out of the occult, I asked him to give his testimony to my crusade team.

In broken English, Luis told how his wife had found the Lord and began praying for his salvation. He wanted nothing to do with God or her religion. But she never stopped praying for him.

While home in California, Luis clicked on the evening news and saw the coverage of preparations for the 2004 Billy Graham Crusade at the Rose Bowl in Pasadena. Luis was intrigued as he watched the news cameras follow my father across the field in a golf cart.

It was my father's custom to make a visit to the stadium the day before a crusade to get a feel for the size and layout. He always enjoyed meeting stadium officials and those who worked hard to make the crusade run smoothly. Oftentimes, while there, he would take questions from the media.

Luis sensed the excitement from the press. He turned to his wife and said, "We need to go!" She was about to witness an answer to her prayer.

Luis and his wife battled heavy traffic the next night on the way to the stadium. By the time they arrived, the crowd was so massive that Luis had to sit in one section and his wife in another. His daughter was in the stadium and called her father on his cell phone to tell him what was happening at the Rose Bowl. "Papa, where are you?" she asked. She was shocked to learn that her father was seated across the stadium. For the remainder of the evening, she prayed that God would speak to his heart.

Luis listened intently to my father's sermon. He was compelled to respond when my father said, "Get up out of your seat and come; we'll wait for you." Luis said, "I ran down several tiers of steps and onto the field and accepted Christ as my Savior."

Through the years I have met hundreds of people who have done exactly the same thing in my crusades, testifying that they ran to the platform and asked Christ to come into their hearts, change them, and make Him Lord of their lives.

Can't Get Away from That Man

There are countless stories attesting to how God has moved in the hearts of those watching my father's telecasts. Every time we air a program, we provide a toll-free telephone number for viewers to call and talk with trained volunteers during or after the programs. Phone centers established in a network of churches across the nation receive life-changing accounts of how God convicts people's hearts during a telecast.

Someone once said, "I was clicking my remote from channel to channel looking for something to take my mind off my troubles. I surfed past a comedy show but didn't feel like laughing. I skipped over a drama because the story was too much like my own. I wasn't interested in watching a documentary about suicide because I was almost there myself. I was desperate to find comfort and peace. I kept clicking. I stopped on a channel long enough to hear Billy Graham talk about sin. I started clicking once more. Lord knows I'm a sinner. But something inside made me go back and find that channel.

"Then Billy Graham said, 'For those watching by television, do you feel hopeless? Do you feel that no one cares? God cares. He wants to forgive you of your sin and cleanse you and make you a new man or woman. Call the number at the bottom of the screen. A counselor is waiting to talk with you and pray with you. And God is waiting to hear you say, "I have sinned against You, Lord. Forgive me. I want to be made new. I want to experience peace in my heart."'"

While attending a banquet at a Christian school, Dr. Donald R. Wilhite shared with me his testimony of how he came to know the Lord through my father's Birmingham, Alabama, telecast in 1964. He said, "I felt a tug in my heart when your dad looked into the camera and said, 'For those of you watching by television . . .' I knew I had to respond to the invitation."

That night in the privacy of his own home, he repented of his sin and received Christ's forgiveness. Dr. Wilhite not only became a Christian that evening, but he later committed his life to serving the Lord as a preacher of the Gospel and senior pastor of Calvary Baptist Church in Columbus, Georgia.

Dr. Wilhite stated, "There is no way to tell how many have been called into a preaching ministry because of the impact Billy Graham has had on young men like me."[8]

Another man described how he had been saved as a result of a Billy Graham telecast. He said, "I was home flipping channels, trying to find something good on TV. When I came across Billy Graham, my wife shouted, 'Stop! I heard he was going to be on television tonight.' So I got in the car and went down to the local bar and ordered a drink. When I looked up on the screen, Billy Graham was on television. I figured I wasn't going to get away from that man, so I went back home to hear what he had to say. The next Sunday, I went to church and was saved. My wife said that television changed our lives."

Dicey Speech

Television can't save anyone, but the message that comes across the airwaves does affect our hearts and minds. And that message can tempt or rescue.

My father envisioned using television as a tool to get the Gospel to as many as possible. He also realized that Satan is the prince of the air (Ephesians 2:2), evidenced by the quick decline television took in program content.

Freedom of speech is a dicey debate. In the early days of television, no profanity was permitted. Entertainment with vulgar language and lewd scenes could be purchased at the box office but not shown on TV. Today, a host of undesirable networks are beamed into our homes, exposing those watching by television to every form of filth and violence. On mainstream cable and network channels, the advertising cutaways are as bad—or worse—as the programming itself. You can't even escape it during the nightly news.

Freedom of speech has evolved into a massive monster. There is a growing industry attempting to combat this stranglehold by marketing blocking and filtering software for parental control. But many moms and dads today are not patrolling themselves, much less the children.

A popular advertising blitz targets parents, raising the awareness of what their children may be watching both on the Internet and television. My mother used to say, "Wrong is wrong and never becomes right!" So why block such filth only for the kids? The Bible says, "Woe to those who call evil good, and good evil" (Isaiah 5:20).

On this subject my father wrote, "The Bible teaches that God is holy, righteous, and pure. He cannot tolerate sin in His presence. However, man has chosen to disregard the divine laws and standards. As a result of man's transgressions, he is called a 'sinner.' Sin immediately breaks his fellowship with God."⁹

Jesus Christ shed His blood to cover sin. Why would His followers want to be entertained by it?

The Evil That Struts

Recently a leading network anchor reported a story called "Culture Collapsing—Can the Youth Be Saved?" The story showed a deplorable scene of two Hollywood female starlets kissing, followed by a battery of clips with barely clothed dancers and twelve-year-old kids imitating them in school. The camera honed in on the reporter shaking his head as he said, "That's teaming up on slime." Even the world shakes its head at the evil that struts around in our culture.

The news story was like a modern-day rerun of Sodom and Gomorrah. I thought of the verse that says, "The wicked freely strut about when what is vile is honored among men" (Psalm 12:8 NIV).

What can we do about it? *Flee.*

That's what Abraham's nephew, Lot, did by command from the Lord. The citizens of Sodom and Gomorrah had become corrupt. Because of the moral perversion and wickedness of these twin cities, God sent two angels to help Lot escape from the vile culture. Would Lot heed the warning and flee to freedom, or would he decide to stay and be destroyed?

Sadly, Lot actually had to think about it. The Bible says, "And while [Lot] lingered, the [angels] took hold of his hand, his wife's hand, and the hands of his two daughters, the LORD being merciful to him, and they brought him out and set him outside the city . . . [and] said, 'Escape for your life! Do not look behind you nor stay anywhere in the plain. Escape to the mountains, lest you be destroyed'" (Genesis 19:16–17).

What a picture for us today. Do we pretend that Sodom and Gomorrah are far from us? With the click of the remote, it is possible to invite Sodom and Gomorrah right into the living room. And for those watching by television, the images are corrupting minds, searing hearts, and feeding fleshly appetites.

When my father preached a message about Lot's wife, who turned into a pillar of salt when she disobeyed God by looking back, he repeated a comment my mother often made about the degradation of our culture: "If God does not judge America for its sin, He will have to apologize to Sodom and Gomorrah!"

Here is a news flash: God won't be apologizing. My mother knew it and would say, "Judgment is on its way." With that in mind, what are we doing to change our pop culture diet that is leading us astray? Do we respond as Lot did? Flip on the TV, click to something that does not honor God, and then linger? The Bible says, "Whoever abides in Him does not sin" (1 John 3:6).

My father quoted the British statesman Edmund Burke, who once said that all it took for evil to triumph was for good men to do nothing. Perhaps all followers of Jesus Christ should hang a plaque over their televisions and computers with this message:

I will set nothing wicked before my eyes. (Psalm 101:3)

A Three-Letter Word

The world's speech is embodied in a three-letter word: *sin*. Profanity on television took root in the late fifties, budded in the sixties, and flourishes today. Heading the list is an assault on the third commandment: "You shall not take the name of the LORD your God in vain" (Exodus 20:7). Yet in most of our schools today, children cannot use the name of the Lord Jesus Christ except in cursing.

The public's initial reaction in the late fifties to vulgar language on television was outrage. Television executives scrambled to put into place stipulations dictating when cursing and foul language would be permitted over the airwaves—never during prime time when kids were still awake.

I suppose the television industry felt they were being moral giants by setting acceptable times for profanity. They waited just long enough for the public to grow accustomed to bad behavior. When the shock value wore off, the industry introduced profanity into prime time and opened up new freedoms for late-night television. Even if viewers did not participate in lifestyles depicted on the screen, those watching by television began infiltrating their minds with the unthinkable.

My father once said, "Because [of] instant communication today, our planet has shrunk to the size of a television screen. A comfortable room can be turned into a foreign battlefield or a street riot with the push of a button."

No wonder Philo Farnsworth later in life said to his son, "There is nothing on [TV] worthwhile, and we're not going to watch it in this household." His son Kent stated, "[Dad] felt he had created kind of a monster, a way for people to waste a lot of their lives."[10] If entertainment was that bad fifty years ago, how would we possibly describe it in the twenty-first century?

Much of society has become flippant about the "colorful" language used in the world of entertainment. It has evolved into the epidemic called mind pollution. Even the Emmys gave warning in September 2003: "Wash your television out with soap. According to a study of the major broadcast networks, the amount of profanity on television has increased significantly since 1998. . . . The study revealed an increase in cursing during every time slot."[11]

As the twentieth century was drawing to an end, my father expressed concern over what he referred to as the raw-language culture. He stated, "It's a four-letter world in movies, on television, in comedy routines, and in real life."[12] Articles from *Time* magazine's "Dirty Words" regurgitated America's foul-mouthed pop culture.[13]

I am thankful that the Lord led my father and others to take the Good News to television. The Gospel will transform people's minds and change their hearts.

Doctors often prescribe purifying the body of toxins. The Bible tells us how to cleanse the mind of corruption: meditate on things that are pure and virtuous (Philippians 4:8). It is God's recipe for having the mind of Christ (1 Corinthians 2:16). Do we?

The Assault That Results

Many churchgoers and ministers are buying into the theory of political correctness. Some say they have to stay engaged with what Hollywood is producing to make their messages "relevant." This is an assault on the Gospel that has resulted in over half of evangelical pastors admitting to viewing pornography, and 29 percent of professing born-again adults in the United States feel it is morally acceptable to view movies with explicit sexual behavior. Focus on the Family stated that 47 percent of families admitted that pornography is a problem in their homes.[14]

"True freedom [in Christ] consists not in the freedom to sin, but the freedom not to sin," my father often said. "Millions of professing Christians are only just that—'professing.' They have never possessed Christ. They live lives characterized by the flesh. Tens of thousands have never been born again. They will go into eternity lost."

Hard-core porn can now be seen in the privacy of one's home through satellite TV, cable networks, and the Internet. This type of programming is a lower pit than that of Sodom and Gomorrah because of its global reach. "Pornography . . . is spewing out a polluted river of filth which can destroy us faster than any chemical pollution we seem so worried about." My father wrote this in 1971.[15]

As we entered the new millennium, Y2K was the big concern, but there was something more troublesome. It was reported that there were 1.3 million pornographic websites—260 million pages. The total porn industry revenue is more than $13.3 billion in the United States and $97 billion worldwide.[16]

The human mind has a great capacity to retain information and images but, like computer hard drives, a lousy track record for dumping. Satan is not only loose—he is terrorizing human nerve centers. His battle plan is drenched in confusion, blurring the lines of demarcation. He has actually found a way to muddle the meaning of porn.

The definition of *pornography* hasn't changed: "Writing, pictures, etc. intended primarily to arouse sexual desire."[17]

Pornography used to be packaged in brown wrappers and sold in stores off the beaten path. Today it infiltrates the Internet and boldly shouts from massive billboards along the interstates. It is found in glossy magazines in waiting rooms. It is seen on television day and night, in movie theaters, in restaurants, and in bestselling books. It is heard on cleverly recorded radio ads, in Grammy award–winning music, and in sold-out concerts. Worst of all, it drenches the mind.

The Bible says, "If anyone . . . does not consent to wholesome words, even the words of our Lord Jesus Christ, and to the doctrine which accords with godliness, he is proud, knowing nothing, but is obsessed with . . . useless wranglings of men of corrupt minds and destitute of the truth. . . . From such withdraw yourself" (1 Timothy 6:3–5).

My father said many times that professing Christians are a far greater number than Bible-believing, Bible-living Christians. This is evident by the many in Hollywood and around the world who profess Jesus Christ as Lord with no testimony to back it up.

Cycle of Civilization

An interesting article appeared in a newspaper a few years ago discovered by the late William W. Quinn, who served as a staff officer in World War II, and later as a colonel under General Douglas MacArthur during the Korean War. Quinn's daughter, Sally Quinn, is a successful writer with the *Washington Post*.[18]

Colonel Quinn sent the following article, included in a letter to a journalist friend of his, before dying at ninety-two—on September 11, 2000. It seemed to foreshadow the somber events exactly one year later.

> The World's Great Civilizations averaged a cycle of 200 years. Those Societies progressed through this sequence:
>
> From bondage to spiritual faith
> From spiritual faith to great courage
> From great courage to liberty
> From liberty to abundance
> From abundance to selfishness
> From selfishness to complacency
> From complacency to apathy
> From apathy to dependency
> From dependency back again into bondage

General Quinn then asked the question: "As the United States has passed its 200th birthday, and in view of the recent epidemic of immorality, I wonder how your readers would assess America's current position in this cycle."[19]

What has happened to our nation? This topic was discussed in a meeting at the White House in 1972 that made headline news more than three decades later.

Billy Graham Said What?

My father always expressed deep concern over issues of immorality, particularly with what television was carrying into American homes. He often preached about it, hoping to raise awareness of the harm caused by society winking at the demonic effect it was having on the culture. He stated, "The moral foundation of our country is in danger of crumbling as families break up and parents neglect their responsibilities." Quoting from the prophet Jeremiah, he said, "Are they ashamed of their loathsome conduct? No, they have no shame at all; they do not even know how to blush" (Jeremiah 6:15 NIV).

This was precisely at the heart of a discussion he had in the Oval Office in 1972 that set off a firestorm three decades later. It became what the media termed "the famed visit" between then president Richard Nixon and my father. I call it the "failed visit."

Interest in the infamous Nixon tapes resurfaced in 2005 when others were released to the public. Some contained comments from my father about immorality and cursing being perpetuated by Hollywood and the press.

The story has been told, but I am not satisfied that Billy Graham's part in it has been thoroughly understood.

When my father first heard the Watergate tapes played on television, he was stunned at the cursing from a man he loved and respected. And my father did blush. He had never heard such abrasive speech from his friend.

Then he heard his own voice on another tape, discussing the state of American culture with President Nixon, who lamented the domination of the press, many of whom happened to be Jewish. My father responded by expressing his own concern that Hollywood moguls were "putting out pornographic stuff." After a lengthy gap in the tape, he went on to say, "This stranglehold has got to be broken or the country's going down the drain."[20]

My father became physically ill after hearing the conversation, though he did not recall the comments. He was criticized for offending the Jews. But he made a public statement asking forgiveness from anyone offended by his statements. As my father's friend Paul Harvey used to say, "Here's the rest of the story."

Hollywood had been courting my father for years. Television and movie tycoons tried to pull my father into their industry. They saw his success in drawing large crowds and perceived him as a magnet to the people, not at all understanding his ministry as being the work of the Holy Spirit.

The "stranglehold" my father referred to was not Jewish dominance (as the media reported); it was the immorality being perpetuated from the industry's sphere of influence. It seems a stretch to say that my father slandered the Jewish people in the meeting with President Nixon. He did not debase them in any way. He was merely pointing out that executive decision makers held the keys to ushering in godless programming and weaving its destructive thread into the moral fabric of our great nation. When the tapes were released, emotion shifted the context of the conversation from the problem to those who could fix the problem but wouldn't.

My father could not ignore this sin or sweep it under the rug. He stated, "They don't know how I really feel about what they're doing to this country."[21]

I dare say that my father spoke as a modern-day prophet. And as he said many times, "The prophets who spoke to their generation for God did not please and conform, they opposed [anything that did not honor the Lord]."

I learned a significant lesson from my father. He believed that the moral foundation of our nation at that time was in serious jeopardy, and he never failed to consistently lift up God's moral standards.

There was a flurry of articles that hit the magazines, newspapers, and headline news: "Is Billy Graham Anti-Semitic?" If these transcripts are eyed within the truth of the context, the conclusion must be that *the preacher* was referring to the sin of immorality.

In 2002, this issue was discussed during a radio talk show hosted by Alan Keyes. He asked Lewis Drummond, a professor at Samford University in Birmingham, Alabama, about this, and Drummond stated, "There was a context that's worth looking into and considering what precipitated [Mr. Graham's] statements. . . . The issue was pornography. . . . I think if you will read the context carefully, [he] really did not say that he was against the Jewish people . . . he was against the pornography."[22]

My father's record is unshakable regarding his love for the Jewish people and the nation of Israel. He never ridiculed Jews privately or publicly.

To some degree, the Jewish community had an impact on my father's decision to hold the 1957 New York Crusade that launched his television ministry. One of the factors that led him to New York in the first place was a conversation with Rabbi Marc Tanenbaum. At that time, one out of four New Yorkers was Jewish.[23]

During his lengthy stay in New York, my father met with Jewish businessmen. Many became lifelong friends and went to hear him preach. Some openly declared their commitment to Jesus as their Messiah.

In fact, during one of my father's trips abroad, he was invited by a rabbi to speak in a synagogue. As he entered, an American reporter asked, "Dr. Graham, are you going in to proselytize these Jews?" My father replied, "No, as a matter of fact, I'm going in to thank them. For you see, I gave my heart to a young Jewish rabbi many years ago!"

My father had many friends within the Jewish community and stood by them, especially in Eastern Europe and Israel. Throughout his ministry, Jewish organizations have honored his steadfast support of Israel. My father was anguished by the misconception of his discussion with President Nixon but took comfort in the fact that God knows the hearts of men.

Plugged into Power

While my father stayed burdened about the moral decline, he said, "At times in the crusades we have conducted, I have looked into the cameras and realized that several million people were watching. I know that many of the things I have said from the Scriptures have offended some, but I cannot afford to tone down the message. I must preach the pure and simple Gospel in whatever culture I am in."

Billy Graham never tired of finding ways to carry God's message of salvation over the air. I well remember when my father felt led to expand his television outreach to include newer technology, using satellite to beam his crusades around the world. His vision was to transmit the meetings to venues in various regions of the continents using skilled interpreters to translate his messages simultaneously as he spoke. It was a huge undertaking. Within a span of six years, my father witnessed remarkable opportunity for the Gospel on every inhabited continent.

BGEA launched Mission World Africa from London in 1989, beaming via satellite to thirty-three countries in Africa. The same thing was done from Hong Kong in 1990, when the crusade was transmitted to thirty-three Asian countries. From Buenos Aires, Argentina, twenty countries in Latin America received the telecast in 1991, and Mission World Europe beamed the crusade from Essen, Germany, into fifty-five countries. All of this represented the Gospel being preached in a multitude of languages.

The climax of the satellite strategy was Global Mission in 1995, from San Juan, Puerto Rico. Via satellite the crusade meetings linked to 185 countries and territories around the world, and people heard my father preach through interpreters in 117 languages, unprecedented at the time.

As dusk fell on the twentieth century, what was left? Was the world evangelized? While God's pendulum keeps ticking toward eternity, the Bible says:

> Beloved, we are confident of better things . . . , yes, things that accompany salvation. . . . For God is not unjust to forget your work and labor of love which you have shown toward His name, in that you have ministered to the saints, and do minister. And we desire that each one of you show the same diligence to the full assurance of hope until the end, that you do not become sluggish, but imitate those who through faith and patience inherit the promises. (Hebrews 6:9–12)

On December 31, 1999, when the lights went out on the millennium of invention, a new dawn opened the door for future generations to build on the faithful work of God's people and the creativity He fused into the human mind.

My Hope

As I thought about how my father used television in his ministry to preach the greatest message ever proclaimed, I wondered how I might further utilize television as a vehicle for the Gospel in areas of the world that had not heard what Jesus Christ has done for them.

For years, people had asked me how they could hear more from Billy Graham. Many who had heard him preach by way of satellite linkups in international cities wanted to know how others in outlying areas could hear my father preach.

The BGEA had been on television nearly sixty years, almost as long as television had been around. I thought back to the stories of when my father had struggled with whether to go on television in 1957. What if he hadn't? The opportunity God gave him to preach in homes across North America, and eventually around the world, unleashed other opportunities to preach the Word of God by means of technological advancement.

Why not transmit the Good News in the smallest of venues—on a massive scale—not in stadiums, but one living room at a time through television?

Many areas of the world are far from city hubs. If television could reach American cities and rural areas for Christ when my father first began televising his crusades, why not use the most powerful communication tool to transmit the Gospel to remote areas of the world house to house? Why not give people something worthwhile to watch—not entertainment to tickle their ears, but a message to transform their hearts?

I recalled when my father convened the International Conferences for Itinerant Evangelists (ICIE) in Amsterdam, Holland, in 1983, 1986, and 2000. What he would have given to walk to the microphone and greet representatives from 174 countries in their own native tongues or dialects! It occurred to me that with today's technology, we could dub my father's taped sermons in multiple languages.

I pictured cinderblock houses scattered across countries such as Mexico, Honduras, and India, dwellings too small for families of six to live in by American standards but room enough for families of ten or twelve, by necessity. Hundreds of millions still live like this today. But in spite of their poverty, they manage to buy, or at least rent, televisions to watch special programs. Oh, they may not have all the bells, whistles, and remotes, but the pictures move and talk. Television captivates the whole world. Why not use its power through which to proclaim the message that God gave to the whole world to those watching by television?

I was inspired by the New Testament story of Matthew, the tax collector. He hosted a great feast in his own house and invited a great number of people to meet Jesus, who said to them, "I have not come to call the righteous, but sinners, to repentance" (Luke 5:32).

As I assembled our team to pray about an evangelism program that would be transmitted into homes through television, the BGEA World Evangelism Television Project *My Hope* was born.

The first step was to put a pilot program together and identify countries that would permit BGEA to purchase airtime. Enthusiasm swelled as we began producing new programs, utilizing local musical artists and testimonies adapted for the local culture.

The next step was to mobilize and train national pastors and laymen who would open their homes to non-Christians, inviting them to a crusade in their home. And God blessed. In 2002, we launched the pilot program in four of the seven Central American countries and called it *My Hope*.

We began by sending BGEA-trained instructors to teach the Christian Life and Witness courses in Spanish. Excitement built as people began to pray and ask God to use them to reach the lost in their towns and villages for Christ. They learned and applied the principles of a program my father called Operation Andrew, based on John 1:41–42, which tells about John the Baptist's disciple Andrew bringing his brother, Simon Peter, to the Lord.

Christians began praying for unsaved friends, neighbors, and family and inviting them into their homes for a meal to watch the telecast together. Hospitality opened the doors of households, turning living rooms into miniature stadiums for the Gospel.

By twos and threes they came. The young and younger squeezed into corners of the room; others sat on steps and peered over the shoulders of others. We had reports of as many as fifty jammed into small storefronts along village streets to watch the programs.

As people sat with their hosts, watching the telecast, anticipation would build as they saw my father walk to the podium and preach God's

Word in their language. After the invitation was given, Christians who had been praying stood and extended a personal invitation to those watching by television. "You can come to Christ right here in this place," they would say. "I join with Dr. Graham in asking that you accept Christ as your Savior tonight." Tears filled the eyes of young and old alike, and God's people rejoiced in seeing loved ones repent of sin and accept Christ's salvation—right in their own living rooms.

In a short period of time, *My Hope* went throughout Central and South America. When we got to Colombia, we had more than seven hundred thousand decisions for Christ during a four-night telecast. By the time *My Hope* aired in India, eight hundred thousand Christians, representing sixty thousand churches, opened their homes to the lost to see the telecasts with unprecedented results.

My Hope has become the model that we use today in countries around the world. The key to the impact of *My Hope* is putting in place the same standards my father established through his sixty years of crusade evangelism: partnering with local churches and providing the same training we have given to church members in preparation of our crusades.

I learned important principles from my father about effective evangelism on a large scale. The Lord impressed on him early in his ministry the importance of proper follow-up—encouraging new converts to become involved in small-group Bible studies and part of Bible-believing congregations. My father felt burdened about leaving crusade cities without a support base for those who had received Christ as Savior. This is what separated him from so many others—partnering with churches to ensure the proper follow-up would be done. It is still an integral part of our crusade evangelism outreach.

Because the World Evangelism Television Project is done in private homes, small groups are already in place, providing the needed follow-up to strengthen people in their new faith.

My father lived long enough to see *My Hope* become effective in places he never had the opportunity to preach the Gospel. He was grateful to God for opening this avenue. Evangelistic preaching has been energized in these countries where crusades would have never been possible.

The results have been staggering and the possibilities unbelievable. *My Hope* telecasts have been received in sixty countries, and the Gospel message, the heart of the program, has given hope to millions of people.

I hope to continue proclaiming to all who will listen what the Savior has done for mankind. And though my father is now in heaven, he is still preaching this same Gospel to those watching by television.

5

Pray, Pray, Pray

For where two or three are gathered together
in My name, I am there.

—Matthew 18:20

Prayer is our lifeline to God.

BILLY GRAHAM

Often we hear that two is company and three is a crowd. Yet the world
seems to be made up of trinities:

- Time, space, and matter.
- Past, present, and future.
- Length, breadth, and height.
- Love, hate, and indifference.
- Heart, flesh, and soul.

- Life, sickness, and death.
- Morning, noon, and night.
- Sun, moon, and stars.
- Even in the beginning it was Adam, Eve, and God.
- There are parents, sons, and daughters.
- Men, women, and children.
- Sin, forgiveness, and eternity.

Then there is the Trinity: God the Father, God the Son, and God the Holy Spirit.

My parents believed in the trinity principle of prayer: pray humbly, pray believing, and pray with thanksgiving. They exemplified the principles of prayer in their home through Scripture and by example.

They were quick to remind us as children that prayer was not asking for things selfishly. My father often said, "I have answered every request my children have made to me. The answer has not always been what they wanted, but it has always been in accordance with what I thought was best for them at the time." This is a true example of how our heavenly Father answers the prayers of His children.

My father taught me a great deal about prayer. If something happened that caused him to rejoice, he immediately wanted to pray and thank God for the blessing. When something tragic happened to others, he felt an immediate burden to pray for them.

While on a Sunday afternoon walk with me in December 2007, my father mourned a shooting that had just taken place at a center in Colorado for young people serving in a ministry known as YWAM (Youth With A Mission). A gunman went into their complex and opened fire. Later as we watched reports on the evening news, he turned the television off and said, "Franklin, let's pray for the families who are going through this terrible crisis." This was my father's way of life, and it made a profound impact on me.

Pray with Purpose

Prayer was also the centerpiece of my father's ministry. He reminded his team often, "Without prayer, this ministry and all of our dreams to spread the Good News of Jesus' love throughout the world would not have been possible."

When I became president of Samaritan's Purse in 1978, I began attending events that preceded my father's crusades. In preparation, my father would often visit a crusade city to address a rally of pastors and laypeople burdened to touch their communities with the Gospel of Jesus Christ. He always welcomed me to these meetings. At twenty-six, I understood clearly that I was to quietly observe and learn from others. And I did. But I learned most by watching my father, asking him questions, and listening for his input.

The cornerstone of my father's ministry was his crusades. The BGEA had become known for its preparation and precision in executing an evangelistic plan. While the philosophy proved successful, many thought that the key to bringing a crusade to fruition was found in partnership with the churches, participation in the community, and promotion of the event using the most modern methods of advertising.

While these are important elements, I learned from my father that the real secret was in something much more powerful.

The first time I went to a prayer rally and heard my father clarify the key to a successful crusade, it seared a lasting impression in my soul. He said, "Prayer is an essential part of evangelism. The most important step in preparing for an evangelistic mission is prayer, prayer, and more prayer."

I understood even better the value of this truth through the eyes of my heavenly Father when I began preaching the Gospel and extending an invitation for salvation in Jesus Christ.

Preaching in Tegucigalpa, Honduras, at the National Soccer Stadium in 1996, I saw the results of utilizing this important key to crusade evangelism. Months before, the crusade prayer committees had been organized, and prayer was covering the city. As I stood to preach the first night with my interpreter Lenin De Janon standing beside me, people began coming toward the platform. I put my hand over the microphone and said, "Lenin! People are responding, and I haven't given the invitation yet. Tell them to go back to their seats while I preach."

Lenin asked the crowd that had gathered to return to their seats. But when the number swelled to several hundred, I looked at Lenin in bewilderment and said, "Maybe I should just give the invitation." Lenin said, "I think so. Their hearts are ready."

It was evident that this was the result of prayer months before the meeting. Those who had prayed for their family, friends, and neighbors invited them to the crusade. One-on-one evangelism through witnessing and prayer had already prepared people to respond to Christ.

My father wrote, "God has worked in a miraculous way in our crusades down through the years. Thousands of men and women have made their decisions for Christ. Their coming was not the result of one man's work or the efforts of a group—it was the product of much prayer by many people."[1]

My father studied the prayers of our Lord and wrote about them often. He always took the opportunity to emphasize this vital aspect of Christian living, challenging men and women to make prayer the center of their lives and ministries.

Jesus Himself gave us a pattern for prayer. "Jesus prayed briefly when He was in a crowd; He prayed a little longer when He was with His disciples; and He prayed all night when He was alone," my father would say. "Today, many in the ministry tend to reverse that process."

When I am asked the key to crusade evangelism, the trinity principle comes to mind:

1) *Pray for an opportunity to plant God's Word.* "Devote yourselves to prayer, being watchful and thankful. And pray . . . that God may

open a door for our message, so that we may proclaim . . . Christ" (Colossians 4:2–3 NIV).

2) *Pray to be used as a vessel to proclaim God's message.* "Pray also for me, that whenever I open my mouth, words may be given me so that I will fearlessly make known . . . the gospel, for which I am an ambassador" (Ephesians 6:19–20 NIV).

3) *Pray for a plentiful harvest.* Jesus prayed to His Father in heaven for those who would spread the truth of His message and for those who would hear: "My prayer is not for them alone. I pray also for those who will believe in me through their message" (John 17:20 NIV).

This is the sole purpose for crusade evangelism—a passion to win souls. The Bible says, "He who wins souls is wise" (Proverbs 11:30).

Prayer is the peg on which we hang every facet of our work done in the name of the Lord Jesus Christ. Our ministry is primed through prayer, for God grants His power through the prayers of His people. Prayer will always be our priority and our source of power.

I thank the Lord for this anchor that was plunged into the soul of the ministry given to my father many years ago and has now been entrusted to my care, under the watchful eye of the Lord. My father pointed me many times to what the Bible says about prayer: the privilege to pray before the throne of God, the blessing received when God answers our prayers, and the faith that grows when prayer is answered differently than we would like.

We are happy when God answers our prayers the way we want. We are not so thrilled when the answer appears to be "no" or perhaps "wait." Our human nature is not bent toward receiving these answers with contentment. But as followers of Jesus Christ, we must not only accept His will but also thank Him for such answers. That is sometimes hard to do.

If we carefully study what the Word of God says about prayer, the Holy Spirit will reveal to us that our heavenly Father has a purpose for every answer He sends to us. What is it? To make us more like Christ. This is the will of God. We are not to pray for what we want. We are instructed to pray for what God wants—His will to be done in our lives. During times of prayer and fellowship, God remolds our desires and brings our hearts into union with His will.

My father wrote often about prayer and stated, "Whether prayer changes our situation or not, one thing is certain: Prayer will change us!"[2] God answers all sincere prayers offered in the name of the Lord Jesus Christ.

When we bring our petitions before Him, we must ask that they line up with the heart of God. For followers of Jesus Christ, the Holy Spirit within will help accomplish this goal. When we brush the Holy Spirit aside and think we can manipulate how we are bringing God around to our way of thinking, we offend the Holy Spirit. He desires to lead us in our prayers, not the other way around.

The great missionary statesman Hudson Taylor wrote, "Shall we not, each of us, determine to labor more in prayer; to cultivate more intimate communion with God by His help; thinking less of our working and more of His working, that He may in every deed be glorified in and through us?"[3]

How many times do we pray asking the Lord to rubber-stamp a decision we have already made? In God's sovereignty He may permit us to walk right into a fiasco of our own choosing. What should we do if we run ahead of God with our own plans and find ourselves in a mess? Repent and acknowledge our disobedience. The sincere follower of Jesus Christ will take extra precaution not to repeat the offense but to be humble before the One who knows best.

Martin Luther preached often on faith and prayer. He said, "Faith prays in such a manner that it commits everything to the gracious will of God; it lets [God] determine whether it is conducive to his honor and to our benefit."[4]

I recall my father saying, "You are denying yourself a marvelous privilege if you don't pray. True prayer is a way of life, not just for use in cases of emergency."

It was my parents' desire for their children to understand the principles of prayer. I did not always like the way prayers were answered, but when I became a father I learned the wisdom to pray about everything, trust the Lord, and accept the answer in obedient response.

Soon after my son Edward graduated from the United States Military Academy at West Point and was deployed on his first combat tour, a friend of mine sent the following prayer to me, with a promise to pray for my son. It was an example of intercessory prayer.

Written by the great general Douglas MacArthur about his own son, the words are eloquent and touching.

Build me a son, O Lord, who will be strong enough to know when he is weak; and brave enough to face himself when he is afraid; one who will be proud and unbending in honest defeat, and humble and gentle in victory.

Build me a son whose wishes will not take the place of deeds; a son who will know Thee—and that to know himself is the foundation stone of knowledge.

Lead him, I pray, not in the path of ease and comfort, but under the stress and spur of difficulties and challenge. Here let him learn to stand up in the storm; here let him learn compassion for those who fail.

Build me a son whose heart will be clear, whose goal will be high, a son who will master himself before he seeks to master other men, one who will reach into the future, yet never forget the past.

And after all these things are his, add, I pray, enough of a sense of humor, so that he may always be serious, yet never take himself too seriously. Give him humility, so that he may always remember the simplicity of true greatness, the open mind of true wisdom and the meekness of true strength.

Then I, his father, will dare to whisper, "I have not lived in vain."[5]

What an expression of a father's heart for his son. MacArthur, with all of his accomplishments, wanted more than anything to be remembered by his family not as a soldier but as a father. He left his legacy in a prayer.

When asked about it later, he replied, "A soldier destroys in order to build, the father only builds, never destroys. The one has the potentiality of death; the other embodies creation and life. . . . It is my hope that my son, when I am gone, will remember me not from the battle field but in the home repeating with him our simple daily prayer, 'Our Father Who Art in Heaven.'"[6]

Not everyone has been blessed with an earthly father who builds him up or prays with him and for him. But the Father in heaven longs for His creation to accept the work of His Son, Jesus Christ, on the cross and to enter into a rock-solid relationship that will endure.

My father exemplified how prayer follows every believer in the small and great decisions of life. Right after I was married, my wife, Jane Austin, and I were living in Seattle. I decided to finish college while my father was still willing to pay for it. I wasn't sure about going to seminary, but I did have a desire to get a degree in business. I reluctantly approached my father about the possibility of business school, thinking he would be against it. To my surprise he said, "Franklin, I think that is a good idea." We prayed about it and asked for the Lord to lead me in making the right decision.

I took two business courses at Seattle Pacific College that spurred my interest, realizing that it would help me in anything I would do in life. I went on to earn my degree at Appalachian State University in Boone, North Carolina, and together with my earlier Bible training, God helped me apply my education in leading Samaritan's Purse.

Twenty years later, my father and I preached our first crusade together in Saskatoon, Saskatchewan, in 1995. For me it was exciting to share the pulpit with him. We spent time during the day visiting and praying together for the meetings. It was during this crusade that my father shared with me how he and my mother had been praying about the future leadership of the BGEA. He told me that the answer to their prayers had been confirmed by close associates like Carloss Morris, Russ Busby, Betty Jane Hess, and others who had also been praying about the ministry and who should assume responsibility to lead the work someday.

"Franklin," he said, "I feel in my heart that God has prepared you for this task. I need to know how you feel about it before I take my recommendation to the board of directors."

Hearing my father express confidence in me was humbling. I told him, "I will do what will honor you and the Lord."

I do not take for granted the fact that I have been privileged to share in my father's ministry. He led the way and set a profound example of serving Jesus Christ with his life. For years my father had prayed, not only for me but for the Lord to prepare the right person to take the reins of his organization. It gave me a deep sense of assurance that my Father in heaven had prepared me along the way in answer to my father's prayers.

Those of us who have experienced the love of an earthly father should reach out to those who do not have that foundation, so that they might see a glimpse of the heavenly Father's heart in us.

The most dynamic prayer was by Jesus Christ to His Father in heaven on behalf of those who would choose to follow Him: "And this is eternal life, that they may know You, the only true God, and Jesus Christ whom You have sent. . . . And I have declared to them Your name, and will declare it, that the love with which You loved Me may be in them, and I in them" (John 17:3, 26).

Jesus exemplifies the meaning of intercessory prayer—because He prays in the Father's name for us throughout time and in love.

Some say I was born with a silver spoon in my mouth. I am not especially partial to silver. When I'm hunting, I am mighty happy to eat from a tin can—and it's a whole lot more fun. But one thing I cannot deny: I was blessed to be born into a home where God was exalted. Because of this enormous blessing, my responsibility is far greater to my fellow man, especially to those who have never known the comfort and joy of a Christian home.

But being part of a Christian home did not make me a Christian. I had to come to Jesus Christ on my own and accept responsibility for my own sinful position before Him. My home environment, however, exposed me to truth and gave me an opportunity to consider the great gift that Christ offers to all. I want to share with as many as possible the Good News that God in heaven desires the souls of men.

This is the heart of the ministry that my father has left behind, and it beats on—calling men, women, and children to Jesus Christ.

Pray in Faith

Prayer was an anchor in our home. I watched my father and mother pray about anything and everything that affected our lives and the lives of others we knew. It was a natural way of communicating with Almighty God. Prayer was not foreign to me as a boy, but the power of prayer did not really hit home until I reached the age of eighteen.

I have written about how my father agreed to let me leave college for a semester and go on a mission trip. He believed that by allowing me to drive a Land Rover from England to Jordan, the Lord might open my eyes to the reality that the Word of God is living and active, penetrating the thoughts and attitudes of the heart (Hebrews 4:12).

And He did. I will never forget the day I learned about prayer by listening and watching.

During my extended stay at the mission hospital in Mafraq, a little desert town near the Syrian border in the Hashemite kingdom of Jordan, I experienced for myself what my father had always proclaimed: "God hears our prayers before they are spoken."

Every Friday, Dr. Eleanor Soltau and nurse Aileen Coleman, missionary founders of the hospital, gathered the small staff for prayer. I wasn't too excited about attending, but I didn't have time to think of a good excuse not to go. When I walked in the room, I slumped to my knees to "fit in" and listened as they laid their requests before the Lord.

When I heard them begin praying specifically for $1,355, and telling God they needed it by Monday, I cringed.

"Lord, this is Your hospital," they said with absolute resolve. "We have a bill for medicines totaling $1,355 that we can't pay, but You have abundant resources. We do not ask for ourselves, but for those we're caring for in Your name. If we do not pay this bill, our witness for You will be weakened. Your name is at stake, and it is in the name of Your Son, Jesus, that we pray humbly asking You to supply this great need—and we thank You in advance for hearing our petition."

For many today, $1,355 would not be cause for despair, but back in 1970 and in the middle of the Jordanian desert, money in any amount was difficult to come by.

Kneeling there on the floor with these sweet, devoted missionaries, I felt embarrassed for them. I sarcastically thought, *Oh sure! Like this is really going to happen.*

As the weekend passed, I lived in dread of seeing the disappointment on their faces. Instead, it was my jaw that dropped in awe. In Monday's mail, there was a check for exactly $1,355, with a note: "The Lord laid it on my heart to send this to you. Use it as you see fit." Eleanor and Aileen did not know the person who sent the check, but they knew the Provider. They smiled with confidence, knowing that

God had blessed the faith they relied on—trusting in Him to answer. "Before they call, I will answer" (Isaiah 65:24).

Walter A. Mueller once said, "Prayer is not merely an occasional impulse to which we respond when we are in trouble: prayer is a life attitude."[7] These missionaries lived in this attitude of prayer. The fact that a check came for $1,355 was miracle enough for me, but when I realized the check was mailed long before the prayer from the faithful few, it sent chills down my spine. I remembered what my father had said many times: "The most eloquent prayer is the prayer through hands that heal and bless."

Not only had I learned through my father's eyes that God works on behalf of His servants, but I learned a lesson through the eyes of my heavenly Father about praying in complete faith. God hears and responds to the prayers of those who are obedient and faithful.

Pray for Others

"At least we can pray." How often have we heard these words from well-meaning friends when we find ourselves in difficult situations? The reality is that the *most* we can do is pray. Intercessory prayer is something very close to the heart of God. He does care about our needs and our desires, but He is moved when prayers for others come from our hearts and lips.

I was with a pastor friend of mine, Mike MacIntosh from California, during the fires in San Diego in 2007. Mike's mother had died soon after my mother had gone to heaven. We shared in mutual grief, not only missing our mothers but realizing that we missed their prayers for us as well. I recalled my father talking about the void he felt after his own mother had died. He said it seemed as though a cloak of protection was gone.

But a friend told me a story about her father's family, ten boys and five girls raised during the Great Depression. Though their mother was busy with fifteen children, she found time to pray for each of them. She died at forty-six while many of the children were still under twelve. Long after she was gone her children were saved, and they grew to love and serve the Lord with their lives. Her testimony and prayers lived beyond her earthly life.

My mother was faithful in praying for her children and grandchildren, and we all sensed the power of her prayers.

At the time my son Edward was first deployed overseas, my mother had become nearly bedridden. When Edward heard about it, he called her from the Middle East. "Tai Tai" (a respectful term in Chinese meaning "old lady"), he said, "I am praying for you." My mother was overjoyed and mentioned it many times when I would visit. She had become the recipient of her grandchildren's prayers.

For those who have been blessed with godly homes where prayer is a regular part of life, there is an enormous responsibility and great privilege in praying for others who do not have such a foundation. Charles Spurgeon preached often on the matter of prayer, saying, "I commend intercessory prayer, because it opens man's soul."[8]

My mother was a prayer warrior, and her prayer focus was others. Missionaries, neighbors, family, and friends often sought my mother's prayers when they were struggling with illness or loneliness, or needed God's direction in their lives. She counted it a great privilege to spend time with them in prayer, and when she said, "In Jesus' name, amen," they knew that was not the end of her prayers. Often they would get notes in the mail long after, assuring them of her continued prayers.

My father often said, "Prayers have no boundaries. They can leap miles and continents and be translated instantly into any language."

Pray with Consistency

We think of prayer as talking to God, but prayer is not a one-way conversation. God listens; do we? There are many facets of prayer, and we are told to listen. "Listen, for I will speak of excellent things, and from the opening of my lips will come right things" (Proverbs 8:6). In the busyness of our world today, listening has become a hurried skill.

All my life I can remember my father exercising. He loved to swim. He also ran years before jogging became popular. He didn't have all the latest gear to make running attractive. He often ran in slacks, a velour shirt, and Hush Puppy shoes. But he understood the importance of staying physically fit and spiritually tuned up. "Unless the soul is fed and exercised daily," he would say, "it becomes weak and shriveled. It remains discontented, confused, restless."

Daily we wake to the alarm clock radio, music blaring or newscasters telling us about the latest tragedy. Our minds kick into high gear and our feet into motion as we head toward the television to watch the latest news flash live as it happens. We rush into the day with cell phones blaring funky tunes. We take the family to a restaurant and attempt to converse over loud music and screeching voices, then rush home to flick the news on again to see what we missed while attempting to connect with those we love.

As we dash through the day, an alarm may be sounding to stop and listen to the still, small voice of God. But we often cannot hear Him until our feet stumble over a tragedy or disappointment; then we run fiercely to God in prayer. The Bible tells us that if we pray always, listening and watching will become natural instincts, whether we are faced with alarm or blessing.

The apostle Paul's instruction to the church was, "Pray without ceasing, in everything give thanks; for this is the will of God in Christ Jesus for you" (1 Thessalonians 5:17–18).

Every parent has said to a child at one time, "Listen when I talk to you!" It is in our nature to want to be heard. A book distributor ran a slogan: "When you talk, God listens." But do we ever consider listening to God? My mother quoted the lyricist Edward Gloeggler, who said, "The polite part of speaking is to be still long enough to listen."[9]

When the prophet Jeremiah spoke to the household of Judah, he preached the Word of the Lord: "I spoke to you . . . , but you did not listen; I called you, but you did not answer" (Jeremiah 7:13 NIV).

Do we realize that Jesus Christ desires to speak to us? Do we realize how often we shun Him? Who would reject a call from the queen of England? Who would not respond to the summons of a US president? Yet the King of kings patiently waits to hear our voices.

The Father in heaven has given us this command: "This is my Son, whom I love. Listen to him!" (Mark 9:7 NIV).

As a boy my mother taught me to listen to my father—no back talk was allowed. My father demanded I give the same attention to my mother when she spoke. If I listened and obeyed, it was to my benefit. If I listened and ignored the words of warning, I paid the price.

I'll never forget, as a young boy, the day my father walked through the kitchen and caught me striking a match. "Franklin," he said, "don't you ever let me catch you playing with matches again, do you understand?" I nodded my head, ran from the house, and shook it off.

The next day when my father found me lighting up another match, he scolded me, "Franklin, I told you not to play with fire!" I grinned and said, "No, Daddy. You didn't say, 'Don't play with fire.' You said, 'Don't let me *catch* you.'" Then I ran—faster than he could. And I recall dreading the next time I had to face him because I knew I had disobeyed. I knew I had twisted his words, and I knew what was coming—punishment.

Isn't this how we sometimes behave before the Lord? We may listen to what He says, but then we run off in another direction and do what we want to anyway, seldom counting the cost. What if we were to listen and meditate on all that His instruction means to us and then heed the warnings? We would never have to run from Him because our fellowship would not be broken. Running from God hinders our prayer life faster than anything. I remember hearing my father say, "Prayer is not just asking. It is listening for God's orders."

Human nature is not inclined to take orders. We often want to rebel and go our own way. Yet imagine a world without orders: highways without directions, vehicles without manuals, classrooms without instructions. Such a scenario would be frustrating and destructive, to say the least.

Many Christians don't make prayer a priority in their lives. But the Bible has much to say about the importance of prayer, the time of prayer, the place of prayer, the posture of prayer, and the people of prayer. Do your prayers reflect the attitude of prayer as demonstrated in the Word of God? The psalmist said, "My heart and my flesh cry out for the living God" (Psalm 84:2).

Time of Prayer

Many people say they just don't have time to pray. For the Christian, taking time to pray is a privilege that should be treasured. It is what fuel is to the automobile. The Bible says, "Evening and morning and at noon I will pray, . . . and He shall hear my voice" (Psalm 55:17).

The psalmist declared that he would pray to God in the morning.

Cornelius prayed at three o'clock in the afternoon.

Paul and Silas prayed at midnight.

Jesus said that men should always pray and not lose heart.

We can experience the comfort of prayer when we realize that the Lord is near us whenever we pray to Him (Deuteronomy 4:7).

Place of Prayer

It is not the place of prayer that is so important. Prayer does not have to be confined to the closet or the pew. "Prayer," my father would say, "is really a place where you meet God in genuine conversation. Prayer is a place where we must spend time if we are to learn its power."

Consider the church at Tyre in Acts 21:5. The early church never hesitated to pray, no matter where they found themselves. They accompanied the apostle Paul to the ship, and on the beach they knelt to pray. When on the sea, Paul dropped four anchors from the stern of the ship and prayed. Paul and Silas even prayed in prison while others listened (Acts 16:25).

Peter went to the roof to pray. When he was freed from prison, he went to the house of Mary, where many people had gathered and were praying.

And what about Jesus? He went to a mountainside to pray. The Bible says that Jesus would go to a certain place to pray. When He prayed for those who followed Him, He looked toward heaven. Many times Jesus withdrew from the crowds and prayed in lonely places, knowing that His Father in heaven would hear. My father wrote about the prayers of Jesus and emphasized that "Jesus was never too hurried to spend hours in prayer."[10]

While preaching in Busan, South Korea, I learned that the local churches gathered in preparation for the crusade at five o'clock every morning for prayer. One church had three thousand people come together every morning to pray for the lost, believing that the Holy Spirit would move in the hearts of the people.

We should always approach the throne of God in expectation. The Bible says, "Listen to the cry and the prayer which Your servant is praying before You today. . . . Hear in heaven" (1 Kings 8:28, 30).

Posture of Prayer

Pray is an action word. The dictionary defines the word like this: "To address God with adoration [worship], confession, supplication, *or* thanksgiving."[11] If I could edit Webster's definition, I would replace "or" with "and."

The Bible says, "Oh come, let us worship and bow down; let us kneel before the LORD our Maker. For He is our God" (Psalm 95:6–7).

"Confess your trespasses . . . and pray" (James 5:16). "In everything by prayer and supplication, with thanksgiving, let your requests be made known to God" (Philippians 4:6).

To most, the image of kneeling comes to mind when prayer is mentioned. But my father said, "It is not the body's posture but the heart's attitude that counts when we pray. The important thing is not the position of the body, but the condition of the soul."

In the early days when my father was a student at Florida Bible Institute (now Trinity College of Florida), he became aware of the need to spend time with God in prayer. Often he would walk along a golf course that bordered the campus, preaching into the air, praying as he walked.

There are many personality traits my father and I share. One is that we are most fulfilled when in motion. So naturally my interest was piqued when I learned as a young man that my father walked as he prayed. There are many instances when my father was driven to his knees in prayer, whether in a time of crisis or a time of thanksgiving, but to think of him praying in motion intrigued me.

It made Luke 18:1 come to life: "Men always ought to pray and not lose heart." As a boy, I wondered how people got anything done if they spent all their time praying.

As I grew and watched my father, I realized that he prayed in many ways: on his knees, on his feet, in a chair, on an airplane, at his desk, and in the pulpit. I'll never forget him telling me that he prayed as he preached. I wondered how that could be done! Then I discovered this verse: "And while they are still speaking, I will hear" (Isaiah 65:24).

Years later when I began preaching, I put this into practice and discovered the power that comes through unceasing prayer. You cannot preach the Word of God with power unless you pray in the Spirit of God. My father gave me some of the best advice a son-turned-preacher could receive: "And take . . . the sword of the Spirit, which is the word of God; praying always . . . in the Spirit" (Ephesians 6:17–18).

My father used to say, "As I sit on the platform and the music plays,

I look into the sea of faces in the upper bleachers from left to right and pray for the souls who are lost in sin. My eyes scan those on the main floor, and I pray to God for the empty hearts that need a Savior, and through it, God prepares me for the message. As I stand in the pulpit and cast the net at the time of invitation, I keep on praying for each one responding, that the Holy Spirit will fill them as they pour out their aching hearts of sin and despair to the only One who forgives completely and fills them with peace."

I also recall my father saying that the greatest battleground is at the foot of the cross, where the souls of men and women hang in the balance of eternity because Satan is there lurking in the darkness of the heart. The Bible says, "Your adversary the devil walks about like a roaring lion, seeking whom he may devour. Resist him, steadfast in the faith" (1 Peter 5:8–9).

My father has told me on numerous occasions, "Every time I give an invitation, I am in an attitude of prayer. I feel emotionally, physically, and spiritually drained. It becomes a spiritual battle of such proportions that sometimes I feel faint. There is an inward groaning and agonizing in prayer that I cannot possibly put into words." I have experienced this myself. Perhaps such weakness is to humble God's messengers as a reminder that their complete dependence must be on God alone.

Paul exhorts us to "stand firm in one spirit, contending as one man for the faith of the gospel without being frightened in any way by those who oppose you" (Philippians 1:27–28 NIV). "For our struggle is not against flesh and blood, but . . . against the powers of this dark world and against the spiritual forces of evil in the heavenly realms" (Ephesians 6:12 NIV).

Many times my father walked to the pulpit when he was physically ill, but the Lord strengthened him as he began to preach. I experienced this myself while preaching in Chisinau, Moldova.

Feverish and chilled, I sat on the platform wondering how I would ever get through the message. I found myself saying what I had heard my father say many times through the years: "Lord, I can't do this." But God renewed my strength and enabled me to preach Christ in that historic city.

If those who follow Christ day by day truly believe that there is a battle raging for the unsaved, they should "pray, pray, pray," until victory is won through the working of the Holy Spirit in broken and repentant hearts.

One of the most thrilling passages about prayer is Romans 8:34, which tells us that as we humble ourselves before the Lord in repentance, worship, and praise, Jesus is sitting at the right hand of His Father praying for those held in the palm of His hand: "Christ . . . who is even at the right hand of God, who also makes intercession for us."

The Savior presents our requests to His heavenly Father, who sees us through the eyes of His Son. *"For the eyes of the LORD are on the righteous, and His ears are open to their prayers"* (1 Peter 3:12). And the prayer that He desires most to hear is, "Lord, save me!" (Matthew 14:30).

I pray that you will sense the assurance that Christ can fill your heart with everlasting peace. "God does not call His children to a playground," my father often said, "but to a battleground."

The Lord is with us in the midst, fighting our battles for us here on earth and in heaven. "Christ Jesus . . . is always wrestling in prayer for you, that you may stand firm in all the will of God, mature and fully assured" (Colossians 4:12 NIV).

Let us say with the psalmist, "I give myself to prayer" (Psalm 109:4).

Tilling the Soul's Soil

I heard someone say once, "When you plant seed, you don't expect to dig it up—you expect it to grow through hard ground." Prayer is no different. We plant the seed of prayer in our hearts and let faith cultivate it through fellowship with our heavenly Father. He listens attentively, and He acts when He knows we are ready. His answers are for our good. If He withholds an answer to prayer, it is because we have lessons still to learn, and the heavenly Gardener tills the soil in our souls until our wills are ready to receive His answer.

My father said many times, "Those who have turned the tide of history have turned it by means of prayer. This should be the motto of every follower of Jesus Christ. Never stop praying, no matter how dark and hopeless it may seem."[12]

There is nothing that will grow our faith more than the three key elements of faith building: *prayer, prayer, prayer.*

6

Preach the Word

And of this gospel I was appointed a herald
and an apostle and a teacher.
That is why I am suffering as I am.
Yet I am not ashamed, because I know whom I have believed.

—2 Timothy 1:11–12 niv

I learned the importance of the Bible
and came to believe with all my heart in its full inspiration.
It became a sword in my hand
to break open the hearts of men,
to direct them to the Lord Jesus Christ.

BILLY GRAHAM

Do you have enough imagination to picture Paul, the aged apostle, sitting in a damp, filthy dungeon somewhere in the bowels of Rome, with death hovering above him? Paul had been imprisoned under the heavy hand of Nero—abandoned and cold; nevertheless, filled with hope. Paul knew that martyrdom would free him from chains of persecution and soon usher him into God's presence.

Some may think that Paul would have listened intently for soldiers' footsteps as they might rattle the iron bars, wondering if that were the day of doom. But not this courageous apostle. As he prepared for certain death for the faith, his thoughts were penned in a treasured letter to Timothy, who was pastoring the church at Ephesus.

I have visited this particular location in Rome, where many believe Paul was imprisoned. It gave me a sense of the raw environment in which he lived his last days.

Commenting on the faithfulness of the apostles in the midst of hardship, my father said, "Christ never told His disciples that they would get an Academy Award for their performances, but He did tell them to expect trouble." And the apostle Paul certainly had his share.

Converted to faith through Paul's ministry, Timothy was close to Paul's heart. Paul took great care to instruct and encourage Timothy, knowing that persecution could also endanger his life and the ministry entrusted to him. What must Timothy have thought when he unrolled the parchment scroll?

> Timothy, my dear son, when I call to remembrance the genuine faith that is in you . . . study to show yourself approved . . . rightly handle the word of truth . . . stir up the gift of God . . . hold fast the pattern of sound words . . . continue in the things you have learned from childhood—the Holy Scriptures . . . which are able to make you wise for salvation through faith in Christ Jesus . . . and I give you this charge: *preach the Word.* (2 Timothy 1:2, 5; 2:15; 1:6; 1:13; 3:14–15; 4:1–2)

This is what Paul wanted Timothy to remember. This is what Paul urged Timothy to put into practice. Paul's inspired letters outlined for the young preacher/evangelist his great responsibility in handling and preaching the Word of God.

> Be ready in season and out of season. Convince, rebuke, exhort, with all longsuffering and teaching. For the time will come when they will not endure sound doctrine, but according to their own desires, because they have itching ears, they will heap up for themselves teachers; and they will turn their ears away from the truth, and be turned aside to fables. But you be watchful in all things, endure afflictions, do the work of an evangelist, fulfill your ministry. (2 Timothy 4:2–5)

These verses encompass the meaning of the word *PREACH*:

Prepare yourself at all times,
Rebuke false teaching,
Evangelize the lost, be
Alert in adversity,
Carry out the work,
Herald the truth of the Gospel.

Timothy must have been filled with deep emotion. He knew that Paul's life was ebbing closer to death. Timothy held in his hands Paul's letter. He sensed the passion from ink-stained words and understood Paul's charge to teach and preach the whole Word of God. He did not tell Timothy to preach some of the words—he instructed Timothy to be "thoroughly equipped for every good work" based on sound doctrine (2 Timothy 3:17).

The urgency of Paul's requests must have tugged at Timothy's heart: "Be diligent to come to me quickly. . . . Bring [my] cloak . . . when you come—and the books, especially the parchments. . . . Do your utmost to come before winter" (2 Timothy 4:9, 13, 21).

Books and scrolls were valuable in that day. It is possible that Paul had left them with Timothy to study. Paul, under the guidance of the Holy Spirit, had groomed Timothy for the work of the ministry and had left Timothy in Ephesus to minister among the Ephesians.

Paul knew Ephesus well—a city filled with idol worship and mythology. He assured Timothy of his prayers for him day and night. Paul was compelled to warn Timothy of the dangers of the godless society, writing, "No one engaged in [spiritual] warfare entangles himself with the affairs of this life" (2 Timothy 2:4).

These words were not written only for Timothy; they are for us today. In spite of the fact that television, radio, print media, and the Internet are flooded with preachers, there is a great falling away when it comes to preaching the Word of God in a society drenched in satisfying human pleasure.

My father often said, "Comfort and prosperity have never enriched the world as much as adversity has." My close friend Sami Dagher, from Beirut, said that during the war in Lebanon, the church grew as people came to faith in Christ. When peace returned to Lebanon, there was a spiritual falling away as people began making money and caring more about living prosperous lives.

Unrolling the biblical scrolls should be an everyday occurrence in the lives of all Bible believers, and particularly for those called to proclaim the treasured message contained in the Gospel. This is what keeps our faith strong in the Lord.

We see this tried-and-tested apostle commending and admonishing Timothy: "You have carefully followed my doctrine, manner of life, purpose, faith, [patience], love, perseverance, persecutions, afflictions, which happened to me. . . . And out of them all the Lord delivered me. Yes, and all who desire to live godly in Christ Jesus will suffer persecution. . . . But you must continue in the things which you have learned" (2 Timothy 3:10–12, 14). Here was Paul, a father figure to his spiritual son, Timothy, teaching him the truths of their heavenly Father.

A well-known author was asked one day the secret to his writing. He looked at the young aspiring wordsmith and said, "Read!" Paul admonished Timothy to devote himself to the reading of Scripture in order to preach and teach—he emphasized that this should not be neglected.

I can recall hearing similar words from another wise ambassador of the Gospel. I had been given good instruction from childhood and lots of pointers from a great many preachers, like the eloquent Dr. John Wesley White, a longtime associate of my father's who had mentored me and encouraged me to preach.

After struggling within myself about whether I was called to such a task, and finally resolving it in my own mind, I went for a walk one day with a seasoned preacher.

Preach It

"Daddy, what is the most important thing I can learn about preaching?" I asked him. He stopped along the wooded trail below the house where we had been walking. His eyes peered into mine and without hesitation he said, "Son, the best advice I can give you is preach! The only way you can learn to preach is by preaching. Take every opportunity to preach. And be sure to always preach the Word."

No longer is it possible to enjoy walks with my father, but his words ring in my ears: "Make use of this tool of communication by which God speaks to us—namely, the Bible. Read it, study it, memorize it. It will change your entire life. It is not like any other book. It is a 'living' book that works its way into your heart, mind, and soul. Read it—then preach it!"

There was an old preacher from the South who was asked how he prepared his sermons. His answer was, "I read myself full, think myself clear, pray myself hot, and then I lets go."

There is no question that down through the centuries, God has placed men in the shoe leather of the Gospel, and they have been beacons of Gospel light. I feel privileged to have been raised in the home of one such man. In following my father's instruction, I am both convicted and inspired to read about preachers whose ministries have been documented in Scripture. "Let him speak My word faithfully" (Jeremiah 23:28).

Preachers generally have mentors—others who have gone before them. I have gleaned treasures from my father, but more than once I heard him say, "I am only one in a chain of men and women God has raised up through the centuries to build Christ's church and to take the Gospel everywhere."

The Bible writers carefully documented that effective preaching comes through God's power. Time and again, the apostles of the New Testament affirmed the prophets of the Old Testament.

Noah, an ark builder turned farmer, was a preacher of righteousness, as Peter stated in 2 Peter 2:5. For approximately 120 years Noah preached repentance, but the people rebelled. I wonder how many preachers would remain faithful to proclaiming God's Word when the results turned up empty, decade after decade? The whole world—save eight people—died in the terrible flood. When God's Word goes forth, the results belong to the Lord, not the preacher.

Ezra, an Old Testament scribe, stood before the people of Israel in a wooden pulpit and distinctly read the Book from morning until midday. They wept when they heard the Word of God and went away having understood the words declared unto them (Nehemiah 8:3–9). What would happen today if God's people delighted to hear His Word read publicly for hours? Perhaps we would go out as they did and do what the Word of God instructed. The result—God was remembered in that generation.

Solomon, a king and son of a king, called himself a preacher who sought to find words of truth to impart to the kingdom (Ecclesiastes 12:10). Many motivational preachers today would not use Ecclesiastes as their textbook. Its final verdict is that "all is vanity under the sun." Solomon's ecclesiastical discourse contrasts human reason to God's wisdom and proves that man's intellect and ability are foolishness apart from Him.

Jonah, a prophet from Galilee, was commanded by God to go to perhaps the most morally decadent city in the ancient world, where the people practiced every perversion known to man—much like our society today.

At first Jonah refused. He ran from God. Jonah wanted God to send judgment on the people of Nineveh (modern-day Mosul, Iraq). But God has a way of getting our attention, and he certainly got Jonah's attention by causing a great fish to swallow Jonah. After spending three days in the belly of the fish and being regurgitated on the beach, going to Nineveh did not seem like such a bad idea after all. When God told him, "Arise, go to Nineveh, that great city, and preach to it the message that I tell you," Jonah arose and went (Jonah 3:2).

Many preachers would not want to be identified with Jonah because of his outward disobedience to God. However, they would happily identify with the end results. In spite of Jonah's weakness, God brought about a miraculous revival as the entire pagan city repented of sin and turned to God—including the king and his nobles. The results belong to the Lord.

Philip, a disciple, and the only one in Scripture called an evangelist (Acts 21:8), was instructed by an angel of the Lord to go toward Gaza. "So he arose and went" (Acts 8:27). He came upon an Ethiopian eunuch of great authority sitting in his chariot and reading Isaiah 53:7–8, a passage that had confounded the Jewish scholars. "Do you understand what you are reading?" Philip asked. The eunuch said, "How can I, unless someone guides me?" (Acts 8:30–31). Then Philip opened his mouth and began preaching about Jesus from the Book, and the eunuch believed (vv. 35–37). Because Philip was prepared in season and out of season and obedient to God's call, he was blessed to lead this influential man to Christ. The result is the Lord's.

Paul, a former Pharisee turned tentmaker, was appointed a preacher by the preeminent preacher—Jesus Christ: "[Paul] is a chosen vessel of Mine to bear My name before Gentiles, kings, and the children of Israel" (Acts 9:15). Immediately, Paul began preaching that Jesus is the Son of God (Acts 9:20). He spoke boldly and preached fearlessly in the name of the Lord.

Jesus said to Paul on the road to Damascus, "I now send you, to open their eyes, in order to turn them from darkness to light, and from the power of Satan to God" (Acts 26:17–18).

One of Paul's great sermons was preached at Antioch, one of the chief cities in Asia. After the reading of the Word of God, Paul rose with command of the Scriptures, rehearsing how the hand of God had moved in the lives of His people: "Those among you who fear God, to you the word of this salvation has been sent" (Acts 13:26). While the Jews rejected Paul's preaching, the Gentiles begged that these words might be preached to them. A preacher may never know the seed that falls on tender hearts ready for the Gospel plow—but God knows.

When my mother was a girl in China, she knew a pioneer missionary by the name of Rev. James R. Graham Sr. (no relation). He preached his entire life to the people of China and did not have one convert that he knew of. When asked if he ever became discouraged, he replied, "No. The battle is the Lord's." Yet today there are millions of believers in China. It has been said that the nation may have the largest Christian population by 2030. I have to wonder how many will come to know the Lord because of this faithful missionary.

This is what Paul spoke of when he wrote about a preacher who had come before him—one who had been called for the sole purpose of announcing the Coming One (Acts 19:4). When John the Baptist came on the scene months before Jesus' public ministry began, people asked, "Who are you?" I love how this earthy preacher answered: "I am 'The voice of one crying in the wilderness: "Make straight the way of the LORD"'" (John 1:23). And John preached repentance for the remission of sins (Mark 1:4).

What a response. He did not say, "I am John the forerunner of the Messiah," or, "I am the cousin of the Promised One." He proclaimed: "I have seen and testified that this is the Son of God" (John 1:34).

This is the message of the Gospel preacher: *proclaim Christ.*

My father wrote, "Some evangelists spend too much time thinking and even planning about how to achieve visible results. This is an easy trap to fall into. Nowhere do the Scriptures tell us to seek results, nor do the Scriptures rebuke evangelists if the results are meager. Let us take note of what evangelists cannot do. They cannot bring conviction of sin, righteousness, or judgment. They cannot convert anyone; that is the Spirit's work."[1]

Canvassing the World

God has spoken His Word down through the centuries through kings and eunuchs, prophets and apostles, scribes and fishermen, shepherds and farmers.

This is true of a young North Carolina boy. My father went from sowing seed in the fields and milking cows, to preaching the pure milk of the Word and sowing the seed of the Gospel throughout the nations of the world for the remainder of the twentieth century—and into the next. He stated many times that he never understood why God called him to preach the Gospel to the world. He also said that there was no greater privilege than to be used by God as a voice proclaiming His love for mankind and calling men to repentance.

Billy Graham preached hell and heaven, sin and salvation, judgment and mercy, Jesus' compassion, the Spirit's comfort, and his Father's great love. I saw this passion in him and it made a profound impact on me. It was always my father's desire to faithfully preach the Word and watch the Lord harvest souls. The testimony he has left behind is this: "O LORD . . . I will speak of Your testimonies also before kings" (Psalm 119:41, 46).

My paternal grandmother held on to a letter my father had written while a student at Wheaton College: "I have but one passion, and that is to win souls."[2] When Mother Graham allowed the letter to be printed much later in life, she said: "Billy's destiny then was decided . . . and it became for him his hour of decision."[3]

The Bible says, "How then shall they call on Him in whom they have not believed? And how shall they believe in Him of whom they have not heard? And how shall they hear without a preacher? And how shall they preach unless they are sent? As it is written: *'How beautiful are the feet of those who preach the gospel!'"* (Romans 10:14–15).

This passage takes me to a scene in the Upper Room when Jesus poured water into a basin and washed His disciples' feet hours before He was crucified (John 13:5). Not only was He serving His disciples, but He was also anointing the beautiful feet that would carry the Good News of the soon to be risen Savior.

Jesus Christ is Preacher, Prophet, King, Husbandman, the Good Shepherd, and King above all others.

On the road to Emmaus after His resurrection, He walked and talked with disciples, expounding to them from the Scriptures—beginning at Moses and the Prophets—all the things concerning Himself (Luke 24:27).

And when He had fulfilled the Scriptures, He commissioned His followers to preach the Gospel to every creature (Mark 16:15); to make disciples of all nations; to teach them to observe all things He commanded (Matthew 28:19–20); and to be witnesses of Him to the ends of the earth (Acts 1:8). He opened their understanding, that they might comprehend the Scriptures, saying, "Repentance and remission of sins should be preached in His name" (Luke 24:47).

"And He led them out as far as Bethany," and the same hands that had washed their feet at Passover were now lifted and "while He blessed them . . . He was parted . . . up into heaven" (Luke 24:50–51).

When I am sitting in the cockpit of a plane, I often wonder what it must have been like for the disciples that day to watch the crucified and risen Lord ascend. There are times I wish I could just point the nose of the aircraft upward, beyond the last layer of clouds, toward the gates of glory. It's an airman's dream, of course, to go beyond the stars—someday I will. For now, God's plan for me is to walk in His presence on earth and carry on the work He places in my pathway—to preach and proclaim the Gospel.

In essence, the greatest Teacher to ever preach the Word is the Word. When Jesus departed He gave His followers—the church—an assignment that would take from His ascension to His return to complete.

For all those who take the Great Commission to heart, consider God's Word: "[The Lord] was received up into heaven, and sat down at the right hand of God. And they [the disciples] went out and preached everywhere, the Lord working with them and confirming the word" (Mark 16:19–20).

The Word of God must be preached with bold confidence, with unwavering resolve, and in godly love. He is working with us and confirming His Word in us. If the Word of God is not at the center of our work, we can be assured that He is not empowering our activity.

Salvation in the City of God

Roy Gustafson was an important part of my life from the time I was a teenager. I traveled with him before I gave my life to Jesus Christ. In 1974, we were on a trip to the Holy Land, staying in Jerusalem on the Mount of Olives, not far from where Jesus died and ascended two thousand years before.

I had become miserable in my sin. One evening I got down on my knees in my hotel room overlooking the Kidron Valley and the Eastern Gate, and I confessed my sin and prayed that God would forgive me. That night I surrendered my life to the Savior.

Roy mentored me in the Scriptures in the early days of my new walk with the Lord. One of his favorite sayings was, "Preach the Gospel, the whole Gospel, and nothing but the Gospel." I often remember Roy's words when I am preparing to preach the Word.

Some years before, my father had asked Roy to write a booklet titled *What Is the Gospel?* To this day I carry it with me in my Bible. Roy had a unique way of communicating profound truths in little nuggets. He wrote:

The word *Gospel* occurs over one hundred times in the New Testament.

It is called the "Gospel of God" because it originates in His love.

It is the "Gospel of Christ" because it flows from Christ's sacrifice.

It is the "Gospel of Grace" because it saves those who are condemned.

It is called the "Gospel of Glory" because in a real sense we have exchanged the Christ of Galilee for the Christ of glory.

It is called the "Gospel of our Salvation" because it is by the power of God unto everyone that believes.

It is called the "Gospel of Peace" because through Christ it makes peace between the sinner and God.

"I declare unto you the gospel which I preached . . . Christ died for our sins according to the scriptures; and that he was buried, and that he rose again the third day according to the Scriptures" (1 Corinthians 15:1, 3–4, KJV).

Jesus Christ did not come to earth to live. He came to die.

He did not come to preach the Gospel. He came that there might be a Gospel to preach.

Turn to Him from your sins today and receive Him as your Lord and your Savior.

Receive Him with your eyes—

"LOOK unto me, and be ye saved" (Isaiah 45:22).

Receive Him with your feet—

"COME unto me, all ye that labour and are heavy laden, and I will give you rest" (Matthew 11:28).

Receive Him with your hands—

"TAKE the water of life freely" (Revelation 22:17).

Receive Him with your lips—

"TASTE and see that the LORD is good" (Psalm 34:8).

Receive Him with your ears—

"HEAR, and your soul shall live" (Isaiah 55:3).

Receive Him with your will—

"CHOOSE you this day whom ye will serve" (Joshua 24:15).

Receive Him with your heart—

"TRUST in the LORD with all thine heart" (Proverbs 3:5).[4]

I thank God that my father asked Roy to come alongside me at a critical point in my young life. And I thank Roy's daughters—Enid, Sonja, and Donnie—for sharing their remarkable father with me.

Evangelizing All God's Creation

My father and Roy met while attending Florida Bible Institute. Not far from campus, the two of them would often hold impromptu meetings. Standing on a busy street corner, Roy would play his trumpet to attract a crowd and my father would give a short—very short—sermonette to passersby. Soon his soul burned for the lost. He often wrote to his mother, and as most mothers would, she treasured every letter.

"Mother," he began, "I think the Lord is calling me to the ministry, and if He does, it will be in the field of evangelism."

According to Mother Graham, it wasn't long before my father began receiving invitations to preach in surrounding communities. He would practice his sermons during the week on the golf course, pretending that the trees were people. When he raised his voice, the squirrels would run under the bushes.

I'm sure my father's preaching never persuaded one squirrel to repent. But all glory is given to the Lord Jesus for the millions of people who have heard God's message and have accepted salvation from the One who died in our place.

A few months later, my father wrote again: "I rededicated my life to the Lord Jesus Christ last night under the stars, Mother, and I've been in tears for weeks under conviction for my past indifference. I want to ask your and Daddy's forgiveness because God has already forgiven."

Until the day my father died, he couldn't let go of a wrong in his life until he made it right—first with God and then with others. I learned from my father that unconfessed sin in believers' hearts hinders their walk, their talk, and their service to God. But when it is settled with God, He restores joy and fellowship.

My parents taught that while God forgives our sin, we still contend with our human natures. My father was more introspective than my mother. She saw life practically and quipped that God's children were under construction from the cradle to the grave. In fact years before, she insisted with a twinkle, that when she died, her epitaph should read: END OF CONSTRUCTION. THANK YOU FOR YOUR PATIENCE. And to the surprise of many, this is exactly what you will see if you visit my parents' graves at the Billy Graham Library.

My father, however, was more somber. He thought frequently about death as his health began to suffer. When he was diagnosed in 2001 with normal pressure hydrocephalus, his doctors at the Mayo Clinic made the decision to insert a shunt into his brain to relieve the pressure. He had put it off as long as he could and, though reluctant, consented to the operation. The night before surgery, he was reflective and even a bit agitated. Whatever was going on in his thinking was between him and the Lord.

Days after the successful procedure, he talked about uneasiness in his spirit. Weak in voice, he said, "Before my surgery I didn't think I would make it through. I knew I was going to die. I've never doubted that I was ready to meet the Lord, but when I imagined myself standing before Him, I knew there were things I needed to settle."

He had hardly slept the night before surgery because he had to "make things right with God." About what? Only the Father in heaven knows. But what I do know is that my father had settled the eternity of his soul with the Lord in 1934 when he walked the sawdust aisle of a pine-framed tabernacle in Charlotte, North Carolina. He surrendered his life to the One who exchanges our burdens for His blessings.

I learned much by watching my father in life and a great deal more by observing him in his twilight years. He never ceased to "settle" things with the Lord and with others. When the Lord called him out of this world, he set aside the shunts, the canes, and the hearing aids. He now rests in the midst of God's peace, waiting for Christ to split the earth wide open, unite the bride of Christ in the air, and bring God's children eternally home.

My grandparents lived long enough to see my father preach around the world. Often they were asked what they thought of their son's preaching. They replied, "Billy takes the Bible and preaches it in simplicity, with clarity and urgency. He has no magic and makes no appeal to the emotions. His indivisible conviction confirms he knows the right way of life . . . that Christ must break down the evil that seeks to destroy the world. Billy Frank punches out the facts—the facts that he reads out from the open Bible in his hand, and which he asks his audience to read again and again from their Bibles."[5]

I have learned by watching and listening to my father the importance of preaching the Scriptures. He often said, "I have used from twenty-five to one hundred passages of Scripture with every sermon and have learned that modern man will surrender to the impact of the Word of God. When we preach or teach the Scriptures, we open the door for the Holy Spirit to do His work. God has not promised to bless oratory or clever preaching. He has promised to bless His Word."

In my own preaching, I have tried to apply a wise observation from my father's years of preaching. He said many times, "When the Gospel of Jesus Christ is presented, with authority—quoting from the very Word of God—He takes that message and drives it supernaturally into the human heart."

I have seen this happen in meetings around the world. God's Word points to the One we preach, and God's Spirit drives it into the barren soul.

The Moody Challenge

I find it fascinating to hear stories about those who have gone before. My father's ministry was greatly influenced by Dr. Dwight L. Moody and Billy Sunday. He patterned many things after their ministries.

Years ago, Rev. J. Wilbur Chapman, an associate of Dwight L. Moody, wrote about an exchange between Harry Moorehouse, the English Bible reader, and Dr. Moody. I would say it took some guts on the part of Dr. Moorehouse to approach Dr. Moody. Thank God for those who are willing to stake their livelihood on speaking the truth, in love, even when it may sting the hearer.

Moorehouse said, "If you will stop preaching your own words and preach God's Word, you will make yourself a great power for good."[6]

To D. L. Moody's credit, he took the good advice to heart.

Reverend Chapman (who had hired Billy Sunday as a teenager years before) wrote, "This prophecy made a deep impression on Mr. Moody's mind, and from that day he devoted himself to the study of the Bible as he had never done before. He had been accustomed to draw his sermons from the experiences of Christians and the life on the streets, now he began to follow the counsel of his friend, and preach the Word. . . . It was by his loving, prayerful, trustful study of the Scriptures that he had acquired his skill as a practical commentator."[7]

In one of Moody's great sermons he posed the question, "How do you suppose you are to have faith in God when you don't know anything about Him? It is those who haven't any acquaintance with God that stumble and fall: but those who know Him can trust Him and lean heavy on His arm. You may say, 'O, we must study science and literature, and such things, in order to understand the Bible.' What can a botanist tell you about the 'Rose of Sharon' and the 'Lily of the Valley'? What can the geologist tell you about the 'Rock of Ages'? What can the astronomer tell you about the 'Bright and Morning Star?'"[8]

God is the creator of science, botany, and geology. How rich and full are the Scriptures that express His creation. He raised the mountains for protection, leveled the plains for food, rushed the rivers with water, set the soul in man, and then hung on an old rugged cross. When Jesus endured our sin, God raised Him from the grave to provide His children with a home in heaven, the bread and water of everlasting life, and His Word of eternal love found in the Scriptures. How boundless are its topics; its studies; its sermons; its warnings; its cures; its blessings; and its promises found in its Subject—the Lord Jesus Christ.

The wealth of wisdom contained in God's sacred library is inexhaustible. The voice of the preacher calling lost sinners to repentance is an instrument unto God. May preachers forsake *all* that sidetracks from proclaiming the greatest message ever told and preach the truth, all the truth, and nothing but the truth that tells of the Lord Jesus Christ:

Our *All*	His *All*
All have sinned (Romans 3:23)	Christ died for *all* sinners (2 Corinthians 5:15)
All our righteousnesses are as filthy rags (Isaiah 64:6)	He forgives and cleanses from *all* unrighteousness (1 John 1:9)
All have turned away—no one does good (Romans 3:12)	*All* who call on the Lord will be saved (Romans 10:13)
All of our sins were laid on Christ (Isaiah 53:6)	Christ washed *all* our sins away in His own blood (Revelation 1:5)
In Adam *all* die (1 Corinthians 15:22)	In Christ *all* will be made alive (1 Corinthians 15:22)
All the days of life are vain (Ecclesiastes 6:12)	In Christ *all* things become new (2 Corinthians 5:17)

The Same Yesterday, Today, and Forever

We are living in an unprecedented age. *Tolerance*, *diversity*, and *relevance* are the buzzwords of the twenty-first century, not only in politics and culture but also in religious circles. Frequently they are bantered about by talking heads.

Many boast that the church has finally stopped preaching sin and learned how to preach love, exchanging fire and brimstone for stroking self-worth. Others fear that the church is getting sidetracked from its true mission—preaching the Word.

Many preach that Jesus Christ is the same yesterday, today, and forever but want to alter His message to fit the ever-changing pop culture. The mission of the church is to win souls for the kingdom and help followers mature in faith. If this were happening, adapting to culture would not have become the driving force it is today.

In his book *Hope for the Troubled Heart*, my father wrote about the popularity cult and the negative influence it can have in the life of a Christian.[9] The church is thrashing about—tossed to and fro by every wind of doctrine. Articles by Christian writers are covering the "identity crisis" in magnified proportions.

In commenting on the term *evangelical*, one Methodist pastor wrote that it "once referred to a theological position. Today, it refers to a political and cultural movement that has taken over much of the church. It has convinced many people that a better day . . . will be achieved through 'engaging the culture' . . . [promising] something that it cannot deliver: the salvation of society. It is depleting the church of spiritual vitality and setting many people up for disappointment. . . . I pray that a leader of wisdom and standing will rise up and call the church back to biblical reality."[10]

Consider the following statements:

- America [has become] thoroughly infiltrated with professors who no longer believe in the complete integrity and authority of the written Word of God.
- The Old Testament, together with much of the New, is considered outmoded and no longer relevant for our sophisticated age. Out of this rejection of the Scriptures have grown some devastating theories. One is that there are no longer absolutes; everything is relative.
- [Students] are forced to substitute: reason for faith, reformation for redemption, a program for a Person. The source of power is thought to be in organizations and numbers rather than in the Holy Spirit.
- [The church] is more concerned with ecclesiastical organization, power and prestige than with the touchy questions having to do with the basic facts of the Christian faith itself. An increasing number have had their confidence in the Bible so greatly shaken

that they hold impaired views with reference to truths which are part of the Christian faith.

- A new religion has emerged that is humanism, not Christianity.
- Unless there is a concerted stand [the church's] witness in America is doomed.[11]

While these statements reflect current trends, you may be surprised to learn that they were written more than fifty years ago by Dr. L. Nelson Bell, my maternal grandfather. In a book he titled *While Men Slept*, he wrote about Jesus' parable of the wheat and tares growing together. "But while men slept, [the] enemy came and sowed tares among the wheat and went his way" (Matthew 13:25). Tares resemble wheat until the wheat head matures, then tares become distinguishable for what they are—weeds.

My grandfather—a medical doctor, church statesman, and lay preacher—carried a heavy burden for Christ's church in the mid-twentieth century. My father considered him one of his closest confidants (second to my mother). Grandfather Bell served as moderator of the Presbyterian Church in the United States. He died in his sleep in 1973 after speaking at a missions conference the night before. He preached on the state of the church and said, "Now in this place there are two groups of people. There are those who know they are saved and love the Lord Jesus Christ, and there are those here who as yet may not know Christ. My hope is that before you leave this place you will come to know [Jesus] as your personal Lord and Savior."[12] With no hesitation he called "the churched" to repentance. There is a great mission field within the church walls.

My grandfather's desire was to see the church strong in doctrine, effective in witness, and fruitful in soul winning. He hoped to wake the church from slumber and sounded the same alarm, as did the apostle Paul: "It is high time to awake out of sleep" (Romans 13:11).

We cannot be sleeping if we are in a state of expectation. The apostles faithfully preached Christ's return for the purpose of motivating the church to action—meaning to live what we preach. "Let us cast off the works of darkness, and let us put on the armor of light. Let us walk properly. . . . Put on the Lord Jesus Christ, and make no provision for the flesh" (Romans 13:12–14).

The apostles preached that Christians must stand apart from the world, not conform to its darkness. My father said it this way: "The way you live often means a great deal more to others than what you say." Having one foot in the world and the other in the things of Christ is living in disobedience.

My father was never one to get involved with denominational skirmishes. However, when it came to the body of Christ, he didn't pull any punches or try to skirt around issues that tampered with the authenticity of the most precious relationship set in place by Jesus Christ—His church.

Every authentic work that is done in the name of the Lord Jesus Christ comes under His authority, whether it is the work of local churches, parachurch organizations, or missionary agencies. Standards are laid out in Scripture, and the power to do the work comes only through obedience to God's Word in all things.

In his book *How to Be Born Again*, my father addressed concerns much like my grandfather had done years earlier. When the church is infiltrated by the world, it breaks down matters of faith.

There is a great counterfeiter [Satan] who adapts himself to every culture, even deceiving true believers at times. He doesn't charge on the scene clothed in red and wearing a hideous mask but charms his way as an "angel of light."

Man suppresses the truth, mixes it with error, and develops the religions of the world.

Substitutes have been handed them in the guise of religious rituals, good works, community effort, or social reform, all of which are commendable actions in themselves, but none of which can gain a person a right relationship with God.

Where there is truth and error there is always compromise. Within some churches there is a movement to reshape the Christian message to make it more acceptable to modern man. . . . From compromise to deceit is a small step. All through the Bible we are warned about false prophets and false teachers.

Thousands of [Christians] are being deceived today. Paul is not gentle with false teachers. Nothing could be more grossly wrong than the old cliché that "any religion will do, as long as you're sincere."

There is a right and wrong way to make contact with God. . . . Idolatrous beliefs have eroded the foundations of truth. Whether ancient or modern, all have posed alternatives to the biblical way of approaching God.[13]

The most sincere act that has ever been done on earth was the sacrifice of Jesus Christ on Calvary's cross. This is the cornerstone of the faith. It is the heart of the Gospel. And everything in the Bible points to this sacrifice for man's redemption.

There is enormous privilege—and great responsibility—in proclaiming what the Bible says. What a heritage is ours to preach the Word.

Writing from Heaven

While still on the dairy farm in the 1930s, my father and his younger brother, Melvin, worked in the fields when they were not milking cows. Uncle Melvin was a farmer at heart. He loved to plant seed, watch God water it with rain, and wait for the crops to break through the rich Carolina soil. He also loved dairy cows. It didn't matter how cantankerous they were, he had a knack with the Holsteins and, like most dairy farmers, knew them by name. For Uncle Melvin farming was hard but satisfying work. To my father it was just a chore.

One day while plowing the field with a team of mules, Uncle Melvin looked to the sky when he heard the buzz of an engine. He stopped and ran over to my father, slapped him on the back, and said, "Billy Frank, look up."

Skywriting back then, especially over farm country, was rare. But for advertisers who believed in their product, it was worth the money to blow a catchphrase onto nature's billboard.

Across the canvas of Carolina blue, a little plane wrote as it maneuvered and twisted the smoky letters into shape: G . . . P . . .

I can just see two farm boys dusting the grit from their brows as they watched the last letter formed: G . . . P . . . G . . .

"Melvin," my father shouted, pointing up as if to spell the words, "that means Go Preach the Gospel!" Uncle Melvin, six years younger, thumped Daddy in the chest and said, "Aw shucks, Billy Frank, that means Go Plow the Ground!"

To this day I remember the rascally look on Uncle Melvin's face as he told the story. He contended that their responses to the sky letters reflected their hearts. To him, it seemed almost prophetic. Uncle Melvin became a successful farmer and landowner, and my father became a spiritual seed sower. No man was more proud of his brother than my father, and Uncle Melvin was grateful that God groomed his big brother to use the Gospel plow throughout the fields of the world.

"That it may give seed to the sower . . . , so shall My word be that goes forth from My mouth" (Isaiah 55:10–11).

Every Soul Won Is God's Ambassador

The Bible says, "We are ambassadors for Christ, as though God were pleading through us: we implore you on Christ's behalf, be reconciled to God" (2 Corinthians 5:20). My father preached, "You and I, God's ambassadors, are called to sound the warning, to call sinners to repentance, to point the way to peace with God and the hope that is in Christ."

God does not call everyone to a preaching ministry, but He does call His followers to dwell on the things that speak of Him, and to tell others what He has done. This can only be done in God's power as we live for Him so that men and women will see Christ in us.

Many have planted, many have watered, and the Great Reaper of the harvest will come soon and gather the wheat and tares before His throne. The wheat He will call by name and say, "Well done, My good and faithful servants." The tares will cower at the dreadful words as the judgment gavel buffets out the verdict: *Sorry, I never knew you. Go and serve the one you served while on earth.*

That is a judgment no Bible-believing Christian wants declared to family, friends, or even foes. Every saved soul should be an ambassador of the Good News. Are you?

There are many standing in your fields of influence. They are lost, they are dying in sin, and they are bound for hell. They will one day stand before Almighty God. The Bible says, "Those who dwell in the wilderness will bow before Him" (Psalm 72:9). Pray that God will give a great harvest from the wilderness that surrounds you, and *preach the Word.*

Paul was weary on his journey, his body frail and weak
The apostle knew the end was near as he dipped his pen in ink
He wrote, Timothy, my son, I have fought the fight of faith
Carry on what I've begun, but most of all I pray

Preach the Word, preach the cross
Preach redemption to a lost and dying world
Lift your voice unashamed of the Gospel of His name
Until all have heard, preach the Word.

Paul and Timothy are gone, but the letter still remains
And the mission that Paul wrote about calls out to us today
Lift the name of Jesus higher until the whole world knows
The story of amazing grace; we are messengers of hope

Preach the Word, preach the cross
Preach redemption to a lost and dying world
Lift your voice unashamed of the Gospel of His name
Until all have heard, preach the Word.[14]

7

Just Write to Me...
That's All the Address You Need

Write, for these words are true and faithful.

—Revelation 21:5

I want to add a few words about my calling....
An evangelist is like a newscaster on television or a journalist writing for a
newspaper ... except that the evangelist's mission is to tell the Good News
that never changes.

BILLY GRAHAM

My father had an interesting—and historical—collection of letters from presidents of the United States and other noted figures spanning nearly seven decades. Media sources have inquired about this correspondence many times. A selection will someday be displayed at the Billy Graham Library.

Some letters were personal in nature; others dealt with social concerns and international affairs. Some presidents offered my father presidential appointments, but he turned them down. His burning concern was for the spiritual climate of a turbulent world. There was no doubt in his heart that he had been called to preach, and he intended to labor for the Lord and water the Gospel seed planted deep in his soul, praying that nothing would deter him.

He did, however, treasure the letters he received throughout his lifetime, whether from the White House, fellow preachers, or the many ministry partners who prayed for him.

My Dear Billy . . .

When he was not traveling, my father often started his days reading through mail. What arrived in the mailbox often dictated the day's agenda. He spent some time in his office at the bottom of the hill, but frequently he would have the mail delivered to the house so that he could work in the privacy and serenity of home—with my mother close by.

His commitment to answering mail remained a priority as he aged, even with bad eyesight. After my mother's death, he had his office staff read letters to him, and then he would dictate responses. For him, the day had been fruitful if he was able to keep up with his mail.

As a young boy I can remember my father talking about the mail. It weighed on his heart. Every letter was unique and yet the same; each letter represented a broken heart or a special request. When I began working, I adapted to my father's style of staying current with daily mail—or at least I try.

In the first year of my ministry, I had a two-person office and used to wonder if the mailman would ever find Samaritan's Purse tucked in the hills of North Carolina. By 1980, I had traveled the world many times; but when it came to running an office, I didn't have a clue. I couldn't wait for the little bag of mail to arrive each morning. Responding to each letter was sheer fun. I stretched the process through the day just to keep busy.

When I tell my staff about the "good old days" now, they can't imagine just a few pieces of mail. They're lucky to get the mail opened by end of day. The letters that come represent thousands of prayers from faithful men, women, teenagers, and even children who support our ministry. Some envelopes contain expressions of thanks from those who have been helped by Samaritan's Purse or BGEA.

Stamp and Mail

During the PC boom of the 1990s, some of my staff lobbied for a paperless office. "We can do away with typewriters, Rolodex spinners, and file cabinets," they said, thinking they could persuade me to declare doom for the tired inventions. I relented to a partial compromise, ushering in the new while clinging to a remnant of the old.

I love gadgets and high-tech electronics, but my comfort zone is still with paper and pen. I might not be able to read my writing once I scribble something down, but if I depended on booting up a computer and logging in to jog my memory, I would never get to my next appointment.

As for e-mail, I have not made that switch from letter writing totally. And I don't believe that my father ever sent an e-mail or read one. I used to tell friends and colleagues, if you need to send me something, stick a stamp on an envelope and mail it—I believe in supporting the United States Post Office!

I have no objection to others in my office communicating via e-mail. It keeps things moving at a fast pace—that part I love. I am glad, though, that this technology was not around when I was younger. I would have never known the thrill of opening envelopes from my father with postmarks from around the world. Or my mother's wise and funny notes received while I was away at school.

The Parental Epistles

My mother was an avid letter writer. When a letter found its way to one of her children, her unique way of getting a point across was unmistakable. My father reinforced her instruction many times through his own letters.

The week following my mother's death, several boxes were delivered to my office. Each box was appropriately marked with my name and a list of contents.

Years before, when my mother stopped traveling for health reasons, she said, "This will be a good time to organize my past." She would climb the narrow steps to the attic and spend hours sorting. My mother defined the meaning of *pack rat*. And "Ruth's Attic" was filled with the evidence. Our family laughed about it often, knowing that surely the rafters were held in place by possessions held dear in a mother's heart. Each item represented a special memory to my mother. She separated each child's belongings, carefully identifying the items, most having no value at all. The fact that she kept it all spoke of her sentiment—a tangible tracking of her footsteps and ours.

One box was marked "Franklin's Trinkets"—old army helmets, used matchboxes and cigarette papers (why she kept these I'll never know), worthless international coins, even my baby blanket that the dog had apparently ripped to shreds (or was it a rat?). As I dug through all this stuff, I marveled that my mother kept such trivial things.

But when I sliced open the box marked "Letters," I found some epistles that were forty years old. Some of the yellow and curled paper crumbled in my hands. The words brought back incidents long forgotten. But as a fourteen-year-old boy in school at Stony Brook,

New York, the lessons were stepping-stones that have led me to where I am today.

My father wrote in 1966:

My dear Franklin, I know there must come times when you get a bit homesick or discouraged. This will be true all through your life. But as you learn to depend on God, reading the Bible and praying, you will find a wonderful sense of fellowship with Him on your own. Mother felt that all the hours she had spent with you since you were a little boy—teaching you the Bible and praying for you and with you—have not been spent in vain.

A little bit homesick? It was more like a major epidemic for me. But letters like this kept me going. I did not want to disappoint my parents. I wanted them to be pleased with my behavior and conduct growing up, but I was not always successful in accomplishing that goal. The letters reminded me that there was a standard expected. When I failed, it caused remorse and great reflection.

My mother wrote in October 1966:

I know there are all sorts of boys there [at school] but you keep your eyes on the Lord, behave like you know He expects you to, pick nice friends, and be nice to everybody. It doesn't take but one boy to make being a Christian attractive to the rest. Just like it wouldn't take but one grub to make others sour on being a Christian. Study hard, be a good sport, be friendly to all—pray and read your Bible. I love you, Mother.

Mail Call, a program on the History Channel hosted by Gunnery Sergeant R. Lee Ermey in 2009, answered questions concerning the military. This guy knew how to turn ordinary mail into entertainment. When I watched the program on television, I remembered mail call as a student. I was always first in line, hoping to find a letter from home.

I could spot my mother's distinctive backhanded script or an air-mail envelope from my father before it would get into my hands. I would hightail it to my dorm to read every line. There was always a word of encouragement, and my parents never failed to express their belief in me—showing confidence that I would do the right thing in every circumstance. Their tactics were packed with psychology that I saw through—sometimes. When I disappointed my mother, I could be assured a letter would arrive sooner rather than later.

Looking back now, I wonder if my mother tried to pattern her letter writing after the apostles. You see, she began with commendation, and then she lowered the boom! One such letter came shortly after a phone call home.

I had mouthed off about being treated less than fairly by some of my peers. Mother just listened. When I hung up the phone, I had justified my position—and was completely miserable. But not nearly as miserable as when I received this letter a few days later:

December 12, 1969

Dearest Franklin:

Boy, I love you. Woke up at 4:00 this morning just concerned for you—and every verse I read was one of reassurance. "All power," Jesus said, "is given unto Me." You need power? You know where to find it. I know you so well, and you wouldn't get ticked off so easily and over such little things if all were right inside. You are really ticked off at yourself and taking it out on the "little squirts." Your "I couldn't care less" gives you away. It takes a big man to ignore little irritations. As Proverbs says: "A wise man ignores an insult." Be big enough to laugh off the criticism and shoulder full responsibility for your actions. You'll never be happy until you're God's man 100%.

I love you,
Mother

Actions? They can serve us well or trip us up.

Whenever I received a reprimand from my parents, it seemed to be underscored by words in Scripture. This is a small example of what our Father in heaven does through His letter to us. Do we open His Word and read it as though He is talking directly to us? We should—because He is.

Letter from a Preacher

Paul wrote many letters to the church at Corinth as instructed by his Father in heaven. Corinth was a metropolitan dynasty of its day, located in Greece. This city was immersed in immorality—sinful behavior was carried into the church by new believers. Paul was concerned that the people seemed unable to break with the culture from which they came.

The Corinthian church claimed to love God and belong to Him. But they refused to separate themselves from worldliness. Does this seem familiar? It sounds like the church today. The Corinthian church flirted with their former pagan ways. Paul had written to them on other occasions, saying: "For out of much affliction and anguish of heart I wrote to you, with many tears" (2 Corinthians 2:4). His desire was for the Corinthian church to cut off association with members, those who would not repent of their worldly actions and associations, and follow Christ. He preached to them that they could not follow the world and follow the Lord.

When Paul told the Corinthian believers to imitate him, he wasn't suggesting that the Corinthians travel and preach as he did. Paul was instructing them to study God's commands and live according to them so that their lives would point others to Christ.

My father wrote, "Following Christ has been made too easy. When nonbelievers see nothing different in the lifestyle of believers, they wonder if our profession of faith is sincere."

The Written Word

My father understood the power of the spoken and written Word. The Bible was his authority to speak the very words of the living God. He spent a great deal of time reading letters and dictating responses—thanking people for their support and responding to criticisms, some of which stemmed from lack of information. Regardless of a letter's message, he always connected to the writer's heart and shared a passage from the Word of God.

I learned by watching how my father handled matters. He was a strong believer in the Proverbs approach: "A soft answer turns away wrath" (Proverbs 15:1). Some might ask, "Who would be upset with Billy Graham?" The answer might surprise you. In the early days of his ministry, some people were offended by his wardrobe, for instance. Not that it was large or expensive. It wasn't. But it was flamboyant—a contradiction to his quiet nature. He would respond to letters and agree with his adversary (Matthew 5:25).

It may be a small thing to some, but etiquette says that first impressions are often the only impressions. My style is not flamboyant at all. I'd rather be in my jeans and denim shirt. Yet the white flag of surrender wins once in a while, and I find my way back to a suit, shirt, and tie. One particular day in August, I was glad I had given in to the flag's warning.

My parents were celebrating their fiftieth wedding anniversary. My siblings and I had made plans to spend the day with them at their home in Montreat for a cookout. The temperature was going to skyrocket that afternoon, so we decided to make it a casual celebration.

On my way out of Boone I got to thinking, *This is a special day for Mama and Daddy.* I remembered how my mother always dressed up when she knew I was coming home. I turned toward home, ran in and threw on a sport coat, climbed back in the car, and headed down the mountain.

When I arrived I was mighty glad of it. My sisters arrived looking beautiful, as usual. My mother didn't disappoint me either. She walked into the room "as pretty as the day I married her," my father said as he squeezed her tight.

My mother had put on her wedding gown—pearls and all. Five kids and fifty years later, the dress fit perfectly. I told her she looked as pretty as she did in her wedding pictures. When she hugged me, she said, "And you look like a preacher—or somethin'." The moment was captured on film, and every time that picture appears in print, I think of that golden day.

My parents weren't big on receiving gifts. They had started passing on heirlooms to their children, grandchildren, and other family and friends. But they did enjoy receiving letters.

All through the day, telegrams and faxes were delivered to the house. And when the mail arrived, it was fun to watch them open cards and letters from across the country and around the world. They enjoyed every aspect, paying attention to the postmark, the stamp, the paper, and the style of penmanship. But the real gift was found in the thoughtful expressions and the signatures that authenticated the messages.

In our fast-paced world, do you ever long to walk to the mailbox and find a friendly handwritten note instead of a stack of bills? *CBS News Sunday Morning* with Charles Osgood featured a segment in 2007 titled "What Happened to Letters?" It bemoaned the lost art of the personal touch through letter writing.

A great deal of history has been documented from letters. Some say it goes back to the medieval era. But as we have seen, the Bible is filled with letters known as epistles. Without them, we would not have much of the New Testament. God, by His sovereignty, preserved these prized documents that we live by today.

A letter more than two pages is an epistle to me. From time to time I get one and wonder why anyone would go to the trouble of trying to duplicate the dictionary.

Our forefathers authenticated much of our nation's history through letters. It took foresight to preserve these rare treasures. The Postal Museum records that early American settlers would write to their families in Europe and "describe the New World as a paradise beyond human imagination." While illiteracy was prevalent in this era, mothers made an effort to learn to read for one purpose: "to give moral instruction to their children by referencing the Bible."[1]

Our nation has drifted far in a short time. Many today don't have Bibles inside their homes, much less its truth in their hearts. A growing minority is destroying the foundational beliefs that established the freedom to worship while rewriting our national heritage.

Our ancestors were eloquent letter writers and diary keepers. We would have only a sketch of American history without their attention to this fine art. The Library of Congress, the largest library in the world, holds the majority of these documents in safekeeping—nearly 142 million items on approximately 650 miles of bookshelves.[2]

Letters and signatures told a lot about a person. Signing one's name to any document signified a personal affirmation that what the letter stated was true.

Becoming Extinct

The letters of Reverend John Witherspoon are among our national treasures. He is sometimes referred to as the forgotten founding father, no doubt because he was the only preacher to sign the Declaration of Independence. He was Scottish-American and a direct descendant of John Knox. And though Witherspoon was a Presbyterian minister throughout his life, he served as president of what is now Princeton University and was a member of the Continental Congress. His collection of letters covers everything from hostilities with Great Britain to how parents ought to care for their children's souls and train them according to God's Word. But his writings will not be found in American history books of twenty-first-century schools.

The art of letter writing is also becoming extinct while the greeting card business booms. We turn to strangers to draw out our deepest thoughts or most frivolous notions.

I am thankful for those who still sit at their desks and write to me. To document all the meaningful letters that have been sent over the years would take at least a miniature Library of Congress to catalog.

When the BGEA was incorporated in 1950, my father began writing letters to those who had supported his meetings or corresponded with him. A mailing list soon developed, and he often expressed gratitude that people were interested in all that God was doing through the revivals, as they were called back then. He conducted much of the business of the ministry through written communication so that instructions would be documented.

I was recently given a copy of a letter my father wrote to George Wilson, who worked with him when BGEA was formed. The letter was dated August 1950, and posted from Portland, Oregon. In it he carefully outlined the steps needed to incorporate the Billy Graham Evangelistic Association, giving particular attention to ensuring that all contributions would be properly recorded and receipted and that office space would be secured at the minimum cost.

It was a good thing that my father had the foresight to take these practical steps because when he and his colleague Cliff Barrows went on the air with *Hour of Decision*, the response by mail was staggering. Because a solid foundation had been put in place, they were able to conduct the business of the ministry with the highest integrity.

It encouraged them that people were tuning in. But the real blessing came when they began receiving letters from people who had been saved through listening to the broadcast. When the crusades went live on television in 1957, the barometer went off the charts. Mail poured into my father's Minneapolis office.

He set in place early in his ministry a priority for handling incoming mail with great respect for those who wrote, giving careful attention to each letter. He always said that the daily mail was the organization's lifeline. Without prayerful and financial support of partners in the ministry, the work would have been impossible to do.

He was aware that there were some ministries soliciting financial support and gladly receiving checks but discarding the letters. My father recognized that it was God who had led people to respond in a variety of ways. He was diligent in seeing that those who sent contributions were properly thanked and those who wrote for prayer received appropriate responses. His heart was touched with the emotion that these letters conveyed, and I believe that God has honored this ongoing commitment.

When the volume of mail became too much to manage personally, my father was careful to hire those who had similar hearts—people who could read between the lines of the letters and, to some extent, identify with people's sorrows and spiritual needs. Many on my father's staff were retired pastors and laypeople who had special insight for such a task.

In the early days when my father was in Minneapolis for meetings, he liked to walk the hallways of his office and shake hands with employees, thanking them personally for their hard work and prayers. He especially enjoyed spending time in the Christian Guidance office. Standing inside doorways, he would talk with committed men and women who prayed over the letters before responding to the diversity of human challenges. This small staff of writers and prayer warriors looked forward to these impromptu discussions with my father. They fired off questions on how to respond to certain inquiries. He would patiently give them his thoughts and suggestions on how to go about dealing with a particular subject. It was inspiring to watch these warm-hearted Minnesotans take notes from the one they liked to address as "boss." Often before leaving, he would sit with them and personally sign letters.

Following one of these meetings, my father felt prompted to compile a handbook that addressed the multitude of questions people asked. With answers he had given in a syndicated newspaper column called "My Answer," which had run for years, a referral book was compiled that would allow the staff to know just how he would answer a particular inquiry.

The most effective mail call for him became an important part of the telecasts. As my father would conclude the invitation, he would turn to the camera and invite viewers to write to him. "If you have accepted Jesus Christ as your personal Savior while watching this telecast," my father would say, "please write to me and tell me of your decision for Christ. I want to send you a little booklet to help you in your new life with Jesus Christ. Or if you have a spiritual need in your life, let me know. Just write to me, Billy Graham, Minneapolis, Minnesota—that's all the address you need, and may God bless you." This sign-off became his verbal signature, you might say.

The names Billy Graham and Minneapolis, Minnesota, were linked together so much that when the BGEA moved from Minneapolis to Charlotte, I was concerned that my father would not be able to transition to the new address. But when he turned to the camera—even at eighty-two—it was as though he flipped a switch in his brain and with ease said, "Just write to me, Billy Graham, Number One Billy Graham Parkway, Charlotte, North Carolina—that's all the address you need."

Dear Mr. Postman

Our hearts were blessed to see thousands of letters pour into the office forty-eight hours after a telecast was aired. In the early days it was more amazing to see how the flood of mail found its way to the BGEA office.

I salute the US Post Office. How they ever managed to properly deliver some of these letters is a mystery. Down through the years the BGEA staff has accumulated an array of envelopes addressed to Billy Graham—some bring a smile to my face and others touch my heart. Often those writing would continue their letters on the envelope flap.

It has been said that Billy Graham is one of a few Americans, like the president of the United States, who can receive mail that is simply addressed: "Billy Graham, America," for example, as it has been borne out through the years by the countless envelopes delivered.

One letter, addressed to "The Rev. Billy Graham," included this note on the envelope: "Dear Mr. Postman, I don't know the address of Rev. Graham, but please try to get this letter to him, it really is important, and thank you, Love Linda." I wonder how many people express love to the post office and show faith in their work?

Letters came by special delivery. Letters came by airmail. They came in every shape and size—from everywhere.

Glory is the one place that isn't covered under that old familiar postman's pledge: "Come rain or shine, the postman delivers the mail on time." My father will no longer see the mail that still comes addressed to him, but the post office is faithful to deliver Billy Graham's mail to our office in Charlotte. And we count it a great privilege to answer those letters in his absence.

A story has circulated about my father as a young preacher arriving in a small town for a revival. He wanted to mail a letter, so he asked a young boy where he could find a post office. The boy gave him directions, and then my father invited him to church that evening. "I'll be telling folks how to get to heaven," he said to the young fellow. The boy looked at him and said, "I don't think I'll be there. You don't even know how to get to the post office."

We may not find the post office easily, but somehow it finds us. The Postal Service processes and delivers billions of mail pieces each day to more than 156 million homes and businesses.[3]

Heart Appeal

Observing my father's own fascination with people's responses to a simple suggestion—"Just write to me"—gave me confidence in my own ministry. Realizing that the public would respond to an invitation to write to my father, I knew they were interested in his work. It also spoke of people's desire to be heard, cared for, and understood.

As time progressed, people who had been saved through my father's ministry began writing and asking how they could help support the crusade telecasts financially.

A monthly newsletter from my father became, for BGEA, the primary source of information to our partners. It was the only way to communicate what the Lord was doing around the world to tens of thousands of people at one time, and the response was overwhelming. He wrote these letters from his heart, telling about invitations received to conduct citywide crusades where the Gospel could be proclaimed. He asked people to join him in praying that God would lead him to the right decisions about where he should hold the next evangelistic meeting. In articulating the need for prayer, people responded eagerly, wanting to be part of what God was doing for the sake of the Gospel.

My father was not comfortable aggressively asking for money. He felt it was important to share the need and leave it to God to direct the giving.

"Dr. Graham," one person would write, "I cannot stand in a stadium in Hong Kong and preach to the masses. That is not my calling." Another would say, "I am running a large corporation, and as a Christian I want to do my part to fulfill the Great Commission by supporting you." My father soon realized that God was stirring people's hearts to join with him in harvesting souls for Christ.

My father's heart was moved as he began to view donors as those who felt a partnership with him. His letters concluded, "If you feel

God is touching your heart to help us minister in this way, your sacrificial gift to the work of the Lord will be blessed by Him."

And God has moved in the hearts of people to join forces in sowing seed around the world in His name. Still today these partners are the backbone of the ministry. "This service not only supplies the needs of the saints, but also is abounding through many thanksgivings to God, while, through the proof of this ministry, they glorify God for the obedience of your confession to the gospel of Christ, and for your liberal sharing with them and all men, and by their prayer for you. . . . Thanks be to God for His indescribable gift!" (2 Corinthians 9:12–15).

Personal, Private, Painful

My father's personal letters remained just that during his lifetime. He was careful not to speak about confidential matters that were shared with him. He felt the trust that people had placed in him gave him a responsibility before God to hold these matters close to his heart and pray earnestly for those dealing with weighty issues and personal dilemmas.

But there were times when well-known people chose to make their private conversations with him public. When a story hit the paper, before my father even knew what had transpired, the telephone lines lit up wanting to know what Billy Graham's response was to the breaking news. A flicker of surprise sometimes became a startling flame.

To make things worse, he seldom knew just how much of a discussion had been revealed, and in what context. He felt obligated to hold in confidence information that had been shared with him, but it raised questions in others' minds as to what my father did, or did not, say. There were also times people remembered my father's words—"Just write to me"—and they did.

Summer Flurries

One such incident was with the late former first lady Nancy Reagan after President Reagan died. The Reagans' special relationship has already gone down in history as one of the great romances of modern time. Their undying love for one another was written about and admired. To say that Nancy Reagan missed the man who had been the center of her everything was an understatement.

Shortly after the former president passed away, Mrs. Reagan phoned my father. He had been asked years before to preach the funeral service, but due to weakened health at the time, he was physically unable to travel.

A considerable time after the state funeral and burial at the Ronald Reagan Library in June 2004, my father was in better health and paid a visit to Mrs. Reagan at her home in Santa Monica. She shared her thoughts with my father on how empty her life was "without Ronnie." My father read some Scripture and prayed with her that God would bring comfort in her loss.

In 2007, ABC aired a special edition of *20/20* with Charles Gibson titled "Pastor to Power: Billy Graham and the Presidents." He interviewed all of the living US presidents and First Ladies, along with Nancy Gibbs and Michael Duffy of *Time* magazine, who had just released a book, *The Preacher and the Presidents*, exploring my father's sixty-year relationships with them. When Charlie mentioned to Nancy Reagan that Billy Graham had comforted her by saying that her husband would be waiting for her when she died, he asked Mrs. Reagan, "How can you be sure?" Mrs. Reagan answered, "Billy said so."[4]

There were some well-meaning Christians who wanted a clarification on this statement, "Billy said so."

They wrote, "Dr. Graham, you have always said that our assurance of heaven comes from our personal relationship with Jesus Christ." People felt that an opportunity had been missed to tell the world the certainty of being reunited with loved ones in heaven and spending eternity with God—to have peace with God according to the Gospel. Our legal system protects attorney-client privilege. The medical community abides by doctor-patient privilege. Clergy can do no less than to preserve confidential discussions with those who seek their counsel.

As a minister, my father was serious about this veil of trust. He learned an embarrassing lesson early in his ministry when he divulged a conversation with President Harry Truman. As a young man, he had no idea that discussions with a US president were kept confidential. He was ridiculed by the press. One doesn't soon forget that kind of public humiliation, and he never did.

When my father died, he took with him a diary of confidential conversations buried deep in his heart. He had no choice but to turn the other cheek when others questioned whether he had been forthright about his private conversations with people from all walks of life. Only they know where they stand before the Lord Jesus Christ.

After the assassination attempt on President Reagan in 1981, the president was asked if he was ready to meet God. The president said publicly, "Oh yes, I'm ready to meet God because I have a Savior."[5] He seemed to understand the necessity of knowing the Savior personally in order to stand forgiven in God's presence.

Few people in life have the privilege of knowing presidents and heads of state for more than a half century. My father often said that he could never understand why those opportunities came to him. He walked through every open door, and no one ever questioned where he stood when it came to the Lord Jesus Christ. So much that when a question arose about spiritual issues, my father's telephone would ring.

"Get Me Billy Graham"

When George H. W. Bush was vice president, George W. was visiting with his mother. They got into a rather spirited discussion about who would be in heaven. "Mom," George said, "here's what the New Testament says." He proceeded to explain. Barbara Bush called the White House operator and said, "Get me Billy Graham."[6]

She told my father that George W. insisted that only born-again Christians would be welcomed into heaven. Mrs. Bush questioned my father on this and then handed the phone to her son. When reports began to drip the details of the spontaneous call, the only part of my father's response that was printed was, "None of us could judge another's soul."

Well, my father was right, but so was George W. Jesus said: "Most assuredly, I say to you, unless one is born again, he cannot see the kingdom of God" (John 3:3). I respect George W. Bush for his witness of Christ's work in the believing heart. And I suspect that on this occasion he was trying out his new faith.

But once again letters of dismay found their way into the mailbags. A few people felt that my father had possibly sidestepped the issue in order to be politically correct. The rest of my father's answer stated, "I agree with what George says about the interpretation of the New Testament."

And my father's position has never changed on this matter. Throughout his life he said, "There is only one answer that will give a person the certain privilege, the joy, of entering heaven, and it is this: 'Because I believe in Jesus Christ and accept Him as my Savior.'"

When it comes to the Gospel of the Lord Jesus Christ, quick answers and sound bites can be devastating, especially when reporters tell only half the story. Leaving unanswered questions can lead someone down the wrong road.

My father always worried about this and often said, "I am constantly concerned about being quoted in the press and perhaps saying the wrong thing or having what I say misinterpreted and bringing reproach to the name of Christ."

When it comes to the most important decision an individual will ever make, we should take great care to never rush through the opportunity of showing someone from the Scripture what God says. Nor should we unfairly question another's response when held in confidence. This is where a person's word is underscored by their character and integrity. My father never wavered on what Jesus said: "I am the way, the truth, and the life. No one comes to the Father except through Me" (John 14:6).

As my father grew older, he was cautious not to wound someone's spirit as they sought the truth of God's Word. He gently persuaded an unbelieving heart to consider Christ's claims.

Christ's ambassadors must not soft-pedal what the Bible says, no matter what answer the listener may prefer. The Gospel does not change with the personality or circumstance. Will the truth offend? Yes, if the offended is not willing to repent and humble himself in the presence of God.

My father never grasped why God had placed him in paths of power. But as his son who knew him well, I believe it was because he never failed to make Jesus Christ predominant.

He Must Increase

Though my father was a very private man, he lived a very public life. He enjoyed quiet moments, but he was energized by meeting people from various backgrounds.

On occasion he was invited to dine with the rich and famous, and he did so without compromising his faith. When he was a guest at social affairs, everyone present knew Whom he represented, as evidenced by the questions people asked.

He grieved when people put him on a pedestal. He knew that no one is immune to a downfall. My father prayed about this a great deal and fought fame when he recognized its seductive power.

I will never forget being with my father in the Netherlands for a gathering of evangelists from all over the world. He had convened a conference for itinerant preachers, predominantly from developing countries. The assembly of delegates was as colorful as the international flag processional into the great hall. The RAI Center in Amsterdam was buzzing with chatter. It made me wonder if the sound was like the days of Babel when God confused the tongues of men.

But when Cliff Barrows led the congregation in "How Great Thou Art" with each one singing in his own language, there was no doubt about the message that praised the Lord—voices were lifted in perfect unison. Then following a song from George Beverly Shea, my father approached the podium to a rousing welcome.

Ten thousand representatives from 174 nations stood to their feet. The applause was deafening. Cheering shrieked across the dome. Flashbulbs were blinding.

My father stood at the microphone. "Please be seated. Thank you for your warm welcome. Please . . ." But his voice could not overcome the adoring welcome. He persisted—to no avail.

My father stepped away from the podium and bowed his head. It seemed impossible to quiet the crowd. Then he moved in close to the microphone and spoke with repetitive gentleness, "He must increase, but I must decrease" (John 3:30).

When the crowd saw my father speaking into the microphone but could not hear him, silence began to fall. Section by section a hush enveloped the dome. My father's face was solemn and unforgettable.

These evangelists had never even heard my father preach. It gripped his soul. While he was humbled by the honor given, he was distressed. When all was quiet, he did what was in his heart—he preached the Word and pointed hearts upward.

When God Wrote

Roy Gustafson once preached a fascinating sermon titled "When God Wrote," in which he pointed out that God did a lot of writing from heaven. The psalmist said, "I consider . . . the work of Your fingers" (Psalm 8:3).

God called Moses to the top of Mount Sinai and gave the prophet His Law—the Ten Commandments. "He gave Moses two tablets of the Testimony, tablets of stone, written with the finger of God" (Exodus 31:18).

God interrupted King Belshazzar's drunken party with a hand-delivered message of warning: "In the same hour the fingers of a man's hand appeared and wrote opposite the lampstand on the plaster of the wall of the king's palace; and the king saw the part of the hand that wrote. Then the king's countenance changed" (Daniel 5:5–6). I bet it did.

Jesus wrote in the dirt as the Pharisees accused a woman of adultery, insisting that Jesus also condemn her. "But Jesus stooped down and wrote on the ground with His finger, as though He did not hear. . . . He raised Himself up and said to them, 'He who is without sin among you, let him throw a stone at her first'" (John 8:6–7). Scripture does not reveal what Jesus wrote, but I believe He wrote about forgiveness.

Throughout Scripture we find a cycle repeated:

- God's pattern for right living
- God's warning when we fail
- God's forgiveness with the command, "Go and sin no more"

Jesus came to pick us up out of the dirt of sin and offer forgiveness as He did the accused woman. When man deals rightly with sin before God, His forgiveness washes our sin away and makes us new creations.

The world today wants answers. People may not like them, but they want the chance to consider their own fates. Our responsibility is to declare to a dying world that Jesus saves. People must hear the full counsel of God—presented unashamed and unedited.

God's Love Letter

My father did a lot of writing throughout his life. He authored more than thirty-three books, the last two at ages ninety-five and ninety-six. He wrote newspaper columns, articles, letters, and sermons—all based on God's letter to mankind. My father penned these words years before he died: "God wants to talk with us through His Word—in fact, it is His 'love letter' to us."[7] The Bible tells us not only that He loves us but that He shows us what He has done to demonstrate His love. It tells us how we should live because God knows what is best for us. Never forget that the Bible is God's Word given to us so we can know and follow Him.

Because of his high profile, my father's ministry has been documented over seven decades from others' pens. My father never considered himself an author, a columnist, or a writer. He was forever the preacher because whatever he set his hand to do, he spoke and wrote, heralding the King's message. He once said, "Believers in Jesus Christ will someday be autographed by the Author."

I believe souls will continue being saved through my father's writings because they point to the Savior of the world. Billy Graham died the way he lived—recognizing his weaknesses and his dependence on God, with the assurance of being transformed into His likeness as seen through our Father in heaven.

Followers of Christ are testimonies in walking shoes. We are testimonies in speech, thought, and action. Are these testimonies reflective of Christ? What testimonies are written on the tablets of our hearts?

"You are our epistle written in our hearts, known and read by all men; clearly you are an epistle of Christ . . . written not with ink but by the Spirit of the living God, not on tablets of stone but on tablets . . . of the heart" (2 Corinthians 3:2–3).

My father once wrote, "Someday you will read or hear that Billy Graham is dead. Don't you believe a word of it! I shall be more alive then than I am now. I will just have changed my address. I will have gone into the presence of God."[8]

My father's ink pen is dry. Someday we, too, will set aside our writing tools. Our lips will be silent, our thoughts still, but God will still be writing. When He picks up His pen at the end of the ages, will our countenances be changed as Belshazzar's was—consumed in awesome fear and trembling—or will we look into His face with joy and adoration?

The Bible says that on that day those who belong to Christ will be written down in glory: "I will write on him the name of My God and the name of the city of My God" (Revelation 3:12).

And that's all the address we'll need.

8

About My Father's Business

If you send them forward on their journey
in a manner worthy of God, you will do well.

—3 John v. 6

*I do not come as an emissary of my government or my nation,
but as a citizen of the kingdom of God ... as Christ's ambassador ...
to preach the Gospel.*

BILLY GRAHAM

Resurrection Bay. You may think that this magnificent body of water flows somewhere in the land of the Bible, but it actually surges through fjords and tributaries in the United States—along the Kenai Peninsula of the great state of Alaska.

Alexandr Baranov, Russian-born explorer and merchant, was sailing the pristine waters when a vicious storm pounded the Gulf of Alaska. Baranov discovered a haven for retreat and hunkered down until the tempest gave way to a welcomed dawning. It was Easter Sunday, 1792. While he was overlooking the calming waters and vibrant sun, relief and hope settled, causing him to declare that place of safety Resurrection Bay. Ringed with majestic mountains and protected from the Gulf of Alaska, this Alaskan fjord has been a place of safety for boats.

When I think of Baranov casting his eyes over this bay and naming it for the greatest work Jesus Christ ever accomplished—His resurrection—I am reminded of the words of the psalmist: "Praise Him for His mighty acts" (Psalm 150:2).

Alaska has become a retreat for me. One summer when my children were still young, I took my family to the Land of the Midnight Sun. No wonder Alaska is known as the last frontier. I began to wonder if we would ever arrive. Once we did, I never wanted to leave. The very next year I announced to them that this was our new vacation destination. Several years ago I was there hunting black bear with some friends. We had chartered a small boat from Seward, which lies at the north end of Resurrection Bay. Late one evening as we chugged out of the bay and into the gulf, our little boat was battered by relentless waves. We tossed to and fro for hours, eventually finding refuge in a protected fjord in Prince William Sound. It gave me renewed respect for those who had experienced storms on the high seas.

I have a history with Alaska. In 1970, my father made arrangements for me to work in Alaska. He called his friend former governor Wally Hickel and asked if he could arrange a summer job for me. I never dreamed that years later I would own a little piece of Alaska wilderness, much less preach my first crusade in Juneau, the state capital, with the late Dr. John Wesley White.

In 1984, my father held a great crusade in Anchorage, Alaska's largest city. Nine years later, I was invited to hold a crusade in the same city where many came to know Jesus Christ as their Savior.

Alaska is a wilderness of fascination for the people who live there.

When December arrives, part of Alaska doesn't see the sun for several months. I have to say that I am glad to be back in the Appalachian Mountains, where winter sunrays shimmer through the trees. But in June, when the sun hangs over Alaska day and night, I can fish from early morning and into the late evening and still get back to my lakeside cabin to put dinner on the grill.

I have wonderful memories of fishing with my father on lakes and rivers. I guess that's why it was thrilling to take my children fishing when we began vacationing in Alaska. My daughter Cissie even enjoyed the outdoor sport. And she should. She stunned me when, at ninety pounds, she hooked a seventy-two-pound king salmon. My boys and I have never lived it down.

Alaska is a fisherman's dream. I have learned much about fishing from the late George Lye, a friend and coworker, during my visits to this magnificent state. Fishing requires performance, endurance, and tact. To be a good fisherman, it is necessary to study the tides and watch the weather carefully.

My father often equated fishing to soul winning. "To 'catch' men effectively," he would say, "we have to study Christ." Jesus told the disciples, "Follow Me, and I will make you fishers of men" (Matthew 4:19). Jesus used the truth of His Word to draw men to Himself. The Gospel is a hook that snags a hungry lost soul.

What a Catch!

When I climb into my little fishing boat and cast a line into the deep, gentle waves lap against the boat as I wait for the catch. The rocking of the waves is soothing to the soul and at times carries my thoughts to another fishing spot located seven hundred feet below sea level. Its history reveals the most amazing and memorable fish stories—not because of its stock, but because of the miracles drawn from its waters.

You can almost hear the water slapping against the wooden vessel—seven fishermen on the sea for a late-night catch. They were in familiar territory, doing a customary deed in a body of water they had traveled in and around most of their lives. But when dawn broke, their nets were empty and they were discouraged.

"Children," a man called to them, "have you any food?"

The husky men shouted back, "No" (John 21:5).

"Cast the net on the right side of the boat, and you will find some." And when they did, they were not able to draw the net "because of the multitude of fish" (v. 6).

Imagine the excitement in the disciple's voice when John said to Peter, "It is the Lord!" (v. 7). There on the shore stood the resurrected Christ.

Impulsive Peter jumped overboard. He was too excited to *try to walk*. His limbs must have propelled through the Sea of Galilee like a two-hundred-horsepower Mercury outboard. He pulled his drenched body from the water and ran to Jesus.

As a frustrated fisherman myself, I can appreciate the responsible disciples who stayed behind to haul in the net. But I'd like to think I would have responded like Peter: *Get to Jesus and forget the fish!*

Peter found Jesus cooking fish and bread over the burning coals. There on the beach the disciples ate breakfast together and warmed themselves in the fellowship of their Master and Friend.

Dropping Anchor

Before Jesus returned to heaven, there were still some lessons these men had to learn about their Father's business. Jesus had called them "children." He had nourished their hunger. He had taught them how to fish for men and feed their souls.

"Do you love Me more than these?" Jesus asked Peter.

Peter replied, "Yes, Lord; You know that I love You."

Jesus said to Peter, "Feed My lambs."

He asked Peter the second time, and Peter replied the same. Jesus said, "Tend My sheep" (John 21:15–16).

Jesus asked a grieving Peter the question for the third time. Peter must have thought about his denial of Christ three times before the crucifixion. He wanted desperately for the Lord to know of his deep love for Him.

But Jesus wanted something greater than just a commitment of human love. It was Peter who would lead Jesus' disciples to be about their Father's business. Jesus wanted Peter to love Him more than fishing. He wanted Peter to love Him at all cost of pleasure and desire. He wanted Peter's complete devotion that would be necessary to feed and tend His sheep. Peter's mission was not only to become a fisher of men but also to feed men's souls with the Word of God and then send them out to fish for others.

My father exhibited what he often preached to those who proclaimed the Gospel. "He who is called to, and set apart for, the work of an evangelist," my father would say, "is to devote his time and effort single-mindedly to this God-given task. He is not to be distracted by anything likely to deflect him from this."

Jesus continued deepening Peter's understanding to the point of telling him that he, too, would lose his life for Christ's sake through martyrdom. When Peter finally realized the genuine love required to follow the Savior, Peter's heart dropped anchor, stabilizing his resolve to follow Jesus no matter what, even to a gruesome death.

Jesus understood His mission on earth, and He wanted His disciples to understand what their love for Him required. "To be a disciple of Jesus means to learn from Him and to follow Him in obedience. The cost may be high," my father often said.

This is what Jesus was telling His disciples. History proves, and the Scriptures document, that the disciples understood to the point of losing their lives for Him.

They Sought Him Anxiously

Even as a boy, Jesus understood His mission on earth. When only twelve, Jesus accompanied His parents to Jerusalem for the feast of the Passover. On the return trip to Nazareth, after a day's journey, Mary and Joseph realized that Jesus was not among the great company of travelers. They made haste and returned to the city and found Jesus in the temple, "sitting in the midst of the teachers, both listening to them and asking them questions. And all who heard Him were astonished at His understanding and answers" (Luke 2:46–47).

Mary said to Him, "Son, why have You done this to us? Look, Your father and I have sought You anxiously" (v. 48).

"Why did you seek Me?" Jesus asked. "Did you not know that I must be about My Father's business?" (v. 49).

Surely Mary realized that a time would come when Jesus would face danger. But her mother's heart could not help but hold on to Him until that awful day.

Our humanity wants to hold tight to what belongs to us. We do not always comprehend what Christ expects of us. But as Peter learned, we must lay aside all things that our wills grip. We must come to Jesus with open hearts and open hands so that we can be about our Father's business, compelling lost souls to seek Jesus anxiously.

Concern of a President

The history of our country has deep roots in missionary work. In civilized America, it is hard to comprehend the day when much of our country lacked exploration and refinement. From the famed explorers Lewis and Clark, the story is told about Meriwether Lewis, who opened the West by following the Missouri River to its headwaters and then crossed the Rocky Mountains to follow the Columbia River, eventually reaching the Pacific Ocean.

I have followed the Missouri River from St. Louis to Montana in an airplane, looking down over its wild and ragged banks. Fingers of land seep into the river, reflecting the monstrous shadow of the Idaho Mountains, where dangers still lurk two hundred years after Lewis and Clark forged through the waters with nothing but paddles and oars.

Lewis had received a commission from President Thomas Jefferson to explore the West, stating that if he was not received with hospitality, he should return to safety.[1]

This reminded me of the great care Jesus showed in His instruction to His disciples as He sent them on their journeys to take the Gospel to Judea. This set the foundation in place to later go into the whole world to spread the Good News.

"Now whatever city or town you enter, inquire who in it is worthy, and stay there till you go out. And when you go into a household, greet it. If the household is worthy, let your peace come upon it. But if it is not worthy, let your peace return to you. And whoever will not receive you nor hear your words, when you depart from that house or city, shake off the dust from your feet" (Matthew 10:11–14).

Jesus left no command without instruction, including how to handle the lack of hospitality from unwelcoming hearts.

When my father began his ministry, major cities had hotels, but there were no Holiday Inns or Marriott Hotels in small towns. The only options were boardinghouses or people's homes. I heard him tell about some of the warm hospitality he enjoyed from laymen and businessmen who opened their homes to him in those early days, their wives cooking breakfast, lunch, and dinner, even washing clothes and ironing shirts for him. Those experiences solidified lifelong friendships.

I, too, have good memories of my early ministry. I was invited by church leaders and missionaries to preach in village churches and open-air meetings in places like Africa and India. These faithful servants carved paths for the Gospel in some of the darkest corners of the world. They welcomed me in Christian spirit that warms the soul and leaves a lasting imprint of the Lord's hospitality on the heart.

But there were times I found myself in hostile territory and had to shake off more than dust. I have crawled from slimy ditches along the border of Cambodia after a mortar attack and have hunkered down along the Green Line in Beirut, known as Sniper's Alley, to escape danger.

Traveling to hot spots of the world gave me a firsthand look at what God's people endure. My work with Samaritan's Purse was built on the ministry of Dr. Bob Pierce, the ministry's founder and a friend to my parents. Dr. Bob had a great and compassionate heart. My father encouraged me to travel with Bob Pierce and learn from him.

I observed Bob Pierce as he walked in the footsteps of other great servants of the Lord, meeting the needs of so many. Dr. Bob fed the hungry—then taught them to plant crops; he clothed the naked—then provided sewing machines and cloth; he provided water in dry lands—then taught people how to dig wells; he sent medicine to the sick—then challenged physicians to consider medical missions. He cared for orphans and widows, just as Jesus commanded.

When Dr. Bob died of leukemia in 1978, I was humbled when asked to take the leadership of Samaritan's Purse—a small organization at the time, with only two secretaries who quit when I took over. At twenty-six years old, I was unsure how to get started. My father pointed me to the footprints of those who had gone before.

Christian relief work has changed drastically, but no matter where I go, the footprints of those before us are still evident today.

I have seen doctors forsake all modern conveniences to follow in the steps of David Livingstone in Africa. I have seen Bible translators follow in the steps of John Wycliffe. I have watched missionaries pack up their families and move to the farthest corners of the earth. Samaritan's Purse has been able to place nurses, physicians, teachers, technicians, well drillers, and a host of volunteers in the steps of the past in order to carry the Gospel into the future.

"Thank You, Bill-ee Graham!"

Encouraging me in all this work were my parents. I had gained significant experience in international travel and had learned a great deal about how international politics could help or hinder our efforts abroad.

So, naturally, I counted it a great privilege when my father asked me to go with him into Eastern Europe on several occasions through the 1980s. He had been outspoken about Communism, which was not much different from the secularism of today, and the threat it posed to the world. He was especially concerned for the state of the church in Communist-bloc countries. Political tensions were at a fever pitch, and persecution of Christians behind the Iron Curtain was widespread.

Russia and its allies had been engaged in an arms race they were losing with the free world, bankrupting their system. President Ronald Reagan had developed a new strategy called Star Wars—a defensive initiative the United States wanted to put in place in order to provide a protective shield against Soviet missiles.

When my father shared with the president that he wanted to go to the Soviet Union to preach, President Reagan supported him. He felt that Billy Graham, as a minister, might to some degree break through the hard shell of Communism and help soften the rhetoric. My father prayed that the result would be religious freedom for those of faith.

When he went to Eastern Europe, he wanted to identify with the persecuted church. Some of the secular media wanted to trap him and tried to get him to say something negative that would undermine his mission to preach the Gospel. They asked him, "Did you see any persecution?" My father replied, "No." He had not seen any, but he knew it was there. He also knew his government host would never allow him to see the persecution.

Everywhere we went, spiritual hunger and openness were clearly evident among the massive crowds that lined the streets and gathered on top of flat-roof buildings. They shouted, "Thank you, Bill-ee Graham!" His visit encouraged them in their dark but hopeful hours to believe that freedom of religion was possible.

I watched, listened, and observed all I could from my father. I walked in the shadow of his footsteps throughout this region. At his side I sat in meetings with heads of state and church leaders in Romania, Hungary, and the Soviet Union.

I learned tremendous lessons from him as he dealt with shrewd thinkers. My father seemed to find points of interest in which to engage those who were opposed to his personal faith in God. He listened intently to their points of view and, when given the nod, nudged open the door for dialogue. He did so with respect; he did so in love.

His ministry in Eastern Europe would have been impossible without God placing Dr. Alexander Haraszti in his life. This Hungarian-born adviser was a brilliant man with five earned degrees, one of them in Communism. He was also a medical doctor trained in surgery, and he spoke multiple languages. Dr. Haraszti became the strategist to open the way into Eastern-bloc countries. He knew the Communist mind and understood just where to place Billy Graham for the sake of the Gospel.

While my father felt privileged to gain entrance into these spiritually starved countries, it came with much fear and trembling. We spent time together with his team, praying for God to reveal specific ways for the Gospel to be presented.

There were uncertainties that my father would be used for propaganda. He had times of anxiety that he might unknowingly compromise the message. What influenced me most was to hear him, without fail, present Jesus Christ. With clarity, he went about his Father's business.

The results were often like what the apostle Paul experienced—some completely rejected the truth, and others were receptive. But we knew that the Word of God had been made known.

I remember being tense when I sat down at the first meeting with our Communist hosts in Moscow. I was amazed at how masterfully my father melted the icy facades of these men. I began to relax as I watched an ambassador for Christ at work, marveling at his gentle and gracious humor, smiling at his ability to relate personally. Whether through questions about their families or about how they might spend their leisure time, he had a way of warming some rather cold hearts.

Tell Us Some New Thing

Paul's visit to Athens was an encouraging Bible passage to my father, especially as he traveled throughout Eastern Europe.

The apostle Paul was staying in Athens, awaiting the arrival of Silas and Timothy. While in this religious hub of Greece, Paul went about his Father's business. He saw that the city was filled with idols—every "god" that man could think up was worshipped in this cultural city of idolatry. The Bible says that Paul "reasoned in the synagogue with the Jews and with the Gentile worshipers, and in the marketplace daily with those who happened to be there" (Acts 17:17).

A big move today in the so-called emerging church is something referred to as "the marketplace of ideas." We haven't seen any idea emerge that hadn't already been thought of in the epic idolatry worship center of the day.

The Bible documents the encounter: "Certain Epicurean and Stoic philosophers encountered [Paul]. And some said, 'What does this babbler want to say?' Others said, 'He seems to be a proclaimer of foreign gods,' because he preached to them Jesus and the resurrection" (v. 18). They took Paul to a court to question him. "May we know what this new doctrine is of which you speak? For you are bringing some strange things to our ears. Therefore we want to know what these things mean" (vv. 19–20).

Paul had to be excited. Nothing thrills an evangelist more than to hear these words: *Tell us what the Gospel means.*

My father once wrote, "Jesus tells us not to be misled by the voices of strangers. There are so many strange voices being heard in the religious world of our day. We must compare what they say with the Word of God."[2]

Paul discerned sincere voices and the words of the skeptics. He knew that the men of Athens and the foreigners in the city spent their time searching to hear some new thing.

So Paul stood in their midst and proclaimed,

> Men of Athens, I perceive that in all things you are very religious; for as I was passing through and considering the objects of your worship, I even found an altar with this inscription:
>
> TO THE UNKNOWN GOD.
>
> Therefore, the One whom you worship without knowing, Him I proclaim to you: "God, who made the world and everything in it, since He is Lord of heaven and earth, does not dwell in temples made with hands. Nor is He worshiped with men's hands, as though He needed anything, since He gives to all life, breath, and all things. And He has made from one blood every nation of men to dwell on all the face of the earth . . . so that they should seek the Lord . . . [who] now commands all men everywhere to repent." (Acts 17:22–27, 30)

When Paul had finished, some mocked him; others said: "We will hear you again on this matter" (Acts 17:32). Paul then departed with some men who believed.

This account is a remarkable lesson in conveying the truth of God's Word in antagonistic territory with uncompromising diplomacy. Paul's careful attention to emphasizing Christ, and my father's application of finding a point of interest, as Paul capably did, is something I always consider when sitting at the table with those who do not believe in the God I serve.

My father spoke many times about persecution, saying, "Jesus warned that the price of believing in Him would be high. Mockery, laughter, persecution, even death would be common, but many would refuse to pay such prices."

You may find yourself drawn into such a time as this. God does the choosing and God does the using, and no authentic follower of Christ wants to fall one step short of conveying God's truth.

Dr. Charles Stanley, who was a great friend of my father's and one he listened to on Sunday mornings, signed off the air with this statement: "Obey God and leave all the consequences to Him."[3]

Something Worthwhile Is Never Old

Men in ancient times longed for some new thing, and our society is no different. Today's culture chases after the same—a new experience, a new thrill, untapped knowledge, and new relationships—but people are looking in all the wrong places.

Reporters run after the latest story to get the exclusive; the paparazzi disguise themselves to get a one-of-a-kind photo; video cameras hover in a helicopter above a social event to capture a private affair. Everyone is looking for that thrilling kick to life.

My mother always enjoyed shopping for antiques. While it is still big business, I have never noticed a crowd outside the antique store. But go to Walmart or Best Buy for the latest and greatest, and it's hard to find a parking place.

Often what people are searching for cannot be bought. They only need to look at the "old, old story" of Jesus' love that becomes new to everyone who believes in Him and follows in His steps.

Every generation encounters the old and the new. My grandfathers' generation experienced the Discovery Explosion, with the inventions of electricity, telephones, gasoline-powered vehicles, and so on. They saw more *new* things than any other generation. When they were born, men traveled by horse and carriage. Ministers at the turn of the twentieth century were circuit-riding preachers who traveled on horseback from town to town, church to church, shepherding many flocks.

Before my grandfathers died, men walked on the moon. Mail delivery went from Pony Express that took ten to twelve days to Federal Express overnight. There is a small fragment of that generation still living who now boasts of communicating by e-mail. The magnitude of changes would have seemed far-fetched in the late 1800s.

My parents' generation experienced the Population Explosion and supersonic travel. The way of life moved from traveling on trains and ships that took weeks and months, to jets that could fly overseas in a few hours. Many say of that generation that they don't like change. The truth is they saw more change than perhaps any other generation. Maybe we should consider their wisdom in seeing that many changes in our culture today are bad for society. Change isn't always good.

My generation experienced the Communication Explosion, with the development of personal computers, cellular phones, social media, and the idea that instant gratification brings happiness.

Today's young generation has experienced the wireless age and the Information Explosion, which has set in motion a culture of disenchantment and leisure. The popular CBS News program *60 Minutes* calls the last generation of the twentieth century the "millennial generation."[4] They want it all and do not know how to cope if they cannot attain it all—and fast. The concept of waiting for anything is foreign to them.

As my father and I sat on his front porch one warm summer's evening, we enjoyed some ice-cold watermelon. He seemed reflective as we looked across the tranquil Swannanoa Valley below the house. "Franklin, the world I once knew as a young boy has disappeared," he said. "I don't even understand the world in which I live today. It has passed me by."

Yet there are many in today's younger generation who desire to understand the meaning of life. Some search in vain; others search until they find that a relationship with God through His Son Jesus Christ fills the empty vacuum of life.

This was the reason Billy Graham never lost his vision for young people. He understood the need for souls to be reconciled to God. Satisfying our desires cannot fill the spiritual longing in the heart. Having spent his early years in Youth for Christ, he made a point to have a youth emphasis during his crusades. Whether it was through a testimony that teenagers could relate to or special music, my father never failed to remember that today's young people will emerge as tomorrow's leaders.

Persecution Swells

My generation has been blessed to have the expediency of supersonic transportation, fast-food restaurants, and convenient hotels lining the highways. For me, they are sorry stand-ins for my pickup truck and mountain home, but they do enable me to cover a lot of territory in short periods of time.

When I began preaching, I can recall sleeping on a pullout couch in the middle of someone's living room and waking to curious little eyes.

To this day when I travel to rugged outposts, roughing it is still a way of life. As we negotiate mined roads in Angola and forge through swamps in Indonesia, we pray for safe arrival. It's not unusual to go to bed at night under a mosquito net while keeping a watchful eye on a snake slithering through the thatched roof above the cot. Such is the case when I travel into remote parts of the world to be about my Father's business.

Like my father, who reached out to the persecuted church through-out Eastern Europe, I have tried to do the same in the Islamic world.

Christians are being persecuted by radical Muslims from the Philippines, Indonesia, and Pakistan, into Iran and all the Middle Eastern countries, including modern Turkey. Christians are being murdered, churches are being burned, and persecution is growing.

"Mr. President, You Missed!"

"As cold water to a weary soul, so is good news from a far country" (Proverbs 25:25).

Samaritan's Purse has been carrying the Good News into Sudan, where civil war raged for more than thirty years, black Christians in the south being slaughtered by Muslims from the north. While fighting ravaged the countryside, it took a backseat to the bloody conflict in Darfur, located in the northern part of the country. For some time I had been encouraging our political leadership to negotiate with the Sudanese government for the sake of innocent lives.

In a place called Lui in the south of Sudan, we built a hospital to serve the local population hammered by years of war. Shortly after our team established a base of operation, the radical Islamic government in Sudan began bombing our hospital. The government tried to run us off, but the incessant attacks strengthened our resolve, and the Lord protected our staff and the building from harm.

One day I received a letter from the Sudanese Embassy in Washington followed by a phone call. The Sudanese ambassador asked to meet me in my Boone, North Carolina, office. I was reluctant at first, due to hostilities from the Islamic government.

When I thought about how my father had met with leaders opposed to his message and remembered the apostle Paul's boldness in speaking to the Greek philosophers about "strange things," I extended an invitation for a Sudanese delegation to come.

Weeks later, the ambassador arrived at my office with his security detail. My staff served coffee, tea, and fresh fruit to our guests. To

Americans, this would not mean much, but to those from African cultures, an offer of refreshments was viewed as extending a hand of hospitality and showing a willingness to meet together in a cordial setting. In other words, to Africans, such gestures mean a great deal. Still, I knew that I could not compromise my message.

After proper introductions were made according to protocol, I invited the ambassador to sit and talk. I listened intently as he spoke about what he saw the problem to be in his country. When he finished, I said, "Mr. Ambassador, your government has bombed our hospital on seven separate occasions. I would appreciate it if your president would stop these attacks. We are Christians helping the people of Sudan in the name of Jesus Christ. Our hand is extended to Christians and Muslims. Mr. Ambassador, I am not taking sides in your politics. Would you ask your president to stop bombing our hospital? Innocent lives of your citizens are being lost. You can be sure I will do everything I can to cooperate with the peace process."

The ambassador's eyebrows raised, and after a few moments of awkward silence, he left, promising to look into it. Weeks later, the Sudanese foreign minister called, and in December 2004, I was on my way to meet Sudan's controversial president, Omar al-Bashir. Some say he is responsible for the death of hundreds of thousands, not only in Darfur but in the south as well.

I was not sure what kind of reception we would receive, but our team prayed that God would put the right words on my lips and plant my feet firmly in His steps. To my surprise, we were invited to stay at the presidential guesthouse. I was thankful to have my trusted friend Reverend Sami Dagher from Lebanon at my side. He served as my interpreter to ensure that the Gospel witness would be clearly translated.

The next day I was ushered into President al-Bashir's office. "Mr. President," I began, "thank you for meeting with me to discuss how we can work together for peace in your country." I told him about our hospital that was caring for the people of Sudan.

With a smug grin he turned to one of his assistants and said in English, "Didn't we bomb that hospital?" When his aide said, "Yes," President al-Bashir laughed.

I looked him square in the eye, smiled politely, and said, "But Mr. President, you missed!"

His smile disappeared.

Then he said, "Mr. Gra-huum, I want to make you a Muslim."

"Mr. President," I said, "I would love to give you the opportunity to try." Then I asked him for permission to preach in his country about my hope for peace. He didn't say yes. He didn't say no. When peace comes to Sudan, it just might be possible.

Two years later, I was with President al-Bashir once again in Sudan's capital city of Khartoum to discuss Darfur. Again he said, "I want to make you a Muslim." He wasn't giving up, and neither was I.

I thought of my father as he dealt with tough leaders. He never disrespected their belief system. By showing interest in their personal lives, he broke down barriers that he hoped some day would open their minds to God's truth.

I presented a petition from churches and schools asking that Sudan's government recognize their work and education among its people. I shared my concern for the innocent civilians in the country, the persecution of the church, and pastors who had been killed.

Christian leaders in Sudan had asked for certain rights: permits to buy land to build churches (until that time Christians were not allowed to buy property); recognition of certificates from Christian colleges (not acknowledged by the Muslim government at the time); Christian education for children; and radio broadcasts of Christian messages in Sudan.

To my amazement, President al-Bashir was cooperative; 512 churches were rebuilt, and today we continue training new pastors to replace those who had been killed.

I had several requests myself on behalf of Samaritan's Purse. I asked for permission to work with the churches and buy airtime to televise a Christmas special. I wanted the governor at Hamesh Khoreb to give us access to a hospital we had built and had been kicked out of. And my last request was for fifteen million dollars from the government of Sudan to help rebuild the churches they had destroyed during the war in the south—part of their plan to eradicate the church.

Sami Dagher capably translated the message, emphasizing that the nobler Sudanese citizens were Christians—those who did not destroy land or people but rather built villages and encouraged their neighbors through peace and love. The president couldn't argue. The facts were evident: wherever a Christian community had a presence, there were hardworking people striving to live quiet and peaceable lives.

The Sudanese president has granted everything we asked for, except for the fifteen million dollars. We trust the Lord to provide. He alone knows just how long the door will be open to plant churches in this battered African nation.

There are people around the world praying diligently for the followers of Jesus Christ in Sudan who have learned, at great cost, what it is to live for Him. The Islamic radicals inside the Sudanese government had stated some time before that it was their desire to wipe out the church across Sudan and institute Sharia law. Nevertheless, the Lord used our visit to open the airwaves across Sudan to the Gospel.

Through our BGEA World Evangelism Television Program, we were permitted to buy time on Sudanese television and broadcast *My Hope*, resulting in nearly three thousand people finding salvation in Jesus Christ. This is a great victory in any country, but especially notable in a Muslim nation. In spite of hostility toward our work, the Lord provided a way for us to strengthen His church in Sudan.

My parents always believed that by extending a hand of hospitality, hardened hearts can be softened. I have seen this work effectively. In contrast, hate can open the floodgate of demonic oppression, as we witnessed shortly after the birth of the twenty-first century.

Gripping Terror

On September 11, 2001, Americans watched in horror as morning news programs broadcast live images of two airplanes crashing into the World Trade Center in New York. Within a couple of hours, both magnificent towers that once reflected financial prosperity in America crumbled, sending plumes of smoke and debris into the sky. The aftermath of the vicious terrorist attack hovered over the free world.

Three years later on December 26, 2004, the world flicked on their televisions to behold the devastation of a great tsunami that swept part of the Indonesian seashore into the Indian Ocean. A northern town in the tip of Sumatra was carried out to sea, leaving eighty thousand dead. An amateur videographer caught the shock on camcorder, and the images were broadcast around the world, bringing the Christmas season to a screeching halt.

The very next year, America held its breath and fixed its eyes on minute-by-minute coverage watching to see if the predictions would come true—that Hurricane Katrina would wipe New Orleans and other cities along the Gulf Coast off the map.

I have learned many things by observing my father at work, going about the Father's business in the name of the Lord Jesus. When tragedy strikes, one thing is always certain: hard times cause people to think about God. For followers of Christ, tough times provide opportunities to share Christ's love and forgiveness with those in distress.

In his book *Storm Warning*, my father wrote, "The entire world is in turmoil. . . . We are living in a time of enormous conflict and cultural transformation. . . . We have been stunned by shockwaves of change . . . all around the globe. . . . While the globalists . . . continue their chant for 'peace, peace,' we are reminded that the Bible says that there can be no lasting peace until Christ returns. So the world remains restless and uncertain."[5]

It has been my desire, through the BGEA and Samaritan's Purse, to be about our Father's business in responding to needs that come knocking at our door at breakneck speed. We can hardly get one response center open before another tragedy strikes. But through it all, God does the enabling by supplying funds through His people and power through the prayers of the saints.

My father wrote that when storms come, "we do not have to be dependent upon the circumstances around us, but rather on the resources of God!"[6] He always prayed that God would open a door for the Word of God to be proclaimed (Colossians 4:3). And many times the open doors led right into troubled hearts and troubled spots.

Samaritan's Purse has supplied practical help in times of distress, and BGEA has provided spiritual comfort through programs like our Rapid Response Teams. We have been overwhelmed with the reaction from across the United States and Canada—people wanting to take their vacations, or a leave of absence, to volunteer with our ministries that serve somewhere each year helping those in dire need.

Days after the terrorist attack in 2001, my father was called on by the president to address the nation, calling people to prayer. While he prepared to speak, I went about my Father's business, preparing counselors and relief workers to go to New York to comfort the suffering—wounded and weary souls who needed assurance that God still loved them.

On September 14, 2001, my father spoke at Washington's National Cathedral in the presence of President George W. Bush and four of the five living presidents: Gerald Ford, Jimmy Carter, George H. W. Bush, and Bill Clinton.

In the wake of the tsunami, Billy Graham sent financial assistance from BGEA to the region, and I dispatched a team from Samaritan's Purse to take relief supplies to the people of India and surrounding countries. We are still seeing God at work through His people, who are reaching out to those who have endured great loss.

I learned from my dad, during times of crisis, the importance of responding immediately. How well I remember the massive cyclone that hit south India in 1977. My father arrived the same week to hold a campaign. He felt the overwhelming need to help the people who had been devastated by this wicked storm. The president of India at that time provided a helicopter, enabling my father to tour the area. When he saw the wreckage, he promised to rebuild one of the villages. I saw firsthand how this opened doors for ministry and hearts to the Gospel.

Samaritan's Purse and BGEA respond within hours to tragedies, working through local churches and Christian partners to rebuild villages, churches, homes, schools, and hospitals in the name of Jesus.

I believe that many times God permits these shocking tragedies to point the lost to Jesus Christ and to keep His own about their Father's business.

From Catastrophe to Crusading

In the last years of his ministry, Billy Graham covered America from coast to coast—Los Angeles to New York. Though his desire to preach never waned, his weakened body could not keep up. He decided to preach his last crusade in 2005 at Flushing Meadows, New York.

I tried to persuade him to stay busy. With a gentle rebuke he would say, "Franklin, you don't understand. I don't have the strength. Wait until you pass eighty." He was wise enough to know that there comes a time to rest.

Every time I was with my father I left feeling feeble myself, wishing I could help him finish strong. Driving back to Boone one day, I couldn't shake the thought: *How can I help Daddy keep doing what his soul longs to do—preach?*

I approached him one day and said, "Would you consider preaching at least one night at each of my crusades this year as you feel able?" He quickly said no. I probably should have backed off right then. One thing about the Grahams: we don't give up easily.

"Daddy," I said, "as long as you are able to preach, you need to keep preaching. It doesn't have to be your own crusade, where the responsibility is on your shoulders."

My father feared committing to something he could not fulfill. He had visions of disappointing supporting churches if, because of bad health, he would have to cancel.

Some time later, when we were together again, he said, "Franklin, I've been praying about what you said. I will try to preach one night in Baltimore, and I really would like to be with you in New Orleans if I have the strength. I am burdened for that city." His heart had been deeply moved by watching the news from the Ninth Ward and parishes in and around New Orleans following the killer hurricane.

I had been invited by local churches to hold a weekend Festival of Hope in the Crescent City to bring a message of comfort to the people of the area who had lost loved ones, homes, jobs, and all hope.

To my surprise, when the time came, my father boarded a plane in Asheville and flew to the recovering city. He expressed interest in touring some of the communities, meeting the citizens and pastors—and he did. People were amazed that this aged Gospel preacher cared enough to come and put his arms around them, assure them of his prayers, and especially remind them of God's love, comfort, and peace in the midst of hard times.

The Bible says, "Blessed be . . . the Father of mercies and God of all comfort, who comforts us in all our tribulation, that we may be able to comfort those who are in any trouble" (2 Corinthians 1:3–4).

When my father stood at the podium in New Orleans Arena, he opened the Bible and preached to the people that Jesus understood their sorrow and their pain; He understood that they had lost everything, and He cared. I believe that as the brokenhearted watched my father preach in a whisper of a voice, their hope was renewed that they, too, could go on, pick up the pieces of their lives, and look to the Lord with hope that they had not been forgotten.

Billy Graham has been called many things in his life—referred to as "Billy the Kid," when he was first starting; the "Pied Piper," when he began to gather in massive crowds; and "God's Ambassador" as he stood tried and proven. It has been said that he preached from the "Billy pulpit" and the "preacher's stump." None of that really matters. His entire adult life was consumed with a compulsion to bring the Good News to those nearby and far away. I am privileged as his son to carry on his ministry, which has been placed in my hands.

While my father was not a businessman, he was a man about his Father's business. He sought wisdom in others who came alongside and put feet and hands to the responsibility that ultimately fell upon him. He carefully chose men and women who shared his vision, and they helped carry the load of running the business end of one of the largest and most respected Christian organizations in the world—to the glory of God.

My father, with the support of his board of directors, entrusted me with leading the BGEA into the twenty-first century. Because of what I learned from him and those who served him faithfully, I have been privileged to couple this experience with my own, discovering other avenues where effective ministry can be accomplished. My father desired to go the extra mile to be accountable at every level, whether in finance or ministry outreach, to ensure the highest integrity to the government and the public, noting the biblical requirement that "stewards . . . be found faithful" (1 Corinthians 4:2). His organization has always sought the highest accountability. He often said, "Our job is not to be successful, but to be faithful."

My prayer is that we, who now give leadership to this ministry, will also be found faithful stewards so all those who are watching will say of the work done, "It is your hand, . . . you, O LORD, have done it" (Psalm 109:27 NIV).

What Is the Son's Name?

God not only spoke the Scriptures into existence, but He also instructs us today. Mankind has many questions, and God has the answers.

There are two Old Testament books written by father and son that contrast man's failure and God's faithfulness. King David wrote many of the Psalms, and his son King Solomon wrote much of the Book of Wisdom—Proverbs. Their writings shed light on being about the Father's business.

The book of Proverbs tells about a man who had many questions. He was searching for truth about creation and about its Creator. Then he asked some startling questions:

> Who has gathered the wind in His fists?
> Who has bound the waters in a garment?
> Who has established all the ends of the earth?
> What is His name, and what is His Son's name,
> If you know? (30:4)

When I read this passage, I want to shout at the top of my lungs, "I do know His name. His name is Jesus! I want to tell you about Him."

This prophetic passage energizes me in the work of evangelism today. Only through the power of the Holy Spirit can I declare the truth.

What is the Son's name? The Lord Jesus Christ! Still today He is about His Father's business. Are we?

9

You're Not Coming to Me...

—Morse Code, Numbers 23:23 kjv

Come and learn more about God and His Word.

BILLY GRAHAM

Coming soon! It's the greatest promotional hook of all time. Advertisers scurry to come up with what should follow these eye-snatching words. Man's relentless curiosity chases the tag.

I can recall, as I sat in a little restaurant, having morning coffee in Kiev, Ukraine, my inquisitive mind followed the newspaper headline: What Is Coming Soon?

The new iPhone to be marketed in U.S. stores
New owners will hold in the palm of their hands a telephone, video

recorder, camera, and stereo Bluetooth all having the ability, by touch screen, to make international calls, showcase videos and photographs, play digital music that syncs with iTunes, send and receive e-mail, and utilize the Safari web browser.

It took several cups of coffee to digest such high-tech capability. No plugs, no cables—a complete wireless system of communication that fits in our pockets and can tap into the cosmos of knowledge.

With me was the current world heavyweight champion Oleg Maskaev, a Russian who rose to fame in the boxing world and had become known as "The Big O." Oleg, a Christian with a powerful testimony, had come to share from the platform in our Kiev crusade, telling about what God had done in his life.

Overlooking the ancient city of Kiev was the golden dome of the Cathedral of St. Vladimir, where my father had preached nineteen years before, with members of the Communist party in attendance. He had hoped to hold a crusade in the city, but in the late 1980s, the political makeup began to change.

It was hard to believe that just a few short years later I was, in a sense, fulfilling one of my father's dreams—to preach Christ in Ukraine's Olympic Stadium. I had met people who had received Christ when my father had preached in the city nearly two decades before.

The weather had turned cold. Organizers were uncertain as to how this would affect the turnout. Many, who had traveled six to seven hours by train or bus, stood for hours in the chilling rain to get into the stadium.

When I took a seat behind the podium, the wind grew blustery, causing the platform to shake. The Ukrainian Army Orchestra, led by a strong evangelical believer, played as though the stars were twinkling in the sky. Their magnificent music thundered across the field and into the stands where several army units were seated.

To be given an opportunity to preach behind the former Iron Curtain, much less to units of the Ukrainian military, was something I never thought would happen. But my father had forged the way, and once again God opened a door to His Gospel message.

This was the first time in Ukraine's history that evangelicals were permitted to hold a national crusade in Olympic Stadium. Christians had come bearing umbrellas and bringing unsaved family and friends.

As I preached, the battering rain did not dampen people's spirits. When the invitation was given, hundreds streamed forward, heads covered by colorful umbrellas and hearts washed with the cleansing blood of the Savior.

My mind began spinning the next day as I thought about the crusade being transmitted to outlying regions by satellite linkup. My mind drifted back to the iPhone and just how far the world had progressed in communication technology and the effect it had in spreading the Gospel abroad.

Wireless Is Nothing New

"Hear ye, hear ye!" Town criers were the original newscasters. Their trade began in ancient Greece. As heralds, they enjoyed royal protection since they were empowered to speak on behalf of the king.

The herald was simply stating the pronouncement of the king. We tend to think the wireless era was invented by modern man, but running through cobblestone streets shouting the latest news is about as wireless as it could get.

Centuries later, when news went to print, young boys were dispatched shouting from street corners. "Extra, extra . . . read all about it!" was their attention grabber.

Read about what? Well, in 1844 you could have purchased a paper on a major street corner for one cent, and the headline might have read:

LONG-DISTANCE ELECTRIC TELEGRAPH LINE
TRANSMITS MESSAGE BY MORSE CODE

Samuel Finley Breese Morse is credited with inventing the single-wire electromagnetic telegraph. But without a language for the telegraph to communicate, the device was useless. With great ingenuity, Morse solved that hurdle by creating a communication pattern using dashes and dots that became known as Morse code. It's believed that his achievements began one of the most important revolutions in American history: the communication revolution.[1]

Morse was the first child of geographer and pastor Jedidiah Morse, a powerful preacher. Young Samuel became a portrait painter. But much later in life, during a transatlantic voyage in 1832, on a ship called *Sully*, his interest turned to technology, and he conceptualized how to breathe life into the telegraph.[2] Troubled by the fact that long-distance communication moved only as fast as horses' hooves, Morse pondered how electric currents could send information through wire. Inspired by Job 38:35—"Canst thou send lightnings, that they may go and say unto thee, Here we are?" (KJV)—Morse's answer was yes; and he concluded that surely messages could be transmitted as "quick as lightning."[3]

Henry Ellsworth, a friend of Morse's from Yale College days, believed in Samuel's dream to create a new method of communication. He reportedly wrote to friends "that if one telegraph instrument were placed in the Capitol and another connected to it in New York City, the people of New York City would know the results of a vote in Congress before it was known at the White House at the other end of Pennsylvania Avenue."[4] Until this time, the quickest way to send word on a congressional vote from the Capitol to the White House was by a messenger on a fast horse.

Morse and Ellsworth lobbied for congressional support to construct an experimental telegraph line. The bill passed the House, though with much opposition, and was sent to the Senate. On the last day of the session, Morse left the Capitol disheartened as the bill appeared to be stalled. He purchased a train ticket to travel home the next day and retired for the night at his boardinghouse—defeated and broke—with one dollar in his pocket.

Henry Ellsworth, however, remained optimistic and did not leave the Senate until the gavel fell, closing the session. It happened that the president was in the building and signed the bill into law five minutes before midnight.

Early the next morning, Ellsworth, commissioner of the US Patent Office, announced the victory to his family. His seventeen-year-old daughter, Annie, pleaded her father's permission to deliver the good news to Mr. Morse. When she arrived at the boardinghouse, she found Samuel Morse in the dining room having breakfast.

"Have you heard the good news, Mr. Morse?" Annie asked with excitement.

"I'm afraid I haven't heard any good news recently," he stated.

When Annie announced that the bill had been passed, Samuel Morse thanked her. And for delivering the message with such enthusiasm, he rewarded her by asking that she select the first message that would be sent over the wire upon completion of building the telegraph.[5]

God Speaks Through the Wire

When the work was completed a year later, Annie told Morse that she and her mother had been reading through the Bible, looking for the perfect message to be transmitted.

From the Supreme Court chambers in the United States Capitol in Washington, DC, to the B&O Railroad Depot in Baltimore forty miles away, the message was tapped through the wire and successfully returned.

._ _ ···· ·_ _ ···· ·_ _ ···· _ _ · _ _ _ _· ·_ _ ⁻· _ _ _ ··_ _ _· ···· _

"What hath God wrought!" (Numbers 23:23 KJV).

The words taken from ancient times inaugurated a new discovery: the telegraph.

God's Word was the first to be sent through the wire! Morse stated, "It baptised the American telegraph with the name of its Author."[6]

Annie Ellsworth could not have selected a more powerful message to send: LOOK WHAT GOD HAS DONE! Samuel Morse took this message, proclaimed three thousand years before, and sent it flowing through cables stretched across miles of timber posts.

While the press carried the news of this successful experiment, many papers reported the experiment but refused to print the actual message that had been sent. But God's Word did not return void (Isaiah 55:11). A century and a half later, when you search any number of websites for "Samuel Morse," "telegraph," or "Morse Code," you will find these words: "What hath God wrought!"

What Samuel Morse accomplished is but a picture of what God has done. He wanted to communicate to mankind. He sent His Son to earth with His message of salvation. But the people did not understand. So the Father lifted the Son out of the waters of baptism, placing Him upon timber, and the message became clear: *Look what I have done for you.*

"Lift up your eyes on high, and see who has created these things" (Isaiah 40:26).

The telegraph transformed how mankind communicates today and has energized the Great Commission—to preach the Gospel to the world.

Come Here—I Want to See You

On the heels of clicking telegraph wires, another invention called out to mankind. Dr. Alexander Graham Bell and his assistant rigged wires inside a home, room to room, and Dr. Bell transmitted a call. When the call was answered, his colleague heard: "Mr. Watson—come here—I want to see you."[7] Instantly, Watson responded. Bell wanted to see Watson so that they could celebrate what had been accomplished—transmission of a human voice through the wire. Acoustic telegraphy became known as the telephone, revolutionizing communication once more.

The telephone has been my connection to family scattered around the world. It has given me the ability to stay in touch with my international offices from home base. Whether I am in my truck or in the cockpit, I am only a phone call away.

This remarkable communication tool was no surprise to God. He has been calling since the beginning of time—"[Adam,] Where are you?" (Genesis 3:9). And He is still calling men and women today.

God's Word to mankind is not passive. God commands "all men everywhere to repent" (Acts 17:30), and He provides what it takes for mankind to receive what God wants to give.

My father was compelled to use every form of modern technology to reach souls for Christ. He did exactly what Bell Telephone advertised: "Reach out and touch someone."[8]

In 1980, my father led the charge for BGEA to develop call centers, allowing television viewers to respond to his invitation by calling a toll-free number that appeared on the screen. At peak times we saw this program swell to forty regional call centers around the country, utilizing more than six thousand trained volunteers and putting approximately six hundred telephones to work when our telecasts aired, averaging fifty thousand to seventy thousand calls per telecast.

Early in my father's ministry, he never dreamed that the Gospel would be preached on television, resulting in people coming to know the Lord by talking with volunteers over the telephone. In God's wisdom He devises ways for mankind to hear what He has done for us.

The Father of Invention

It is said, "Necessity is the father of invention." Ben Franklin, Thomas Edison, and the Wright brothers, among a host of others, have shared the title "father of invention." While their historical legacies have shaped the present and will enjoy longevity into the future, none of them can claim the singular title Father of Invention.

What is a necessity? My mother used to say necessity was bread, water, and a warm bed. We might say in years gone by that it was the need to see better, thus applauding the inventions of Ben Franklin's bifocals and Thomas Edison's lightbulbs. Today we should all salute the memory of Henry Ford when we climb into our family automobiles, thankful that he devised a way to mass-produce what many would claim as their most prized possession. We stand in awe when we see airplanes transporting people and cargo across the oceans. But when one need is filled another is usually created. Man is never satisfied.

Discoveries seem to create more need, and someone is standing in the wings prepared to outdo the last.

So, who is *the* Father of Invention?

Who will invent a method to calm a storm or hush the wind?

Who will create an all-knowing being?

Who will give birth to a never-to-die body?

The Bible answers these questions. "You do not know what is the way of the wind, . . . you do not know the works of God who makes everything" (Ecclesiastes 11:5). Mankind marvels at its own brilliance but casts doubt on Creator God, who graciously allows man to discover the works of His hands at various times.

"Is there anything of which it may be said, 'See, this is new'? It has already been in ancient times before us" (Ecclesiastes 1:10).

God is the Great Communicator and the Father of Invention, not bound by electrical current or technology. He speaks the world into space. He opens His mouth and shuts the jaws of lions. He commands and opens the mouth of a donkey to speak. He breathes and the wind sails. He thunders and waves rush to shore. He whispers and souls come alive.

A Wireless Method for a Timeless Message

Our God is the Creator of everything. But more important, He *is* the message that goes forth through ways that He makes available to mankind. Each man, woman, and child has the opportunity to receive the message with great joy, or delete it with pending doom.

Annie Ellsworth couldn't wait to announce good news to Samuel Morse. Why should we hesitate to proclaim the greatest news to ever reach man? My father grasped the message and preached it his entire life. The Bible says,

> God . . . accepts men from every nation who fear him and do what is right. You know the message God sent to the people of Israel, telling the good news of peace through Jesus Christ, who is Lord of all. . . .
> They killed him by hanging him on a tree, but God raised him from the dead on the third day and caused him to be seen . . . after he rose from the dead. . . . All the prophets testify about him that everyone who believes in him receives forgiveness of sins through his name. (Acts 10:34–36, 39–41, 43 NIV)

This is the Gospel that hundreds of millions have heard. This is the Gospel that billions more need to hear.

You're Not Really Going to Preach . . .

When I began preaching years ago, the media took an interest in interviewing me, in part, because I had once been identified as Billy Graham's rebel son and because I had already spent several years traveling to hot spots in conflict around the world. For years, I had watched my father interact with reporters, and I learned many things from his vast experience. But it wasn't until I put all these lessons into practice that I realized the impact of having my comments appear in print.

One of the first interviews I did resulted in the headline: BILLY GRAHAM'S SON PREACHES HELL.

Some said that no one would come to hear me preach a negative message. Others thought it meant I would speak about my past rebellion. But my father would say, "If we had more hell preached in the pulpit, we would have less hell in the pew."

The speaking circuit is booming today with positive Gospel presentations, productive goals, and prosperous living. There is nothing wrong with any of these when put into the right perspective. However, the Bible is a book of contrasts.

Many claim that the Gospel is exclusive (for a select group), not inclusive (for everyone). I disagree. Jesus did preach an *exclusive* Gospel—a message especially designed for mankind, the whole world. Jesus also preached an *inclusive* Gospel—a message about everything mankind does—and I mean everything.

Jesus preached exclusively that all people could experience forgiveness of sin. He preached inclusively that all people would be given a life sentence: heaven or hell. I cannot think of a message full of hope and love more than this because He leaves the decision with us. The conclusion will be ours to live and die with.

No one can read the Bible in its entirety and claim that God left any stone unturned. He exposes man's heart for what it is: corrupt, vile, selfish, and crude.

The wonderful thing is that God does not leave man in this hopeless state. He promised that He will "give you a new heart and put a new spirit within you" (Ezekiel 36:26). He wants to give man a heart transplant. You might call it OR—Operation Repentance. He wants to perform a heavenly procedure: remove the sinful heart and replace it with His heart. Not only will the Great Physician do the surgery, but

He has already paid the price with His own blood. But we have to walk into the OR. This is elective surgery man enters into by faith.

When God transforms a heart, He fills it with an around-the-clock companion—the Holy Spirit—and the patient walks into newness of life. His new heart gives him a new way of thinking that will guide his every step. The work of the Holy Spirit will help him "be renewed in the spirit of [the] mind" and "put on the new man which was created according to God, in true righteousness and holiness" (Ephesians 4:23–24).

Many times Jesus spoke in parables, contrasting light and darkness. He preached to Pharisees and peasants, lawgivers and lawbreakers. Jesus preached about demons and divine beings, the destructive life and the disciplined life.

God's wrath and His love go hand in hand. He wants to save man from His wrath and wrap him in His love. His message is for everyone, and this truth became my father's rallying message. I am privileged to have learned through him the effectiveness of proclaiming God's Word.

My father said many times, "Too many Christian programs have been geared to please, entertain, and gain the favor of this world. The temptation is to compromise, to make the Gospel more appealing and attractive."

While my father preached God's love, he did not shy away from preaching that man's nature is evil—that's the bad news. The flip side is that the truth of the Gospel offers mankind the opportunity to exchange our evil nature for His nature—that's the Good News.

There was a young preacher on television recently who said, "My grandfather has been criticized for not preaching about sin." He said, "There are enough people doing that. I am going to preach the positive side." This philosophy collides with the Gospel. Salvation cannot be imparted until sin has been dealt with; therefore, it must be preached.

The Good News has the power to turn bad to good and darkness to light. It provides an escape from the anguish of hellfire into the glory of heaven's light.

So if I care for lost souls bound eternally to the father of lies, how can I not warn them of their sentence? As Paul said, "Woe is me if I do not preach the gospel" (1 Corinthians 9:16). If I preach the Gospel, I must preach sin and its everlasting verdict.

Keep It Simple

I am frequently asked when I go into a city to preach, "Mr. Graham, what are you coming to speak about this week?" In the early days, I gave a lengthy answer, trusting that I would say something to pique the interest of those who would hear or read the story and come to the crusade. My father always encouraged me, "Franklin, keep it simple." So as time went on, I shortened my response.

I recall one reporter asking, "Mr. Graham, what will you be speaking about?" I smiled and remembered what my father said, "Well, I won't be *speaking*, but I will be *preaching* on sin."

It took the reporter aback somewhat. "Sin? What sin?" he asked.

My answer? "Not *what* sin, but *whose* sin. I will not be speaking about a sin; I'll be preaching about mankind's sin. The Bible says, 'All have sinned and fall short of the glory of God'" (Romans 3:23).

Life stands between bookends:

> Birth and death; beginning and end.
> Sickness and health; weariness and rest.
> Rebellion and obedience; lies and truth.
> Greed and generosity; sin and forgiveness.
> Repentance and salvation; sorrow and joy.
> Man's hatred of God and God's love for man.

Many say that the Gospel can be preached without mentioning hell. They insist that love must prevail. Prevailing speaks about winning *over* something. So if love is to prevail, what is it prevailing over?

Jesus answered this many times. "Love covers all sins" (Proverbs 10:12).

My Father Was a Newshound

Preparing for a crusade was important to my father. He arrived in the city several days, perhaps a week, early in order to acclimate himself to the area. Until the last few years of his ministry, he always enjoyed walking down the streets and through the parks, visiting with people, chatting with storekeepers and shoppers, and enjoying the local restaurants with church leaders and businessmen.

As he prepared his sermons for the week, one thing he never failed to do was pore through local newspapers. He characterized the term *newshound*. Throughout his ministry he sharpened his eye for a headline that was sure to capture attention or a sound bite that might catch the listener's ear. It was not unusual to walk into his hotel room and find news clippings scattered on the floor and coffee table. He loved the challenge of looking to Scripture to expound on what God might say about a topic that would speak to a current event.

"I do not have to make the Gospel relevant," my father would say. "It is always relevant in any part of the world. Don't let the newspaper headlines frighten you. God is still sovereign. He is still on His throne."

Our society has become saturated with news. Seldom do you see a headline that shouts J-O-Y. Generally, the headlines growl trouble— *bad* trouble. Wherever I go, whether domestically or abroad, the headlines can be summed up in three letters: S-I-N.

Selfishness. Insecurity. Need.

I have become a bit of a newshound myself. When I am traveling, I look for the morning paper at my door and have news apps on my iPhone. However, when I peruse the headlines, it leaves me asking, "Is there any good news?" Then I recall God's truth: "Love covers all sins."

While preaching crusades over two decades, I have accumulated quite a collection—from Canada to Ecuador, from Japan to Scotland:

DOCTOR CONVICTED FOR DRUG TRAFFICKING

TRUCKER JAILED ON FEDERAL CHILD PORN CHARGES

MAN INTOXICATED WHILE ON CELL PHONE DURING FATAL CRASH

POLICE OFFICERS FIRED FOR CHEATING ON LEADERSHIP TEST

FOUR ARRESTED AFTER WOMAN IS SHOT, ROBBED

MAN GETS LIFE SENTENCES FOR MURDERS

LYING FOR A JOB—JOB SEEKERS CAUGHT IN THE ACT

Lying to conceal evil, killing out of jealous rage, cheating to get ahead, drug trafficking to get rich, drunk driving out of despair, abusive behavior due to pornography—all expressions of man's sin. Convictions, life sentences, arrests, fines levied—expressions of man's judgment.

The world says, "Live as you choose." But the Bible says, "Be sure your sin will find you out" (Numbers 32:23).

Evil deeds, however, are not what send people to hell. These deeds are the outpouring of the human heart. The Bible says, "The heart is deceitful above all things, and desperately wicked; who can know it? I, the LORD, search the heart, I test the mind" (Jeremiah 17:9–10).

The majority of the world's population are proud to be law-abiding citizens, as long as the law is on their side. Man wants to live a care-free life, with no thought of God, no thought of consequences—unless, of course, someone else violates him; then he wants justice. He wants the perpetrator to be held accountable for his actions, with consequences applied.

A child predator goes on trial, and the world sighs relief as the jury reads the guilty verdict. Cheers erupt in the courtroom when the judge passes sentence: death! But we balk at a ticket when caught speeding down the highway.

The law is the law, and it applies to all.

We are all too happy to let a judge—a mere man or woman—pass a verdict on someone the jury finds guilty. Mankind accusing mankind—we're okay with that. Yet men reject the fact that God has the power, and the right, to judge man's heart. We have the audacity to kick and scream, "What kind of God would send someone to hell?"

The truth is that God does not want His judgment to send anyone to hell. Jesus said, "For judgment I have come into this world, that those who do not see may see" (John 9:39). That decision rests with only you and me. God in His mercy and grace allows mankind to make such an eternity-altering decision. We walk blindly, but Jesus will open our eyes if we let Him.

The only sin that keeps us from eternal life in heaven is rejecting Christ. Not too many years ago this was preached with passion. But today we don't like to hear the truth. We want to be affirmed in our actions.

The Wilderness Called Sin

Men struggle with the subject of sin. Some even laugh at it—but sin is no laughing matter.

Let's look at this tyrant called sin. Just what is sin? What does sin do? And who sins? Psalm 51:5 says that we are sinners from birth because our flesh is sinful. If you don't believe that, you've never been around a baby.

Parents do not need to teach babies to cry, whimper, kick, and scream—it just comes naturally. Toddlers don't need lessons on disobedience or meddling. Teenagers don't have to be taught to sass or rebel. There is no need for mankind to take Life 101 to learn the art of lying or cheating; these behaviors follow the path from infancy right into adulthood.

But when people are confronted personally with this thing called *sin*, they rename it to soothe their minds. Every person is born with a conscience—it is a general revelation from the Creator. But when they ignore it year after year, the conscience becomes hardened and they no longer hear it warning, *Do not partake.*

Followers of Jesus Christ have within us the Holy Spirit, who breathes life into our consciences and will not leave us alone. If we habitually commit sin, we must honestly ask ourselves if we really ever were in Christ Jesus.

Some say, "If we just had a sign that God was really with us, we would not fall into sin." Well, let's suppose that we were held against our wills in a foreign country. No way of escape. Suddenly God sends someone to the rescue, and we pack our few belongings and head out. Then we notice our former captor is approaching. He's decided not to let us escape after all.

Sound a little far-fetched? This is the story of the children of Israel fleeing Egypt. They begged God to free them from slavery. Moses led the way across the sandy desert with the angel of God behind the host of Israelites. Pharaoh's chariot went after them with his army in hot pursuit. Suddenly, the Red Sea rolled back, and God's chosen people passed through a massive corridor of water on dry ground. The moment the last Israelite foot reached the shore, the waters roared back into place, drowning Pharaoh and every Egyptian soldier who entered the warring sea.

Wouldn't we jump for joy? Wouldn't we tap replay to witness that miracle once more? Wouldn't we fall on our faces and glorify the saving hand of Almighty God?

This is just what the children of Israel did. After they considered God's moving hand upon them, they turned their backs to the sea and their faces to the Promised Land. They rehearsed the victorious defeat of the enemy, and it energized their long journey—*for three whole days.* But as they crossed the parched, desolate terrain, they began to fuss and complain. About what? Of all things, *water!*

Poor Moses. God had just delivered them through the sea, and now they want water? What was Moses to do with all these thirsty men, women, and children? Moses just couldn't win. And because the people bickered and doubted God, they wandered forty years right into the Wilderness of Sin. "And they journeyed . . . to the Wilderness of Sin, which is between Elim and Sinai" (Exodus 16:1). And there the whole congregation of Israel complained against Moses and Aaron.

You would think that after witnessing what God had done, they would do what He commanded. But the Bible says, "They sinned even more against Him by rebelling against the Most High in the wilderness" (Psalm 78:17).

Let's not be too hard on God's people. We all do the very same thing. God blesses—we rejoice. God is silent for a time—we complain. We sin—God disciplines. We repent—God forgives.

Can you imagine the nightly news covering such a story as this? I remember going to Indonesia following the 2004 tsunami. It was an epic disaster in modern times. It was caught on videotape and beamed around the globe. Certainly there were stories of breathtaking escape, but nothing can compare to the Red Sea triumph. My imagination sure loves to wander around that vision: How would a news anchor report this drama today?

A MILLION SLAVES ESCAPE THROUGH RED SEA ON FOOT
ARMY DROWNS IN RUSHING WATER!

Reporters on the ground would not know how to cover such a miracle. They would not be positioning their cameramen in strategic places for interviews. I believe they would be on their faces with God's people, bowing in reverence to the invincible Deliverer.

A Powerful Network

The media is no doubt a powerful force—a daily source of information that molds our thinking in many ways. It continually feeds our minds with news.

There is another type of network that mankind loves more than this—it is a composite, you might say, of every sick thing Satan and his demon-producers can think up and carry out through their correspondents. Let's tune in for just a moment to his network: SIN—Satan's Influential Network.

What is the purpose of this network?
- **S**eparate man from God (Isaiah 59:2)
- **I**nhabit the body and mind (Ephesians 2:3)
- **N**egate righteousness (Psalm 52:3)

Who tunes into this network?
- **S**elf-
- **I**ndulgent
- **N**atures

What is the effect?
- **S**alacious appetites (Ephesians 2:3)
- **I**nclined toward evil (Jeremiah 17:9)
- **N**eeding to fulfill fleshly desires (James 1:14)

What can we do about it? All we have to **S**ay **I**s **N**o!

When I was a boy, one of the first verses my mother helped me memorize was: "My son, if sinners entice thee, consent thou not" (Proverbs 1:10 KJV). But my mother paraphrased the verse to make sure I understood its message. "Son, when bad boys want you to do bad things, say *no*." I got that!

My father once wrote, "The world is seething with demonic energy. Only supreme inner strength can resist its ceaseless hassling."[9]

When man connects his heart and soul to SIN, he pulls the shades, locks the door, and says, "There's no room for You in here,

God." He becomes entangled with every wretched thought and action. The Bible poses the question: What do darkness and light have in common (2 Corinthians 6:14)? God cannot look upon sin (Habakkuk 1:13).

Turn the channel. Obliterate it. We can say no to sin if we call on the Greater Power.

Today, almost everyone understands the new language of high tech: blogging, surfing, browsing, and so on. It is almost impossible to move around in cyberspace without understanding its language.

Samuel Morse wrote Morse code, but if he had not demonstrated it to others, if they had not comprehended the language, they would have missed the message.

This is what my father did his entire ministry. In God's power, he preached,

> If your heart is not attuned to God, it will become a catch basin for every device of the devil. Yes, Satan is at work in our world. He exists and he has control over hearts that have never been captured by Jesus Christ. [Satan] has hundreds of agents writing pornographic literature and producing movies to pollute [the] mind. He has intellectuals in high positions teaching a hedonistic and permissive philosophy. I come in contact with men and women caught in the anguish of their own unpreparedness . . . and I long to take every one of them by the hand and lead them into the presence of the One who said, "Come."

Shouldn't we ask God to open our hearts to comprehend His language of love, His forgiveness, and the meaning of sin and how to block it out through His power?

I do not know anyone who wants to spend eternity in hell. Everyone wants to go to heaven, but many do not want to change the condition of their darkened hearts in order to enter eternal light.

If we want someone to do something for us, we generally call and ask. This is what Christ wants man to do. He is waiting to hear the call. And He will answer. The Bible says to call on the name of the Lord, and He will wash away your sins (Acts 22:16).

Accept the fact that we are sinners and repent of our sins;
Believe that Jesus died for our sins and rose to new life, and
surrender our lives to the Master;
Confess our sin to Christ, who forgives, and turn away from
sinful deeds.

The Bible says, "Repent therefore and be converted, that your sins may be blotted out" (Acts 3:19). This is what it means to be converted—transformed. "For He has clothed me with the garments of salvation, He has covered me with the robe of righteousness" (Isaiah 61:10).

Valley of Decision

Early in my father's ministry, he began partnering with local churches in cities where he would hold crusades—canvassing surrounding communities and encouraging involvement for the purpose of evangelism, opening the way for churchgoers to invite friends and neighbors to hear the Gospel.

He believed that evangelists should work hand in hand with the local church. Over his seventy-year ministry, God honored this approach. The church edifies the evangelist in his mission, and the evangelist channels converts back into the local body of believers.

Every Bible-believing church today, and every follower of Jesus Christ, has the greatest calling—to live a testimony that points lost souls to the Savior. Many local churches have been a tremendous encouragement in our work. They have opened their doors to Samaritan's Purse and partnered with us through Operation Christmas Child, reaching out to children around the world. They have invited BGEA to come into their communities and hold citywide evangelistic crusades while supporting us with volunteers, prayer warriors, and financing—all for the purpose of preaching the Gospel to the lost, channeling new believers back into their congregations to be discipled and nourished in the Scriptures. This strengthens both the church and community.

Before we go into cities for crusades, careful attention is given to cultivating church support. Without this, our meetings would be ineffective. We often hold advance rallies in an effort to garner support for volunteers who will help in our endeavor—to see a great harvest of souls for the Lord.

An important component of our strategy is through Operation Andrew. This program was used by my father to motivate Christians to identify lost friends, relatives, and coworkers, encouraging Christians to pray and invite others to the crusade.

He wrote, "All around [us] are people who need Christ. . . . Are we praying for them? Are we asking God to use us to tell others about Christ? . . . You may never meet them in this life—but in heaven you may discover that your prayers had a part in bringing about their eternal salvation."[10]

A colleague of mine wrote a song for use in our ministry as we prepared for a crusade in the great state of Texas. Later the song was recorded in California by the Tommy Coomes Praise Band.

> People all around us today need Jesus,
> They need to hear He died to make them new,
> Let's keep working to fulfill the Great Commission,
> Lord, we ask You now to bless this work we do.
> So come together now, church of Jesus,
> Hand in hand we'll reach out to the lost,
> Lord, break our hearts for the ones that do not know You,
> Help us show them the way to the cross.[11]

We brush shoulders with lost souls every day. Oh, they may wear smiles, and they may laugh and joke, but we don't know their hurt inside. They are in deep, dark valleys next door, down the street, in the office cubicle next to you, or perhaps on the pew or chair beside you in church.

You may think it strange to reach out to someone who is lost. If they know you are a Christian, they may think it strange that you don't.

There are people all around us today who need Jesus. Ask the Lord to help you identify someone who may need you to lead them to the cross. Don't put it off. The Bible says: "Exhort one another daily, while it is called 'Today'" (Hebrews 3:13).

My father has said, "Mass crusades, in which I believe and to which I have committed my life, will never finish the Great Commission; but a one-by-one ministry will." The Gospel is an urgent message. There are "multitudes, multitudes in the valley of decision! For the day of the LORD is near in the valley of decision" (Joel 3:14).

The Father's Effective Call

I am often asked how I best remember my father. If I sit quietly, I can hear his soft-spoken voice—a word of encouragement, a word of caution. Visually I can recall him in a variety of settings: sitting with him at home laughing and enjoying meals, watching him tenderly embracing his grandchildren, talking and walking with him along the ridge of the mountain above the house. This is Billy Graham the father, grandfather, and great-grandfather.

But I have to be honest; the most compelling vision engraved in my memory is my father—the evangelist—standing at a podium in an outdoor stadium, his voice booming through the microphone: "*Thus saith the Lord!*" Then I remember how he would step from behind the pulpit, stoop over the platform's edge, and stretch out his arm—as though to sweep everyone into heaven.

If only he could.

I learned an important lesson from my father about giving the invitation. At the start of his sermon and many times throughout, he said to all who listened, "In a few moments I am going to ask you to come forward and stand in front of this pulpit to receive Christ's forgiveness. There is only One who can forgive sin. Listen to the prompting of the Holy Spirit and get ready to respond." It was important to let people know at the beginning of his message what he was going to ask them to do.

The image of my father extending the invitation is vivid—his big, old Bible in hand, wide open—pages blowing in the evening breeze as though God were gently whispering, *Come. Come to Me, all you who labor and are weary. I will give you rest* (Matthew 11:28, paraphrased).

This is where the preacher in him fell silent, and a prayer warrior emerged to plead for lost souls of the young and old. A hush would fall over the crowd, as though to acknowledge a heavenly host waiting, watching, hoping.

The shuffling of feet and the murmur of voices would blend with the music as my father sent out the call, and the choir would sing:

> Just as I am, without one plea,
> but that thy blood was shed for me,
> and that thou bidst me come to thee,
> O Lamb of God, I come, I come.[12]

Throngs of people coming, filling the floor with counselors standing near, my father gently persuading those who delay to answer the Savior's call—*Come!*

"When you hear my voice coming through the speakers," he would say, "all around this vast complex, don't delay; don't ignore God's plea. *Get up out of your seat* and come to Christ. He is the One who is calling. He is the One pleading for your soul. He is drawing you near. Don't resist.

"He is waiting with open arms. The arms that stretched across the beams of the old rugged cross to draw you near. Don't listen to Satan's ploy that says, 'Perhaps tomorrow.' Listen to the still, small voice that speaks this promise: 'Now is the day of salvation'" (2 Corinthians 6:2).

"You're not coming to me," my father would say. "You're not coming to man; man cannot save you. You're not coming to Billy Graham; I cannot save you. I am a sinner saved by the same grace that is offered to you. I am only God's messenger. Come to Christ. We'll wait for you—come now."

This picture of a Gospel preacher calling sinners to repentance sweeps through my thoughts every time I walk to the pulpit. This is my father's portrait framed in the old rugged cross.

I may not preach like him and I may not be used by God in the same way, but I have learned through his example that we must allow God to speak through us to communicate the Gospel.

The Lord has given us wonderful tools to use, and His message is being heard through the wire and the wireless. More important, the message is penetrating hearts and calling souls, "Come to Me" (Matthew 19:14).

My father proclaimed this Gospel unashamedly as he stood before kings and before paupers. He preached in his own tongue and through interpreters before the masses in foreign lands. He stood in the sweltering sunrays of African jungles and torrential rains of the Amazon. He stood in the corridors of the Kremlin and in the Oval Office, and he peered into the grandstands of American stadiums and Canadian arenas to say, "Come and hear . . . I will declare what [God] has done for my soul" (Psalm 66:16). My father wrote, "God is sending forth His message of love, but you must tune in. You must be willing to listen and receive His message and then to obey it."[13]

How have you responded to God's invitation? Do you scoff at His claim? Or have you accepted the message that has traveled through your ears and eyes, into the depths of your soul, and said, "Yes, I do believe that God's message can cleanse my soul and allow His love to flow within"? Have you acknowledged Him?

Christ **C**alls; are you listening?
Christ **H**ears; are you praying?
Christ **R**edeems; are you repenting?
Christ **I**s near; are you drawing close?
Christ **S**aves by grace; are you accepting?
Christ **T**ransforms; are you willing to be made new?

Mankind scoffed at the message and killed the Messenger, silencing the language of love—they thought.

God's code of love taps on the doors of our hearts. And God waits. He listens from heaven for our response. When we cry out in mercy and accept His grace, He sends back a message: *I will forgive and cleanse you. I will transform you and make you My own.*

This, my friends, is the Good News; it is the best news; it is the only news that communicates God's language of love.

Coming soon! Yes. Jesus is coming soon. Will you be ready for your journey into eternity? For those who cannot answer yes, I echo my father's call. I cannot do anything for you. But look at what Jesus has done—He has given His life for you.

Perhaps today will be your hour of decision.

10

In His Steps

Christ also suffered for us, leaving us an example,
that you should follow His steps.

—1 Peter 2:21

*Godlikeness of character is the Christian's proper heritage
in this earthly walk.*

BILLY GRAHAM

Walking is the original mode of transportation.

Before planes, trains, and cars, it was four-legged horsepower pull-ing wagons and chariots. But in the beginning there was man—with two feet. Even if man traveled on the back of a camel, donkey, or horse, the only way of arriving at any destination was step by step.

When was the last time you walked to get anywhere? Some in big cities walk a short distance to public transportation. Imagine walking from New York City across the George Washington Bridge to New Jersey just to get home. It would change your lifestyle.

Johann Wolfgang von Goethe, the German poet, said, "The heights charm us, but the steps do not."[1] Sir Edmund Hillary probably thought about this on his historic climb to conquer Mount Everest.

Many want to bask in the glory of scenic travel, but they don't want to go on foot. Why do we dislike taking one step at a time? For me the process is too slow, I have to admit. Hiking step by step to the top of Mount McKinley, the crowning jewel of North America's highest peak, or walking the perimeter of a lake to get to the other side would not excite me as much as climbing into the cockpit of a plane and soaring above the mountain peaks or boarding a float plane and skimming the glassy surface of the Alaskan lakes that flow beyond the front porch of my cabin.

Why is walking, as a form of transportation, drudgery for many people? It seems tedious, for one thing, and it makes reaching certain goals impossible. One may walk across a river but never a sea—unless, of course, you're Moses. An astronaut may take one small step for mankind on the moon, but he will never get to the moon by walking.

When my dad was younger and in good health, he would walk down the mountain to our gate and back up, about a mile, at a blistering pace. Sometimes he would do it three times a day. In his latter years he used a walker and went a shorter distance, but he still pushed himself to walk. Following my mother's death, his walks became reflective as he recalled the memories of how she had chosen that mountain on which to live and raise their family.

Though he was gone much of the time, my father made a profound impact on my siblings and me by his example. We looked forward to his homecomings, knowing that he would find something special for us to do together. Sometimes he would gather us up, grab his walking stick, and take us on a hike up the mountain above our home. He always made it fun. He used his walking stick to check out the ground in front of us, warning of what was ahead. He led the way, and we followed in his steps.

This is what God does. He walks before us with warnings and also encouragement to follow in His steps.

My father walked in every country he ever visited and learned much about people and their way of life. He often walked with those who traveled with him—men like T. W. Wilson, Maury Scobee, and David Bruce. He reflected on these walks and said, "I used to walk the trails around my home and pour out my heart to the Lord. In some of the darkest hours, I could feel the touch of His hand [through prayer]."

My mother used to laugh about a walk my father took when they were in Europe working on a book. She was sitting on the beach when she spotted a man some distance away. She thought, *Oh my, who is that man walking toward me? He must be an American.* He wore big sunglasses, a golf hat, no shirt, plaid baggy Bermuda shorts, black socks, and Hush Puppy shoes. *That is the most ridiculous-looking man,* she thought. As he drew closer, she gasped. *Oh no, it's my husband!*

He came up with some pretty wild disguises, but it enabled him to get his walks in each day without being recognized.

I will never again take an afternoon walk with my father in this life, but the steps he left behind will always guide me.

There would be slow progression in our physical lives without steps. It is the same when it comes to our spiritual lives. Maturing and falling into step with the Lord require feasting on His Word. Christians should look back at how far we have come in our spiritual walks. Do we see a progression of growth in our daily steps?

The world has turned the most basic exercise—walking—into a booming business. There are product catalogs that target walkers: walking shoes, walking sticks, walking meters, and walking sensors. Publishers produce books and magazines about walking trails. There's even a walking dictionary. Who would take time to read that? The answer, I suppose, is someone who wants to be the best walker he can be. Pick up a magazine in just about any office, and you'll find advertisements that promote walking for fitness, walking for charity, or walking for recreation. You can buy a membership in a walking club—or even hire a walking buddy.

Walking, as an action word, means to place one foot in front of the other with one foot always making contact with the ground, step by step. It speaks of movement and progress. Many people make walking part of their regular exercise routines, yet they forget to apply the same principles to their spiritual walks. Walking with Christ will make us fit for the kingdom, will help us reach out to others, and will refresh our spirits. The best part is that we can take every single step with Him.

A feature film based on the book *One Man's Wilderness* tells the story of Dick Proenneke, who retired at age fifty and moved to the shores of Twin Lakes, west of Anchorage, Alaska. There he built an inconspicuous log cabin and lived out his remaining thirty years alone in the frozen north.[2]

I met Dick once before he died. He used to walk from Twin Lakes to Lake Clark, about fifty miles through rugged terrain, bogs, raging rivers, and deep ravines. It took him hours to reach his destination—the log cabin of his friend, former governor Jay Hammond, at the mouth of Miller Creek on Lake Clark.

I asked my friend Glen Alsworth how Dick made that treacherous journey. Glen said, "I asked him the same question one time, Franklin. Dick said, 'I just put one foot in front of the other.'"

While we may not elect to walk for pleasure, all who are able-bodied walk every day. For me, I would rather run. Some say I am speeding my way to knee deterioration. The point for me is that I'm *speeding*.

I began jogging a few years before I turned fifty. A friend of mine, Dr. Richard Furman, convinced me that it was good exercise. It was dreadful at first, but the discipline energized and whipped me into shape.

Clipping along mile after mile, whether you are running or walking, you see things you don't see when in a car or on a motorcycle. It gives me a new appreciation for leaves on the trees, blades of grass blowing with the breeze, and the realization that every sprint begins with a first step. The regimen helped me see what I was missing in my dash through life.

Consider, then, the apostle Peter's command that we should follow in the steps of Jesus. We should pause to carefully look at what that means. Doing so will give us a glimpse of what Jesus is commanding us to do as we follow in His steps.

Notice that Jesus did not send twelve men out into the world when He initially called them. You could say He put them through spiritual boot camp. They walked with Him for three years, observing His steps and practicing all that He commanded. He instructed them. He trained them. He loved them.

Making Every Step Count

Other than an occasional boat trip across the Sea of Galilee and His triumphal entry into Jerusalem on the back of a colt, Jesus walked everywhere—absolutely everywhere. The Son of God came into the world and walked among sinners.

His first steps recorded in the Bible led Him as a boy to the temple in Jerusalem. The next time we encounter Him in Scripture, we see the Man Jesus stepping into the River Jordan. Isn't it interesting that as soon as Jesus was baptized, the Spirit led His steps immediately into the wilderness to be tempted by the devil? After Jesus rebuked Satan and sent him away, He began His public ministry, step by step, according to His Father's will.

Jesus walked the dusty roads every day. His feet trudged rocky ridges. He crossed the hillsides laden with lily of the valley—His very own creation of immense beauty.

As Jesus walked, everything He taught His disciples foreshadowed His steps. As they walked through pastures, He spoke about the shepherds and their flocks of sheep. Successful fishermen learned from Him the real secret of catching fish—and men. When their feet grew weary, they sat beneath the trees and ate of the fruit. I would imagine that when Jesus walked through the forests, He looked at trees differently than the disciples did. He must have thought about which trees would make good beams and which type of timber would make a strong table or bench—after all, He was a carpenter.

This is how God looks at us. He knows what we are made of. The Bible says, "We are His workmanship" (Ephesians 2:10). Perhaps He says, *She will make a good writer or mother,* or *He will make a good soldier or pastor.*

The disciples did not realize at first that this is what Jesus was doing in their lives. He was making them effective fishers of men. They did not fully comprehend, though, that He was the Good Shepherd who must first lay down His life for His sheep on an old rugged tree of His own creation. They did not have the big picture at first, but in time it was revealed that each step of Jesus was purpose filled. Each step was a teaching tool. Each step led His disciples into a deeper understanding of Him.

What do our steps teach us about ourselves? What do our steps teach others? Do they make an impact for good? They're supposed to. Every day our steps carry us along. Each step exposes us to something. Do we walk a thin line nudging the edge of compromise? Are we content placing our steps right down the middle of the road so that no one really knows where we stand at all? Or do our steps consistently follow Christ's, leaving others no doubt where we stand? There is an old saying: *Make every step count.* Do we?

The Bible says, "The steps of a good man are ordered by the LORD" (Psalm 37:23). Jesus set the example as He walked along the shores of Galilee and called fishermen to follow Him. His steps carried Him up to the magnificent scenery atop the mountain where the greatest sermon was preached, the Sermon on the Mount. Footsteps took Jesus through towns and villages like Tyre and Sidon. He walked the narrow streets of Capernaum, healing the sick; raising the dead in Bethany; casting out demons in the region of Tiberius; and rebuking scribes and Pharisees in Jerusalem. As He walked, He called individuals from the highways, down from treetops, and out of caves.

Many times I have crossed the Sea of Galilee in a small tour boat and thought about Jesus walking on the water. When Peter wrote that we should follow His steps, I wonder if he was reliving the moment he stepped out on the black midnight waters of Galilee to walk to Jesus. Can you imagine a robust fisherman navigating the boisterous waves? Peter did just fine. Then he took his eyes off the Master of the sea, and down he went. I would imagine those faltering steps taught Peter to *fix his eyes on Jesus.*

Did you know that if you watch your feet as you walk, it can throw your equilibrium off? If you want to stay balanced, keep your eyes focused on what is ahead of you. If you are walking in His steps, your eyes will be fixed on the One who said, "Follow Me."

A Walk with Jesus

We like the idea of following someone exciting. Who would not want to walk along the shores of Galilee? Who would not want to walk on the water? But step by step Jesus was working His way to Calvary's cross. Who is willing to walk with Him to the foot of the cross?

My father often said, "Living for Christ, walking in His way, will not be an easy path, but true faith and suffering frequently go hand in hand."

For three years Jesus' steps dotted what we now call the land of the Bible. Where did they lead next? Back to Bethany. Jesus' feet had walked many times to the home of Mary, Martha, and Lazarus. But on the night Jesus dined with Simon the leper, Mary anointed the feet of the Lord.

Then Passover came. Jesus climbed the staircase to the Upper Room. Step by step He ascended to the place where He had the Last Supper with the disciples. That evening He took a walk with them. The disciples followed Jesus' steps across the Kidron Valley into the Garden of Gethsemane, where He agonized in prayer.

After Judas betrayed Him, Jesus took another walk—this time as a prisoner. Just as He had walked obediently into the garden to be betrayed, He walked in obedience to the courtyard of the high priest to stand trial. Jesus was ushered into Pilate's presence, and His sentence was pronounced: "Crucify Him!"

An entire garrison (about six hundred men) led Jesus to the Praetorium, the governor's palace. There He was clothed in purple and crowned with thorns—scourged, mocked, beaten, and spit upon. Then, step by agonizing step, Jesus, bearing our sin—symbolized by the burden of His heavy cross—ascended Mount Calvary.

In the presence of His disciples, His followers, His enemies, His prosecutors, His mother, and all of heaven, Jesus was stretched out on the old rugged cross. His precious feet that had walked across the land, hands that had healed the lame, were nailed to the tree. The soldiers thought they had ensured that His steps had been halted forever. And those who loved Him never really believed that those feet would ever walk again.

Think about it. Jesus Himself said that He would be raised after three days, but not even the disciples who had followed His steps day by day fully comprehended His claim that His temple would be raised in three days. If they had, their feet would have carried them to the tomb on Easter morning—to welcome Him back and to worship at His feet. Instead, after His crucifixion, they fled, terrified that their lives were endangered for believing in their King—now dead.

But then . . . steps.

More steps.

Up from the grave He arose.

And the risen Savior took a morning walk—alone.

Can you imagine?

Along the way, Jesus saw Mary Magdalene and Mary the mother of James. They worshipped at His nail-scarred feet. He hastened the women to go tell the disciples He was alive—then He continued walking, step

> by

> > step.

There were others walking that glorious morning, but they were filled with despair, not jubilation. Two men walked the road to Emmaus, heavyhearted and probably heavy-footed, all hope gone. Jesus heard them talking about what had transpired. They had heard the tomb was empty. But still they did not comprehend the promise.

Then Jesus came.

Walking beside Him, they did not recognize Jesus in His risen and glorified body. In time, Jesus asked them why they were so sad. They answered, "Are You the only stranger in Jerusalem, and have You not known the things which happened there? . . . We were hoping that it was He who was going to redeem Israel" (Luke 24:18, 21).

Step by step, Jesus walked and talked with them, all the way to the village of Emmaus, seven miles from Jerusalem. When the men insisted He join them to eat, Jesus took the bread and blessed it. And then their eyes were opened; they realized that they had been in step with the Savior.

During the forty days after His resurrection, Jesus appeared to nearly five hundred people. Then the disciples followed His steps up to the Mount of Olives and watched His feet leave this earth as He ascended.

Are you following Jesus? Are you abiding in Him? Are you walking step by step with Him?

Which Step to Take?

Do we pause long enough to consider that misdirected footsteps can lead us right into temptation? They may not lead us into sin, but they could lead us down a diverted path from God. My father was faced with this reality at various times in his life.

Casual acquaintances tried to persuade him to become a Hollywood actor. Others insisted he run for president of the United States. I don't think my father ever had time to consider the possibilities. If he had, my mother would have put her foot down—believe me—and that was always a huge step. Not that my father would have ever given it serious thought, but the influence of my mother's steps in his life were powerful.

I have a friend who speaks often of his struggles with giving in to temptation. He keeps one foot in the world and the other foot in the faith, always falling back on God's grace. "I'm forgiven when I sin," he says, "but I wish I could overcome."

The wonderful answer is that he can. The absolute answer is that he must. Can he do it in his own strength? No. But God's Word promises that "the Lord knows how to deliver the godly out of temptations" for those who walk in His ways (2 Peter 2:9).

Temptations will come. But if our steps stay in His pathway, we will be so mindful of His power in our lives that we will make the right choice.

The Bible has a lot to say about our steps. "I have led you in right paths. When you walk, your steps will not be hindered, and when you run, you will not stumble. . . . Do not enter the path of the wicked, and do not walk in the way of evil. Avoid it, do not travel on it; turn away from it and pass on" (Proverbs 4:11–12, 14–15).

How can we determine whether a path is good or evil? Many find this difficult. The Bible makes it clear: anything that does not glorify the Father is evil. The Bible says, "Let us lay aside every weight, and the sin which so easily ensnares us, and let us run with endurance the race that is set before us" (Hebrews 12:1).

Over the years I observed my father avoid snares. I learned, by watching his steps, that I can't do everything. I get invitations all the time to be part of various causes—many that are good but wrong for me because they distract me from what I was called to do.

I grew up in the country. When I was hunting squirrel, I didn't want my dogs running rabbits. Roy Gustafson often reminded me when I was struggling about some opportunity before me, "Don't get off on rabbit trails, Franklin. Keep the main thing the main thing."

What is the main thing? What has God called us to do? For me, it is to preach the Gospel. These are the steps He has ordained for my life. And the heavenly Father gave me the great gift of an earthly father who exemplified this throughout his lifetime.

Joseph and His Two Coats

Early in my father's ministry, he and his team were concerned about the snares that entangled ministries and caused men to fail and get out of step with God. He and his close-knit team developed their own standards of accountability to live by. Other ministries, through the years, have adopted these standards. In the Christian life, it is vital that we anchor our standards to biblical principles laid out in God's Word.

We see in Scripture an upstanding young man whose footsteps led him into a place of power because he walked uprightly. My father preached many times about Joseph and his coat of many colors and how his brothers stole it from him. After Joseph was sold as a slave to Potiphar, an officer of Pharaoh and captain of the Egyptian guard, Joseph found favor in the kingdom and became the overseer of Potiphar's household where he acquired—and lost—another coat.

Joseph was given the finest of everything; he was dressed in fine robes and given full authority over his master's house. One day while his master was away, Joseph encountered Potiphar's wife, who tried to seduce him. The Bible says she "cast longing eyes on Joseph" (Genesis 39:7). But Joseph, not yet thirty years old, walked wisely. He understood that the steps of an adulteress are unstable and lay hold of hell (Proverbs 5:5–6). And he knew God's solution: "Remove your way far from her" (v. 8).

That is exactly what Joseph did. When Potiphar's wife clasped Joseph's coat in an effort to trap him, he split and left her alone, holding his cloak.

The Bible says that Joseph fled. His exit was so immediate that Mrs. Potiphar had no power over him. There she stood dejected, humiliated, and angry. She must have looked at that empty coat wondering why her charms had fallen short of their magic. Joseph did not linger to consider the pros or cons. He put his feet into motion. He took the right steps at the right time.

The Word of God has given us examples to guide us. The Christian life is designed with a greater purpose than just going through the motions. How precise are our steps?

Body of Evidence

A true-to-life documentary TV series called *Body of Evidence* was about a female criminal profiler who solved crimes on difficult case files. She compiled facts, based on profiles of suspected perpetrators, by examining their patterns of life and, literally, their footsteps. One step at a time she created prototypes of criminals by using DNA, what scientists call "the blueprints for life."[3]

How many followers of Jesus Christ can be profiled so accurately? How does our spiritual DNA match up to the precious blood that

Jesus shed on the cross for our sins? Our walk should be so clear to others that they see a body of evidence with an unmistakable link to the Savior of the world.

Some people live their lives as jet-setters—always looking for a buzz because their lives lack depth. But walking is a lifestyle that can bring stability and a deep sense of belonging. Do we walk the talk? Do people watch our steps and know what direction we are traveling? They should. It is our outward testimony that reveals our inward belief.

When a true follower of Jesus Christ stumbles into sin, the Holy Spirit living within will immediately convict him. As my father always pointed out, "Do not ignore that still, small voice inside. That is the Holy Spirit's convicting power."

God is concerned about the steps we take. His Word is not just printed in a Book. It is the instruction manual about how to walk:

- Walk humbly (Micah 6:8).
- Walk decently (Romans 13:13).
- Walk orderly (Acts 21:24).
- Walk worthy (Ephesians 4:1).
- Walk by faith (2 Corinthians 5:7).
- Walk in truth (3 John v. 3).
- Walk in integrity (Psalm 26:11).
- Walk in the Spirit (Galatians 5:16).
- Walk in the light (Ephesians 5:8).
- Walk in wisdom (Colossians 4:5).
- Walk in love (2 John v. 6).
- Walk in newness of life (Romans 6:4).
- Walk in Him (Colossians 2:6).

"My little children, these things I write to you, so that you may not sin. And if anyone sins, we have an Advocate with the Father, Jesus Christ the righteous. . . . He who says he abides in Him ought himself also to walk just as He walked" (1 John 2:1, 6).

A Father's Footsteps

We have all probably used catchphrases to communicate a thought, like "take one step at a time" or "he's one step ahead." Another familiar expression is "following in another's footsteps."

There are people who follow in the footsteps of successful businessmen, acclaimed entertainers, decorated soldiers, or victorious athletes. Others choose to follow the footsteps of a criminal or a swindler. Then there are those who retrace steps that leave indelible marks that must be explored.

I read one such story on the fiftieth anniversary of the infamous World War II battle at Iwo Jima. A man by the name of David told how his father had served in the US Marine Corps and survived the bloodbath. The marine-father had returned home to a son he had never seen. As David grew he seldom heard his father speak of his military feats. David was busy growing up and, well, he never thought to ask.

When he reached adulthood and realized that his father had been a significant part of American history and a victorious war hero, he wished he had taken an interest in his father's life, which was marked by darkness in the wake of the conflict.

As his father's health failed, David fired off riveting questions—like an automatic weapon—but the answers were buried deep within a man no longer able to communicate. It was too late to listen to the blow-by-blow accounts of his service to the country he loved, served, and had been willing to give his life for.

After his father's death, David announced to his family and friends that he was "going to a place he'd never been, to commemorate a battle that occurred before his birth."[4]

But as he recalled the few things he had learned from his father, he made this decision. "If Iwo Jima was important enough to die for, it was important enough to remember."[5] And with that, David traveled to Iwo Jima to walk in his father's footsteps.

What he said was well said. Iwo Jima made an impact on his life before he was born because it ensured his future freedom as an American. It is the same for followers of Jesus Christ. If Jesus cared enough to die for us before we were born—and He did—it should be important enough to remember, and it should make a life-changing impact on how we walk through life and into eternity.

I have been able to retrace some steps taken by my great-grandfathers who fought in the Civil War. I have also retraced some of my parents' steps. I have walked where they walked as children, from North Korea to North Carolina. Today, I walk often to their gravesides to reflect on the steps they took through life.

Walk the Suffering Path

Those privileged to live in the West do not realize that the mode of transportation in many countries is still by foot—to go anywhere.

I have been to Bangkok, Thailand, many times. If you get stuck in a traffic jam, you may not move more than one block in an hour's time. If an accident should occur, it may take hours to untangle the tie-up. When that happens, walking isn't so bad.

A few years ago, heavy bicycle traffic crowded Beijing, China, thousands pedaling their way through the streets. It is the same in Vietnam. Hanoi has experienced massive economic growth, and hundreds of thousands have upgraded to motorbikes. But in Pyongyang, North Korea, I saw something for the very first time in a big city. The roads were not jammed with cars or bicycles. There were thousands of people walking. There are few personal automobiles. Men, women, and children still walk.

I will never forget my father walking among the ruins in the San Martin Jilotepeque region of Guatemala in the wake of the 1976 earthquake. He said it was important to identify with people in their time of trial. To fully comprehend the sorrow of others, one must walk the suffering path with those affected by storms of life. My father taught this by example. I vividly remember the impact it made on him as he came alongside those in Guatemala. He sought ways to reach out in compassion to people devastated by such tragedy.

In my work with Samaritan's Purse and the BGEA I have been exposed to people's hardships on nearly every continent. I learned great lessons of God's compassion by observing my father's footsteps.

This is the reason Jesus came to earth: to identify with mankind in their hour of need. He came to show us a better way—a better path. He left an example of how to walk in His steps.

I've lost count as to how many times I have crossed the Jordan River or flown to Amman to visit the small tuberculosis hospital in northern Jordan at a place called Mafraq—meaning "crossroads." North will take you to Damascus; east will lead you to Baghdad; south will take you toward Amman; and west will lead you into Haifa, Israel.

I have already talked about my trip to Jordan in 1971, made possible by my father. Still to this day when I ride into the desert toward the clinic, I see many walking toward the Annoor Sanatorium. Travelers, sick unto death, walk from Syria, from Iraq, and from the vast Jordanian desert, where Abraham, Isaac, and Jacob would have crossed from the land of Ur, in present-day Iraq, into present-day Israel. They crossed the same desert step by step. We have been able to undergird the ministry there through the faithful giving of God's people.

On occasion, I have walked with African tribesmen escaping the heat of battle or simply looking for a better way of life—their feet bare, calloused, and scorched by the sun.

Think back to the beginning of time and what it must have been like to be one of the only two people on the entire earth. No voices, no machines, no radios, no televisions, no construction, no industry, no traffic jams, no police sirens, no fire alarms, no air or noise pollution, no shoes—just the rustle of God's footsteps. I would imagine the keen ears of two people would pick up the slightest shuffle among the lush grass blades that carpeted Eden.

"And they [Adam and Eve] heard the sound of the LORD God walking in the garden in the cool of the day" (Genesis 3:8).

You have to wonder if Creation's first couple had enjoyed evening walks with their Maker. Perhaps they followed behind in His footsteps as He instructed them about all that His hands had formed: the sunny days, the moonlit nights, and the stars peering from the drapes of the heavens like angels' eyes.

Celebrity Status or Called Servant?

There is a kind of walking that can mislead a sincere heart. It has to do with walking after something else instead of walking in the one distinctive path. Steps that chase after fame and acclaim do not mark the steps of a true servant of God. Nor are they marks of one walking in the footsteps of Jesus.

Celebrities are modern-day idols, put on display like idols of old in our cities filled with sports complexes, concert halls, and movie theaters. Homes harbor things that can become idols: televisions, computers, and the latest and greatest of whatever is new. Time is eaten up with idols: working to amass fortunes; living for entertainment and leisure. Hearts are overrun with idols: the love of things, the love of busyness, the love of pleasure.

Years ago my father wrote about Alan Redpath, who had once served as pastor of the Moody Church in Chicago. On the wall of his study he posted this plaque: "Beware of the barrenness of a busy life."[6]

How do we spend our time, and what example do we leave for the young generation? My father used to say, "Young people are yearning for a leader they can trust and worship." They look in all the wrong places and often immerse themselves in the arts.

Music bands are the rage these days and have been for decades. When I was a teenager, it was the Beatles and Rolling Stones. In the first decade of the twenty-first century, the band U2, which has been around for forty years, leads the pack. These cultural icons have power to effect change, especially in young people.

I would like to introduce to you a band chosen personally by Jesus. Even those who were against them had to admit, "These [men] have turned the world upside down" (Acts 17:6). But the leaders of cities did not roll out the red carpet for them—instead, they drove them out of town.

This band of men known as the disciples knew what it was to go against the trendy tide. They were not afraid to be different. They had the distinct privilege of walking in the steps of the Master of miracles. But they also walked in the steps of the Man of Sorrows. The footprints He left behind led them to carry out the command of taking His Word to the ends of the earth.

When their work was done, they walked in the footsteps of the crucified Lord to martyrdom. They were beheaded, stoned, dragged to pieces, thrust through with a spear, hanged, had their brains dashed with a fuller's club, and crucified.[7]

There was no glamour, no comfort, no ease. Bright lights? There were none. Welcomed as celebrities? Hardly. There were agony, hardship, and suffering—and a promise from Jesus: "I go to prepare a place for you" (John 14:2). Our treasure is stored up in heaven, not down here on earth (Matthew 6:19–20).

When preaching about the disciples, my father said, "The men who followed Christ were unique in their generation. They turned the world upside down because their hearts were turned right side up . . . and the world has never been the same."

There are many who desire to walk in Billy Graham's footsteps. The question has to be asked: Why? Are they allured by the thought of traveling around the world, going from place to place, preaching in arenas, in stadiums, on television and webcasts? Do they desire to follow in his steps to preach before massive crowds? Do they envision being pictured on magazine covers or being quoted on the evening news? My father would say this is not what preaching the Gospel is about.

Do they really want to preach around the world, no matter what? Are they willing to do it God's way? Are they so passionate, so committed, so called by God that they will depend on Him in everything? What if financial support is hard to raise? What if only small crowds gather? What if only a few—or none—respond to the invitation?

Yes, my father did become a world figure. Yes, Billy Graham did attain status that opened doors to royal palaces and seats of power. But when he began preaching God's Word, he had no idea what was in store.

My father would be the first to say, "Let God speak to your heart and then be obedient to His call." Many have been inspired to consider God's call to the ministry because of my father's steps.

Countless numbers are pastors, missionaries, and evangelists because God used my father's life to challenge them. But Billy Graham preached, "Follow the steps of Christ. Accept the burdens that come, for God will carry them on His shoulders. Accept the blessings that come, and humbly give them back to God."

"If anyone ministers, let him do it as with the ability which God supplies, that in all things God may be glorified through Jesus Christ" (1 Peter 4:11).

Consider a response from some of God's choice servants when confronted with men's adoration.

Paul and Barnabas were preaching in Lystra, a city in the province of Galatia. Paul had healed a young man who had never walked. When the people saw what he had done, they shouted that the gods had come to them in the likeness of men.

The people began to clamor for Paul and Barnabas and treat them as gods. When they saw this outpouring of idolatry, Paul and Barnabas "tore their clothes and ran in among the multitude, crying out and saying, 'Men, why are you doing these things? We also are men with the same nature as you, and preach to you that you should turn from these useless things to the living God, who made the heaven, the earth, the sea, and all things that are in them, who in bygone generations allowed all nations to walk in their own ways'" (Acts 14:14–16).

Paul cried out and said that men are not to be worshipped. Men are not to be acclaimed. Men are to walk in the steps of Jesus. He alone is to be worshipped. All followers of Jesus Christ have but one step to take—walk with Him.

Observing My Father

Sons tend to follow in their fathers' footsteps to some degree. Often doctors beget doctors, lawyers beget lawyers, farmers beget farmers, and preachers beget preachers, so to speak.

When it comes to preaching the Gospel, the call to preach cannot be handed down from one generation to the next. Many times preachers follow generation after generation, but one must be sure of his call so that he may receive God's power to faithfully proclaim the Word. While there is nothing wrong with desiring to serve as a minister of the Gospel, often men do it for the wrong reasons.

The power to preach comes from God's call. There is a requirement for those who preach God's Gospel. The Bible says that we must walk as Christ walked. His steps are plainly laid out in His Word. It is a great honor to preach in His name, but riding on the back of honor is something called responsibility—heavy responsibility—that many ignore. For those hearts that are pure and genuine, the responsibility is seen not as a duty but as a humble privilege.

A close friend of mine had a pastor years ago who counseled young men desiring to preach the Gospel. He encouraged them from God's Word but painted a dismal picture of what they might encounter. Many walked away from their decision to serve the Lord. Why? Because their minds were calling them, not their hearts. But a few left the session with absolute resolve of their calling from the Lord Jesus Christ—to serve Him with all of their hearts, no matter what.

My oldest son, William Franklin Graham IV (Will), felt God's call in his life as a young man. I did not want him to be pressured to follow in my footsteps or his grandfather's. But Will studied and sought God's direction, and after several years of Bible school, seminary, and pastoring his own church, he joined me in ministry and has begun preaching evangelistic crusades himself.

Steps Taken

The most important steps a person can take are to the foot of the cross of Jesus Christ. It is there that we lay aside our earthly cloaks of sin and step into robes of righteousness. Perfection in our bodies will not come in this life, but we can walk in newness of life by following in the steps of Jesus.

Chasing the culture means we are following trendsetters instead of leading the culture to the foot of the cross. The fact is the world will not recognize us as followers of Christ if we are steeped in the things of this world. But Jesus promised that if we follow His steps on earth, we will follow His steps in the life to come.

The reality is that one great day Jesus Christ will come back to this sin-sick world and eradicate sin. He will break through the gates of glory, and hoofbeats will pound the wind.

My father wrote a wonderful book many years ago titled *Approaching Hoofbeats*. He would agree that these coming footsteps couldn't be told more vividly—or more thrillingly—than right from the pen of John the Revelator:

Now I saw heaven opened, and behold, a white horse.
And He who sat on him was called Faithful and True,
and in righteousness He judges and makes war.
His eyes were like a flame of fire,
and on His head were many crowns.
He had a name written that no one knew *except Himself.*
He was clothed with a robe dipped in blood, and His name is called
  THE WORD OF GOD.
And the armies in heaven, clothed in fine linen, white and clean,
  followed Him on white horses.
Now out of His mouth goes a sharp sword,
that with it He should strike the nations.
And He Himself will rule them with a rod of iron.
He Himself treads the winepress of the fierceness and wrath of
  Almighty God.
And He has on His robe and on His thigh a name written:

KING OF KINGS
AND
LORD OF LORDS.
(Revelation 19:11–16; emphasis and formatting added)

Jesus is the One I want to follow on that day. I long to see my Savior mounted on that majestic white stallion, thundering to earth in all of His glory.

A Walk with My Father

I am so glad that in 1974, on my twenty-second birthday, I took a walk with my father along Lake Geneva in Lausanne, Switzerland. It became for me a pivotal walk—one that led me to do an about-face.

There was a spiritual battle raging within me that I did not completely understand until my father gently confronted me. As I walked beside him, he said, "Franklin, your mother and I sense there is a struggle going on in your life." The truth of his words startled me. I thought I had been covering up my sin well. He said, "You're going to have to make a choice either to accept Christ or reject Him. You can't continue to play the middle ground. Either you're going to choose to follow and obey the Lord or reject Him."

I wondered how he could know what was in my heart. But he was my father, who had prayed for me and taught me about living for Christ. However, I could not do it without acknowledging my own sin and asking forgiveness.

With a pat on the shoulder, my father said nothing more as our walk drew to an end. But several days later, while in Jerusalem, it was the walk with my father that caused me to fall on my knees before the Father in heaven and accept His Son, Jesus Christ, as my Lord and Savior.

My father had preached to moms and dads, daughters and sons. He had invited millions to repent of their sins and accept Jesus Christ as their Savior. I am so glad my father did the work of an evangelist with his own son that afternoon in Switzerland, giving me the opportunity once and for all to turn from a life of sin to Jesus Christ and walk in His steps.

II

From Stepping-Stones to Milestones

I have proclaimed the good news of righteousness
In the great assembly.
I have declared Your faithfulness and Your salvation.

—Psalm 40:9, 10

If you remember me at all, remember me as a preacher
of the Gospel of the Lord Jesus Christ.

BILLY GRAHAM

Now that my father is in heaven, I can see clearly the path God led him on, each step of the way—from beginning to end. Reading the opening of a sermon titled "A Memorable Milestone" that Charles H. Spurgeon preached in 1904 to his congregation in London helped me understand why my father often quoted from this prince of preachers.

I have preached righteousness in the great congregation: lo, I have not refrained my lips, O Lord. (Psalm 40:9)

Here is . . . a continual testimony. . . . But all of us who are the Lord's servants have, I hope, borne our testimony according to our opportunities and abilities.

It has been imperfect, but it has been sincere. In looking back upon our testimony for God . . . we can truthfully say that it has been sincerely borne up to the measure of the capacity given to us. It has been borne . . . because it could not be silenced. I have preached the Gospel to you . . . because I have believed it—and if what I have preached to you is not true, I am a lost man! For me there is no joy in life and no hope in death except in that Gospel. . . . It is not to me a theory. . . . It has become matter of absolute fact to me! It is interwoven with my consciousness. It is part of my being. Every day makes it dearer to me—my joys bind me to it, my griefs drive me to it! All that is behind me, all that is before me, all that is above me, all that is beneath me— everything compels me to say that my testimony has been borne with my heart, mind, soul and strength—and I am grateful to God.[1]

Ninety and More to Come

This is also my father's testimony, and as he approached his ninetieth birthday, he had another opportunity to deliver the message of God's love to those around him.

A year after we buried my mother, my father traveled to West Virginia for a ministry meeting with his longtime associates and many new and younger people who had come to help me in the work of the Billy Graham Evangelistic Association. Family members and faithful donors joined us for a special evening to celebrate my father's ninetieth birthday—one he never thought he would reach.

It was November 2008. He addressed those in attendance and thanked his team who had faithfully served the Lord with him. His stirring comments encouraged everyone to press on and, above all else, preach the Gospel.

Then with a spark of humor and a twinkle in his eye, he invited guests to his ninety-fifth birthday, among them Fox News anchor (at the time) Greta Van Susteren and her husband, John Coale. In his weakened condition I did not see how he could live much longer. But during the span of years that followed, Greta and John often remarked, "We're looking forward to your Dad's ninety-fifth birthday!" They believed him. And when the time came, they were there.

Hand Still on the Plow

The year leading up to this moment was challenging for my father. When I assumed the leadership of the BGEA in 2000, there were two primary things that motivated me. First, to keep the ministry on the track of proclaiming the Gospel of Jesus Christ to the world—the vision my father had built the ministry on; and second, to help him finish well.

There were times that he grew stronger; they seemed to always be connected to opportunities for ministry, even to the point that he talked about wanting to stand behind the podium in a stadium one more time to deliver a final message to the nation about repentance.

We set his pulpit up at The Cove, along with a large screen so he could see his notes clearly. There were lights, camera—but no action. My father just did not have the stamina to stand. He looked at me with those steely blue eyes and said, "I thought I could do it, but I just can't."

The next time we were together, I wanted to encourage him and asked if he would consider putting his message in a book—something that would last long after he was in heaven.

"I thought I had written my last book, but I would like to try," he said. Stirred by the world's hopelessness, he was compelled to press on.

"Franklin, I am concerned that the message of salvation has been watered down. I would like the chance to put my message into a book for people to understand that salvation in Jesus Christ brings about a life transformation. There are times I feel that in the last years of my ministry, I did not emphasize this truth enough. This message is heavy on my heart. I want to preach a message to the church, a message to those who would never walk in a church, a message to the nation, a message from God's Word to the world. What do you think?" I heard a strain of enthusiasm in his voice.

"Of course you can do that, Daddy. It sounds like you have it worked out in your mind. We'll help you."

"I need a writer who will work with me," he said, and inquired about someone we had both worked with for many years.

"I'll call and work out a time to discuss it," I encouraged him. That made him happy, but still I was bent on recording his message so that others could hear his voice proclaim, once more, God's Gospel.

The Reason for My Hope: Salvation

Within days he began putting his message into manuscript form with the instruction, "I want to title this book *Salvation*. I have a deep concern for those who say they believe in Christ but do not live for Him. I feel the Lord would have me deliver a message to dispel the idea that we can truly be saved without living according to His Word. People need hope—Christ is the only hope for the world!"

He was invigorated and worked through the winter months and into the summer and fall, always looking to the Scripture for fresh thoughts about the unchanging message that Jesus Christ came to earth to live among us, die for us, and be raised to life; and to prepare a home in heaven for those who put their trust in Him.

The preacher in him was emerging once again as he mulled over the sermon that had burdened his heart. He may have been sitting in an easy chair, but his voice and the resolve in his eyes were that of a prophet with a burning message. His longing to share God's Word once more with the world was as fresh and forward-bound as it was when he first grasped the Gospel plow as a young Bible student. In his nineties, Billy

Graham was still the soldier wielding the sword of truth that changes lives. "This," he said, "is the reason for my hope—salvation."[2] And so the book was titled.

He began and ended each session in prayer. It was the spark plug that ignited him.

Lord, we pray that the message of this book will speak to those who do not know you, and to those in the church who think they are saved but are deceived, claiming to belong to Christ without knowing the change that is brought about when the Holy Spirit of the living God dwells within.

As he outlined the main points of what the book would contain, Scripture guided and enriched each topic about God's rescue mission and His great redemption plan, what the world thinks of sin and of heaven and hell, and the price Christ paid to forgive sinners and give us victory over "sin which so easily ensnares" (Hebrews 12:1).

"I want an entire chapter on the cross, and one on the resurrection of Christ, because without the resurrection, there is no salvation," he said. "Then I would like to end with a chapter on the return of Christ! I regret I didn't preach more on the resurrection and the last days when Jesus will return." His comments revealed that God was not finished with him. There was another sermon—maybe more—yet to preach.

"I want to anchor the message to 1 Peter 1:3–5," he continued; then he quoted, "In his great mercy he has given us new birth into a living hope through the resurrection of Jesus Christ from the dead . . . who through faith are shielded by God's power until the coming of the salvation that is ready to be revealed" (NIV).

The Living Room Pulpit

He seemed so encouraged by working on the book that I asked if he would like to try again to tape the core message.

"I would like to, but I just can't do that, Franklin." His voice was emphatic.

"Try, Daddy," I urged him. His longing caused me to persevere.

"I do have a burden to preach at least one more time, but I just don't have the strength," he said with a tone of regret. His eyes told me that he had the will, but his lips carried the disappointing words. "No, I just can't. Franklin," he said, "you don't understand. When you get to be my age, you'll realize why I cannot do this." A few years ago I couldn't quite understand, but now as I begin to feel the weight of the years myself, I comprehend his frustration with a little more compassion.

Nevertheless, I encouraged him to hold tight to the message that was driving him onward. "Let's pray that the Lord will show us how you can do this." I think my father was pleased that prayer was the cornerstone of seeking God's guidance on the matter. After all, he taught me by his example to pray about everything and commit it to God's sovereign will.

Telling me one day about the progress on his book, his voice seemed stronger, and he started talking again about preaching one more time.

A friend has told me that I redefine the word *persistence*, so I decided to live up to the reputation. "Daddy, I agree that you do not have strength to stand before a crowd and preach in a stadium, but you can preach right here from home. Will you try it?" Quite honestly, I was prepared to hear him say no with evangelistic vigor.

Instead, he thoughtfully asked, "How could that work?"

"Here's what we can do." I leaned up to the table's edge. "You choose the points you want to make, and we'll send a videographer up here to the house. Why not preach the living message of the living Savior right from the living room? You can tape the message in segments right here at home as you have the strength. We can build a program around the message that can be aired to the nation as *"My Hope America" with Billy Graham*, like we've done around the world through the BGEA World Evangelism Television Project." He didn't say no and agreed to proceed.

Daddy waving goodbye to our family at Black Mountain Train Station, not far from our home (1950s)

Welcoming my dad home (1955)

Mama welcoming Daddy home (1950s)

I always sat on Mama's lap when she read
Bible stories before bedtime (1954)
(Left to right: Anne, Gigi, Ruth [Bunny])

Daddy and me, sitting on the woodpile
outside our log home (1958)

Daddy demonstrating the proper golf swing (1950s)
(Left to right: me, Mama, Bunny, Daddy, Gigi, Anne)

My father's New York Crusade, Yankee Stadium (1957)

Daddy playing baseball with his staff at a picnic in Minneapolis (1950)

Daddy with his Minneapolis staff, reading letters from listeners (early 1950s)

My father with the US troops in Korea the year I was born (1952)

Richard Nixon visiting with Mama and
Daddy at home in Montreat (1960)

My father's parents at their home in
Charlotte, North Carolina (1954)

The team: my father joins his colleagues George Beverly Shea and Cliff Barrows for a lighthearted moment at his crusade in Nashville, Tennessee, in an often-requested performance of "This Little Light of Mine" (2000)

My father's most trusted adviser, Dr. L. Nelson Bell (Mama's father) (1972)

President Ronald Reagan presents my father with the Medal of Freedom award at the White House (1983)

Daddy invites me to sit with him on the platform at his crusade (1971)

Roy Gustafson reads Scripture to my boys while in Israel. My son Roy was named after this great Bible teacher (1980s)

Mama enjoys watching Daddy with some of the grandchildren as he teaches them to fish with a cane pole (1980s)

Daddy and me at the Great Wall of China (1988)

Sharing a crusade with my father in Saskatoon, Canada (1995)

Sami Dagher, on my right, interprets for me during a meeting with Sudanese president Omar al-Bashir (2004)

I sit next to my father as he presents the Gospel to Communist leaders during a trip to Eastern Europe; Dr. Alexander Haraszti stands behind us (1985)

Touring Beijing Temple of Heaven with Mama and Daddy in the People's Republic of China (1988)

Christians throughout North America invite friends into their homes and yards to hear my father's message of hope and salvation found only in Christ as part of *"My Hope America"* *with Billy Graham* (2013)

My Hope Television Project in Asia (2007)

My father's message is translated by satellite to 185 countries during Global Mission, San Juan, Puerto Rico (1995)

On the occasion of my parents' fiftieth wedding anniversary (1993)
(Left to right behind them: Gigi, Anne, me, Ned, Bunny)

My father questioning my son Edward about conditions at the military academy at West Point when he was a cadet (1999)

After five children, my mother wears her wedding gown, without alterations, on her golden anniversary (1993)

My family contributing to the cleanup effort after Hurricane Katrina in New Orleans (2006) (Left to right: Son Edward and his wife, Kristy; son Roy; my wife, Jane Austin; daughter, Cissie, with her fiancé, Corey Lynch)

Daddy in deep discussion with my two-year-old daughter, Cissie (1988)

Four generations: William Franklin Graham V (Quinn), William Franklin Graham IV (Will), William Franklin Graham III (Franklin), and William Franklin Graham Jr. (Billy) (2007)

My father extends an invitation to receive Christ, Indianapolis, Indiana (1980)

Prayer service after 9/11 at the National
Cathedral, Washington, DC (2001)

Preaching at my crusade in Tegucigalpa,
Honduras, with my interpreter, Lenin De
Janon (1996)

BG Personal Collection

The British ambassador and his wife share a moment with my parents, following a ceremony at the British Embassy in Washington, DC (December 2001)

BG Personal Collection

The White House chef presents a birthday cake to my father (first lady Laura Bush on his left) (November 2001)

BG Personal Collection

President and Mrs. George W. Bush graciously honor my parents by hosting a private dinner for our family at the White House on the occasion of my father's eighty-third birthday (November 2001)

My father's last crusade, Flushing Meadows, New York (2005)

At age ninety-four, WWII POW Louis Zamperini does a book signing at the Billy Graham Library (2011) and then travels to Montreat for a visit with my father. Louis was saved at my father's 1949 tent meeting in Los Angeles.

Taking one of many walks with Daddy at home in Montreat (2007)

My father warmly welcomes former president George W. Bush and former first lady Laura Bush to the Billy Graham Library for lunch and a book signing (2010)

Praying at the Library Dedication (2007) (Left to right: Franklin Graham, Billy Graham, and former presidents George H. W. Bush, Jimmy Carter, and Bill Clinton)

The last picture of my father with his children, grandchildren, and great-grandchildren at the Billy Graham Library Dedication two weeks before my mother's death (2007)

My father's final goodbye as he places a rose on Mama's casket (2007)

Metropolitan Hilarion of the Russian Orthodox Church brought birthday greetings to my father at his home in Montreat (2014)

My family with former president and Mrs. George H. W. Bush and former president Jimmy Carter at the Library Dedication (2007)

BGEA/Russ Busby

My father attends my crusade in Wilmington, North Carolina (1995)
(Left to right: My first cousin Mel Graham, my son William Franklin Graham IV,
Daddy, and me)

BGEA/Russ Busby

On the occasion of my father's ninetieth birthday, a year after my mother's death, he
greets his guests and invites them back for his ninety-fifth birthday (2008)

My son Edward escorts my father at the *My Hope America* celebration and evangelistic outreach in honor of his ninety-fifth birthday on November 7, 2013

In an impromptu exchange between my father and his longtime friend and colleague, Cliff Barrows says, "Happy birthday, dear Bill . . . I praise God for the journey we've had together." Donald and Melania Trump, future president and first lady, look on. (2013)

Greta Van Susteren brings birthday greetings on the occasion of my father's ninety-fifth birthday and carries a microphone to him to address the guests while Donald Trump and Rupert Murdoch look on (2013)

Recording artists gather to sing "Happy Birthday, Billy Graham" (2013)
(Left to right: Lecrae Moore, Lacey Sturm, Ricky Skaggs, Michael W. Smith, and Kathie Lee Gifford)

My father enjoys seeing old friends and meeting some new friends who honor him on his ninety-fifth birthday. Among them, standing left to right, are J. W. "Bill" Marriott Jr.; my wife, Jane Austin; Melania and Donald Trump; John Coale; Greta Van Susteren; me; North Carolina governor Pat McCrory; and Sarah and Todd Palin; and seated, left to right, are my son Edward, my father, and Rupert Murdoch (2013)

Delivering a prayer at the inauguration of the forty-fifth president of the United States, Donald J. Trump (January 20, 2017)

A warm blanket around him as he listened to the news through his headset, Daddy joined his furry friend, Cat, in an afternoon nap. This is the last picture taken of my father, February 18, 2018

My father's casket—appropriately placed behind the pulpit—at The Cove, where his longtime staff, friends, caregivers, and family gathered to pay their respects, February 23, 2018

Neighbors and well-wishers waving goodbye as the ceremonial motorcade made the journey from Asheville and Black Mountain to Charlotte

Thousands paid their respects, including former president George W. Bush and former first lady Laura Bush, as my father's body rested in his boyhood home

The Graham family was moved by the outpouring of love expressed by President and Mrs. Trump, Vice President and Mrs. Pence, Speaker of the House Ryan, Senate Majority Leader McConnell, and every branch of the US government that paid tribute to my father

A Gospel preacher is saluted as he lies in honor under the dome of the US Capitol Rotunda

My wife, Jane Austin, and I stand with our four children in the Rotunda
(Left to right: Roy, Will, Cissie, and Edward)

President Trump and Vice President Pence read the engraved names of the prisoners who built my father's casket

Daddy asked that the Gospel of Jesus Christ be preached at his funeral; it has been my great privilege to "honor thy father and mother"

Edward escorts President Trump, first lady Melania, Vice President Pence, and second lady Karen to the canvas cathedral for the funeral service, March 2, 2018

A simple fieldstone covers my father's grave in the prayer garden at the Billy Graham Library. Even in death he wanted to preach the Gospel of the Lord Jesus Christ (John 14:6)

My dad loved his children and grandchildren. What an honor for all his grandsons to serve as pallbearers

Together again

I called Dr. Don Wilton, senior pastor of First Baptist Church in Spartanburg, South Carolina. A few years earlier my father had begun listening to his Sunday morning broadcast and invited him for lunch. Because he could no longer attend church, Don became his pastor. For the remainder of my father's life, this faithful preacher of the Gospel would drive a three-hour round trip every week to my father's log house.

When taping began, Don was there to prompt him with questions that made it easier to respond in a setting that was comfortable—right from his home that overlooked the mountains of the Blue Ridge.

The Cross That Breaks the Chains

The powerful message that emerged became the centerpiece of a thirty-minute program titled *The Cross*, giving BGEA the tool to embark on the greatest evangelistic outreach in (at the time) its sixty-three years of ministry. It seemed fitting for my father to preach in a way that was unimaginable—from his living room to living rooms all across the world in *My Hope* fashion!

He looked forward to each taping session. His message came together, and supported by music and testimonies that followed the model of his crusades, *"My Hope America" with Billy Graham* was ready for broadcast.

Meanwhile, BGEA registered and trained more than twenty thousand church congregations to participate. Church members learned how to best utilize the program to influence lives with the Gospel. Plans were put in place to air the message on television, in churches, and in homes across North America, as we had done around the world. Massive training took place, helping people use Scripture to be witnesses for Christ, giving guidance on how to extend an invitation and lead people to the cross of Jesus in repentance and faith.

Testimonies from Christian artists Lecrae Moore and Lacey Sturm were used to demonstrate how God takes broken and anguished hearts and transforms them by His amazing grace. But there was no question that the power point in the program was the proclamation of the Word of God from my father's lips:

> The Bible says that we are all sinners, that we have broken God's law and His commandments. We have turned our backs on Him. That is a very dangerous thing for our country, for us as individuals, and for our families. People don't want to believe they are sinners. Sin is a disease of the human heart. It affects the mind, and the will, and the emotion; every part of our being.
>
> This is why the cross offends; it directly confronts the evil that dominates so much of the world. We deserve hell, we deserve judgment and all that it means. How can we break this bondage? How can we be set free?
>
> God helps us break these chains. I want to tell people about the meaning of the cross—not a cross that hangs around our necks. The cross is where Jesus Christ took upon Himself the sins of the world. God can make us totally new. God's Word demands—it doesn't suggest—it demands a new life in Christ—and He will help us overcome sin. The Bible says, "Therefore, if anyone is in Christ, he is a new creation; old things have passed away; behold, all things have become new" (2 Corinthians 5:17).

The process began with television networks to negotiate times to air the program on November 7. We asked Christians across the country to invite people into their homes and churches to show the program. We thought it would be wonderful for my father to do what we were asking others to do—invite people for a meal and use it as an evangelistic outreach—on his ninety-fifth birthday!

Six weeks before, I had asked the family, board members, staff, and friends to each host a table, inviting their unsaved neighbors and business associates. My father liked the idea of his team doing this together, and it seemed to be a greater reason to gather—not for his birthday but for a Gospel presentation. But he made it clear that he did not want to commit to speaking at the dinner. I agreed that we would only use his message that had been digitally recorded. His fear was that when the day arrived, he wouldn't feel up to attending. Nevertheless, he was excited about people coming to see the program and began praying for each one who would attend.

His fear was almost realized when, one week before the event, he was taken to the hospital for a bronchial infection. It was doubtful that he would recuperate in time to be part of his own birthday celebration.

Cable News Airs Good News

I shouldn't have been so surprised when my father's health steadily improved; people around the world had been praying for him, and he returned home. His book *The Reason for My Hope: Salvation* had just been released by Thomas Nelson Publishers, and many who read the book declared that it was his "masterwork."

Days later, amid family members, friends, and hundreds of invited guests, Billy Graham entered the Omni Grove Park Inn in Asheville, North Carolina, just a few miles from his home, to a rousing ovation as my son Edward, a US Army major, escorted him to his table. He joined with more than eight hundred guests to watch the debut of the program *The Cross.*

Among many well-wishers were dignitaries and longtime friends: Rupert Murdoch and J. W. "Bill" Marriott. Donald Trump (entrepreneur at the time) and his wife, Melania, were also there. Who knew that we had the future president and first lady in our midst?

Greta Van Susteren and John Coale were there, just as they had promised. Former Alaska governor Sarah Palin and her husband, Todd, and North Carolina governor Pat McCrory also joined the many supporters, along with an array of leading pastors from across the country who had stood with us in this unprecedented evangelism effort.

We planned to air the broadcast only in North America but did not realize that the week we chose happened to be "sweeps week" for the networks—all vying for viewer ratings. Buying network time was prohibitive.

We learned that cable news networks have their own ratings battle at a different time. So when my father wrote to Rupert Murdoch and told him what we hoped to do, he graciously responded that he would air the broadcast on his cable station and asked that I get in touch with Roger Ailes, who ran the Fox News Channel for him.

When we talked by phone, Mr. Ailes said that Fox would give us a good time. He kept his word and confirmed that the program would air on November 7 at 10:00 p.m., during the new time slot for *Hannity*, hosted by Sean Hannity. Because of this, the program aired everywhere in the world that carried the cable network. It was more than we could have asked for, and God blessed my father's desire to preach one more time.[3]

"There have been times when I have wept as I've gone from city to city, and I've seen how far people have wandered from God," he said. "There is only one message in any generation and in all times, and that is Jesus. Jesus came to save us, and there is no other message in the world that offers eternal hope." Then he prayed, "We are in need of a spiritual awakening, Lord. With all my heart I want to leave others with Your truth."

The Lord answered that prayer. No gift could have thrilled my evangelist father more than to proclaim to the world the Gospel, one more time.

Billy Graham Turning Ninety-Five Is News

Governor Palin brought personal emphasis to this when she addressed him and the guests assembled that evening. "My mother heard about how to have a personal relationship with Christ [through a Billy Graham crusade in the 1970s]. She made a decision to follow Christ, and it rocked her world and changed her life. She then led her family to Christ, including me. We need Billy Graham's message now more than ever . . . and thanks to today's technology, this message will be heard across the nation."

Her comments warmed my father's heart as he sat praying that many in that very room would come to Christ. And they did. We found out later that more than 180 guests indicated their decision to make this life-changing commitment to the Lord.

Governor Palin brought smiles to faces in the audience when she looked at my father and wished him ninety-five more years so that he could continue preaching the Gospel.

But as the clock ticked toward the ten o'clock hour, it seemed doubtful he could last ninety-five more seconds. My father was deeply moved to be surrounded by family and friends. He was also honored to have his longtime friend Rupert Murdoch at the gathering and expressed appreciation to him for airing the program.

That very morning I had been in New York and visited with Roger Ailes to express gratitude for supporting us in this strategic way. He told me that some people had questioned why Fox, a news network, would carry a program like this. I liked his answer when he said, "Billy Graham turning ninety-five is news, and Fox is in the news business." I thought about that as I flew to Asheville that afternoon.

Later that night, as I visited with Mr. Murdoch and told him about my meeting, I thanked him for allowing the greatest news channel in America to broadcast the greatest news in the world—that God loves sinners.

Governor Pat McCrory had opened the evening, wishing my father a happy birthday and welcoming guests to North Carolina. To bring the evening to a close, I asked Greta, who had conducted my father's last interview a few years before, to say a few words. She walked enthusiastically to the lectern. The pro that she is, she coaxed well-known musical artists in the room up front. "Come on, Michael W. Smith, Ricky Skaggs . . . Lecrae, Lacey . . . come on. Let's sing 'Happy Birthday' to Mr. Graham." She even persuaded NBC *Today* cohost Kathie Lee Gifford to join them as her husband, Frank Gifford, looked on.

I had never seen Greta perform a musical number, so when she led these artists and the guests in a robust rendition of this iconic song, my father was touched when she suggested that we might all gather again for his one hundredth birthday! The lighthearted moment prompted my father to join in singing, and when it ended with "Happy Birthday to you," he pointed to himself and sang, "Happy Birthday to me," with a tired, but amused, chuckle.

While everyone enjoyed the moment, guests were most pleased to hear his impromptu remarks.

Though he had not planned to speak, his heart was overflowing with gratitude to be surrounded by those who encouraged him and made him glad to be sharing in the special moment. Greta could sense his desire to address his guests in the room. She left the platform with cordless microphone in hand and walked to my father's table. "You look like you want to say something, Dr. Graham!" And he did.

Unplanned, Unscripted, Unforgettable

Sitting with him at the table was longtime friend and associate Cliff Barrows. Typical of my father, he had been listening to those giving honor to him. It always bothered him when his team was not mentioned because he knew that his ministry would not have been possible without the committed team God had assembled beside him every step of the way.

Cliff, and the late George Beverly Shea, had labored with him since the beginning. I know my father well, so it was not a surprise when

Greta handed the microphone to him. He began speaking, and a hush fell as ears strained to hear his weak voice: "I want to thank you, Cliff, for all you've meant to me through all these years. You've traveled with me every step of the way. God bless you, and we love you."

The emotion of his words touched the hearts of the guests who sat spellbound, watching the rapport between these two valiant friends. It was only right to give Uncle Cliff an opportunity to respond. With a break of emotion in his own voice, he said to my father for all to hear, "We struggled in those early days what we should do with our lives . . . that was sixty-eight years ago, dear friend. I praise God for the journey we've had together. Thank you with all of my heart. Happy birthday, dear Bill. Let's pray the Lord will keep us together till He calls us home or until He comes again. I thank God for every remembrance of you."

The exchange was more than just words, as demonstrated by the tears in their eyes and in the eyes of many others in the room. The brotherly love between these two stalwart men spoke volumes of what they had spent a lifetime watching God do around the world.

For many that night, they felt they had witnessed a personal moment in time that would not soon be forgotten. I had to wonder what others in the room thought as they watched an overwhelming demonstration of what happens when people share in the work of Christ, full of love and grace. For many in the world, they cannot comprehend the fruit of such loyalty and camaraderie. It was an unplanned, unscripted, and unforgettable moment because God's faithfulness was glorified. I never would have imagined that night that Cliff Barrows would be called to heaven before my father, but he died three years later (November 15, 2016), at ninety-three years old.

No Better Gift than Souls Won for the Kingdom

Guests lingered to greet one another following the program while my father quietly slipped away and headed for home. The outing had depleted his strength, but the interaction with old friends had encouraged him. His body wanted to rest, but his mind wanted to relive the evening, and he did until the stroke of midnight when he finally settled in for a peaceful rest.

The following Sunday I drove down to see him. He was still invigorated from the event and rejoiced as I shared with him the number of people who had responded to the invitation. No birthday gift could have brought him more joy than souls won to the kingdom of heaven. I shared with him that 2.5 million viewers across the nation had watched the broadcast. In the coming weeks we would learn that the program had been viewed on other outlets by over ten million people and aired on fifty-three network affiliates, not to mention subsequent airings on the Fox News Channel and the multiple thousands who watched it from around the world via YouTube and the BGEA website.

He was overwhelmed at the coverage and was delighted to hear that BGEA was going to mark his birthday for at least the next five years by establishing Evangelism Week in America with new *My Hope* initiatives.

He thanked me for the vision and for the birthday party and commented on how wonderful it had been to see so many there. "I wish I could have talked to everybody." I was certain the excitement had been a boost. He had already started work on another book, and I encouraged him to make it his new priority.

"Who knows," he said with a grin, "maybe I'll really live to see one hundred!" He was in good spirits as I left that week for China and Thailand, and I chuckled to think he may just reach that milestone.

Am I in Heaven?

So it seemed like whiplash when I got a call from David Bruce, my father's executive assistant. With a fifteen-hour time difference, I didn't have a particularly good feeling to hear his voice at ten o'clock in the evening, North Carolina time.

"Franklin, your Dad has been taken to the hospital," David said. "He is exhausted from battling this bronchial infection. The doctors don't think it is serious, but at ninety-five they are going to monitor him for a few days."

I knew what the call meant. Even a minor cold could have deadly repercussions. Between meetings and flights, I checked in daily for the latest report. But by the time I returned home, so had he. I was tired from my trip but not nearly as exhausted as my father was from fighting a nagging cough that kept him weak and frail. He made little progress in the days that followed and remained in bed, seldom speaking. It was startling to think that just days before, he seemed full of life and was looking forward to Christmas with the family.

December 25 came, and so did the family, but there was no fellowship with Daddy. It was difficult to see him unable to get out of bed. Sunday after Sunday, and more frequently when I was home, I went to see him. Walking into his room was reminiscent of the days before my mother went to heaven. His room was quiet, and so was he. His thoughts seemed distant. Because of his bad eyesight and hearing, I did what I could to let him know I was there.

"Daddy, this is Franklin. I've come to see you." He would reach out, as he had always done, for a hug. His arm would flounder, searching for a touch. Grasping his hand, I would pat it with assurance that he wasn't alone. But he already knew that.

Others who came to see him would say, "Billy . . . or Mr. Graham . . . this is . . . ." His eyes would open slightly, and in a whisper he would ask, "Am I in heaven?"

"No," would be the answer. "You're right here in Montreat," others assured. He seemed disappointed. Many wondered what he might be thinking. But as I looked through my father's eyes, it was clear to me: his mind was on heaven—God's country.

Where I Am

To my surprise, my father rebounded once again, expressing his desire to complete another book he had already started. In earlier conversations with Donna Lee Toney, who had been working with him on his last several books, he had said, "Many people today do not understand the fundamental truths about mankind's eternal destinations and that each person has a choice to make concerning the most critical matter of life—where they will spend eternity after death.

"The more I listen to the news of what is going on in the world, and in the church, the more I can see there is great confusion about the end times. Some people wonder how to get to Heaven and others don't seem to care if they wind up in Hell. God has a lot to say about this. . . . I would like to shed some light on what the Bible has to say about the subject of eternity for today's generations."[4]

So my father gave instructions for the book to be completed. "Do it quickly," he said, "because I am an old man.

"I just may live until my one-hundredth birthday!"[5]

No matter how my father grew older by the year, his aim was to point others to Jesus Christ. And he wrote about it once again in his last book, *Where I Am*, released in 2015, making it his thirty-third and final book.[6]

In it he posed the question, "Who would not want to be where Jesus is?" My father's calling was to answer this question from God's Word, and it is the same calling on my life. He always preached the truth of heaven and hell and wrote, "Heaven is where Jesus *is*. Hell is where Jesus *is not*. But the citizens of hell will spend eternity remembering Jesus Christ, the Savior they rejected."

But he also wrote about the hope of heaven for those who receive Him as Savior and Lord. When asked, "Where is heaven?" he wisely answered, "Heaven is where Jesus Christ is, and I am going to Him soon!"

I thank my Father in heaven for the example of my father on earth who has faithfully proclaimed the message of the cross and the good news of the hope of heaven. One of these days I will join my father there. Death for the Christian is the last milestone on earth, and it leads to the place Jesus promised, "I go and prepare a place for you . . . that where I am, there you may be also" (John 14:3).

My father said with resolve, "When I die, tell others that I've gone to my Lord and Savior Jesus Christ—that's *where I am*."

12

High Noon:
The Hour of Decision for America

Render a decision.
. . . at high noon.

—Isaiah 16:3 NIV

As long as we are on this earth, we possess dual citizenship. On one hand we owe allegiance to our nation and are called to be good citizens. But we are also citizens of the kingdom of God. Our supreme loyalty is to Him.

BILLY GRAHAM

Stepping into unchartered territory has never bothered me. When I believe my footsteps follow God's pathway, I press forward. Throughout his life my father often said, "I will travel anywhere in the world to preach as long as there are no strings attached."[1]

So when I found myself standing on the steps of every state capitol in America, during a hotly contested national political showdown, I thought about my father's unprecedented steps around the world.

I knew such a plan could be risky. I knew it would draw some criticism. I also knew God would bless the plan because we were going to call the nation to prayer. Therefore, I embarked on the most aggressive tour in my lifetime, inviting people to stand with me on the steps of every capitol in the US during the 2016 primaries and presidential campaign; it is a year that will go down in history as the "Year of the Outsider," with an outcome that disrupted the status quo.

My eye was on the rapid decline of our nation. Dr. Ross Rhoads, a longtime friend and board member who died in 2017, had been encouraging me to preach at least one night in all fifty states. Society had lost its footing, and the church was growing weaker by the year as godlessness reigned. Our nation was heading into the most divisive political campaign in history. Headlines on television and the Internet began to blaze with fiery rhetoric and combative points of view as people rushed home in the evening to catch the latest political skirmish.

My thoughts turned to the idea of holding prayer rallies in America's capital cities to preach the Gospel of the Lord Jesus Christ and to challenge Christians to pray for our nation; to live out their faith at home, in public, and at the ballot box; and to consider running for office.

I drove down to see my father and shared with him the evolving plan that I believe was from God. It was an evangelistic outreach for certain. After all, the evangelist calls for a decision for people to receive salvation offered by Jesus Christ that leads to eternal citizenship in heaven. Many followers of Christ had forgotten that God set us on a journey of faith as pilgrims and earthly citizens in a strange land. He has called us to be the light of the world and walk daily with Jesus Christ.

The Right to Have Our Voices Heard

By the time my father was ninety-six, just getting up in the morning and having breakfast was a big deal for him. This globe-trotter for seven decades had slowed down for sure, but he listened as I laid out a vision to gather people from churches and communities to pray for the United States of America, asking God to halt the collision course it was on. He didn't understand how I would have the strength to take on such an aggressive schedule and said, "Too much!" I chuckled. To be honest, though, I wasn't sure I could do it either. But when he assured me of his support and prayers, I resolved to move ahead, and he was pleased to know that the Billy Graham Evangelistic Association would take the lead in calling people to prayer.

Some people tried to discourage me, saying that I was stepping into the political arena. But through the eyes of my father and watching his steps decades before, I had recognized for some time the destructive path our country was on. He had said on many occasions that it was not only the responsibility of citizens to participate in the business of our nation but also the rights of citizens to have their Christian voices heard. Years before, he had said:

> I believe America has gone a long way down the wrong road. If we ever needed God's help, it is now. Spiritually, we have wandered far from the faith of our fathers . . . no nation which relegates the Bible to the background, which disregards the love of God and flouts His truth, can long survive. We have so many battles going on in our country today, that we should be a people of prayer. Our government needs prayer. Our leaders need prayer. Our schools need prayer. Our youth need our prayers. Our families need our prayers. The secret strength of a nation is found in the faith that abides in the hearts and homes of the country, and such faith is found in no other—only the Lord Jesus Christ.

My desire was to challenge people to pray fervently and live boldly for Jesus Christ in the midst of the nastiest primary season and election year of my lifetime.

Gathering just the right team to put this plan into action was no small task. I called my friend Jerry Falwell Jr., president of Liberty University in Lynchburg, Virginia, and told him what God had put on my heart. His father, the late Jerry Falwell Sr., had done something similar by touring many US states to heighten awareness of moral decline across the nation. This eventually led to the founding of the Moral Majority in 1979, which made a profound political impact in the 1980 presidential campaign. Dr. Falwell's aim was to stir up the conservative base and energize the Republican Party, and it worked.

Igniting a fire in the hearts of God's people and lifting up the Lord Jesus Christ and His truth was my aim. Jerry encouraged me and gave me the names of key people who had helped his father years before with the Moral Majority. I sought advice from many of them. One man that proved to be the key to putting things into motion was Lawrence Swicegood, a very sharp guy. He had helped Jerry's father and had an excellent reputation. If anyone could pull it off, it was Lawrence.

The challenge was trying to figure out how I could secure his help. He was serving as executive director of media at Gateway Church in Dallas, Texas, one of the largest churches in the country. Some of the best praise and worship music comes out of that church. I put out a fleece: *Lord, if you want me to move forward, give me Lawrence Swicegood.* So I called him. It didn't take long for me to know the Lord had already been working when Lawrence said, "Franklin, this is really something. Our pastor, Robert Morris, was asking just this week what we as a church could do to wake up America. This might be the answer."

Lawrence called a couple of weeks later and said, "Franklin, the church and the pastoral staff have given me the green light to help you." I told him that we would reimburse the church for his salary for two years. Immediately Lawrence said, "No, Franklin, the church wants to be part of this." Talk about answered prayer!

Years before, I had worked with Lawrence and always appreciated his insight, work ethic, and love for the Lord. With his incredible abilities, he led the energetic team at BGEA that assembled more than twelve thousand volunteers and chaplains.

Securing permission from each state house to hold rallies on the capitol steps at *high noon*—on weekdays no less—was a bold petition. But, after all, the state capitols are "for the people." In some cases we were met with opposition, but the Lord went before us and smoothed the rocky roads. Watching the logistics come together increased our faith. The Bible says that the Lord "will go before you and make the crooked places straight" (Isaiah 45:2). We were on our way to running not a political campaign but a campaign for God from the capitol steps across the nation. We named the outreach *Decision America Tour 2016*. The purpose was to call people to prayer, asking God to turn our country back to Him.[2]

Peering Through the Bus Window

Taking a stand for Christ in all fifty states was received with protest by a few and celebration by many—in fact tens of thousands. Tour buses were prepared and made ready for our team to trek across the nation.

I flew to Des Moines on a bitter cold winter's day in Iowa— January 5, 2016. NBC's political reporter Hallie Jackson was there to interview me and asked, "How many people will show up?" The team had originally pulled permits for a crowd of five hundred people. To attract this many people in the middle of the day, we thought, would be huge; I figured we might have one hundred people. But Jackson's question was answered when we rolled into the snow-covered capital city and Christians showed up in a big way, not hundreds but thousands.

The frigid 16-degree temperature and gusty winds did not deter the more than twenty-five hundred people who had bundled up and stood for hours prior to the rally. As I peered through the bus window, my heart soared to see prayer answered more powerfully than what we could have ever imagined. Swallowing lumps of emotion, I watched with amazement at the elderly on walkers, the disabled in wheelchairs, and young mothers with toddlers in strollers, all there and ready to pray.

To my surprise, as we advanced from capitol to capitol, we averaged nearly five thousand people per stop. It was obvious they had not come to hear me speak; they came to unite in prayer and take a stand for our nation. When we finished in my home state of North Carolina ten months later, more than fourteen thousand people became the landscape for the grounds surrounding the state capitol in Raleigh.

Every place we went I thanked the swelling crowds of people for caring so much about their states and our country that they would come and pray.

"Our nation is in trouble spiritually, racially, economically, and politically," I said, and then I led them in prayer: "Father, our nation has sinned against You. We need to turn our face back to You and Your Son Jesus Christ."

Multitudes of Americans stood shoulder to shoulder at each stop on this fifty-state tour, repenting of their sins and asking the Lord to heal our land. I was deeply touched to look into the faces of the people and see their concerns for America because of its sin, the church because of its lack of obedience to God's Word, and the breakdown of the family due to the godless culture that seeks to diminish and eradicate spiritual influence in the home and society in general. It was evident that they were there for one reason—to pray. And did they pray.

At each of the one-hour rallies, we paused to join hands and lift our hearts and voices to almighty God, asking that He would forgive our sins and that He would draw the lost to His salvation. I led them in special prayer for those serving our country, that they would fear God and not man. At times the collective prayers caused a sacred murmur.

In some cities, as prayers went up, a solitary voice echoed above all the other voices, repenting of sin. This happened in Portland, Oregon. While leading the people in prayer, I waited longer than normal to conclude because of a praying man in the very back of the crowd. His voice grew stronger as he pronounced, "In the name of Jesus . . . in the name of Jesus . . . in the name of Jesus." It gave me chills as I listened to this lone voice rising above the others and glorifying the Son of God. I did not want to hinder His work in people's hearts. To this day I can hear that man's voice. I will never forget the impact it had on me and all those listening. The Spirit of the Lord was among us.

It was touching to see little ones fold their hands, the aged bow their heads, and all the others call on the One who hears our prayers. Groups of people would huddle together. Some would stand alone whispering a plea; others were on bended knee or extending hands upward as prayers stormed the gates of heaven. Regardless of how the prayers were expressed, the Lord was listening. People prayed out loud, confessing the sins of our nation and silently confessing individual sins as God brought them to mind. I believe the very heart of God was moved. As my father always said, "Persistent, prevailing, pleading prayer can halt the rising tide and the spread of evil."

Engraved with God's Blessings

With this in mind, I stood on the steps of our nation's state capitols and thanked the Lord that our Constitution gives us the right and privilege to proclaim His name, and He honors this testimony of faith.

The history of our nation is richly engraved with God's blessings because its people looked to Him as their Creator, Ruler, Legislator, Judge, Savior, and almighty God. The Pilgrims and forefathers spoke

His name, sought His direction, and studied His Word. As with the nation of Israel, when the people obeyed Him, He blessed. When they defied His truth, He judged. The saga continues to this day. God's Word asks: "Who would not [revere] You, O King of the nations?" (Jeremiah 10:7). Today the world demonstrates that no nation reveres the King of Glory.

America is in a time of judgment because obedience to God has taken a backseat to exalting godlessness. We have forgotten our roots. Most Americans do not know that in all fifty state constitutions God is acknowledged. The early settlers understood that He is the source of freedom, justice, liberty, and preservation. God's law reflects His judgment as well as His love, grace, and mercy. This is the law that is written on the hearts of mankind and can be found on our national monuments and in our state houses.

Our forefathers never intended for Christians to leave our faith out on the capitol steps. No matter the city, I stood before concerned citizens who understood the perils of our nation.

The Bible says, "If My people who are called by My name will humble themselves, and pray and seek My face, and turn from their wicked ways, then I will hear from heaven, and will forgive their sin and heal their land" (2 Chronicles 7:14).

The Enemy Has Come Through the Gate

This is what the prophet Nehemiah understood in the ancient days of his homeland, Israel. Nehemiah was a slave to a pagan king in a foreign nation, but his heart was moved with compassion for his people when he learned of the destruction that had come to them because of their sins and disobedience to God. The cherished city of Jerusalem, once protected by a mighty fortress, had come under siege; its towering wall had fallen in defeat, and the gates had been burned. The enemy of God had terrorized His people.

Nehemiah gives the account:

> Hanani, one of my brothers, came from Judah with some other men,
> and I questioned them about the Jewish remnant that had survived
> the exile, and also about Jerusalem.
>
> They said to me, "Those who survived the exile and are back in
> the province are in great trouble and disgrace. The wall of Jerusalem
> is broken down, and its gates have been burned with fire."
>
> When I heard these things, I sat down and wept. For some days I
> mourned and fasted and prayed before the God of heaven. Then I said:
>
> "Lord, the God of heaven, the great and awesome God, who
> keeps his covenant of love with those who love him and keep
> his commandments, let your ear be attentive and your eye open
> to hear the prayer your servant is praying before you day and
> night for your servants, the people of Israel. I confess the sins we
> Israelites, including myself and my father's family, have commit-
> ted against you. We have acted very wickedly toward you. We
> have not obeyed the commands, decrees and laws you gave your
> servant Moses" (Nehemiah 1:2–7 NIV).

Nehemiah resolved to go back to his nation and call on the Lord
to heal its land. His first step of action was to turn to God in fasting
and prayers, repenting of his sins, the sins of the people, and the sins
of the nation. God heard Nehemiah and moved in the heart of the
pagan king to grant Nehemiah favor and permission to return to
Jerusalem to rebuild the wall of the great city of God. The king sent
provisions and a detachment of soldiers to protect him along the way.
The task was perilous. Nehemiah was confronted by enemies and
grumblers. But no matter the opposition, God performed a miracle,
and the wall was rebuilt in just fifty-two days, an impossible task if not
for the Lord. The lesson for us is that it is never too late to turn to
God in prayer.

Campaign for God

To prepare my message for the tour, I studied this remarkable passage in the Old Testament. The similarities were startling. America's *walls* have been crumbling for decades, leading to the vicious attack on 9/11. Planes slammed into skyscrapers, shattering our symbolic crowned jewel; the dynasty that held the hopes of a prosperous people fell into heaps at the hallowed site that became known as Ground Zero. The wake-up call should have lasted more than just a few days—but it didn't. The disaster that rocked New York City, Pennsylvania, Washington, DC, and our nation, drew us together just long enough for the US Congress to gather on the steps of the Capitol and in breathtaking unity sing, "God Bless America . . . stand beside her and guide her, through the night with the light from above." The dramatic performance was short-lived, and politicians reverted back to politics as usual.

Friends, the enemy is not at the gate—the enemy has come through the gate. It did not take long after the shock and awe of 9/11 for citizens to settle into a deeper apathy than ever before, leading up to the fierce election of 2016.

My message echoed across the land, "Folks, it is time for action. We cannot afford to stay home on Election Day as millions of Americans have done in the past. We have a God-given responsibility to vote and encourage others to do the same. There is a price to be paid for apathy. Will we choose leaders who fear and follow God, or will we allow godless candidates to continue to steer our country into moral anarchy and open rebellion against God and His ways?"

It was time for God's people to consider what we can do to turn the tide. Faithful citizens stood strong and cheered with surprise and relief when I declared, "I have no hope in the Democratic Party!" All the Republicans applauded. But I smiled and said, "Now, before you Republicans start high-fiving each other, I have no hope in the

Republican Party!" Then the Democrats would clap louder. I continued, "The only hope for our nation is almighty God!" The crowd responded with thunderous applause.

I am not willing to lose our country without a fight, are you? Let's stand for godly principles and biblical values. Fighting for souls for God's kingdom and for the soul of America is my strong conviction. The disgrace of America due to persistent, willful, rebellious sin is shameful. This rebellion cannot continue any longer if our children and grandchildren are to live in a country that still recognizes and honors God, as virtually every generation has done since settlers first set foot in America.

Fox News Special Report—The Evangelical Vote

We need more people like Nehemiah—men and women who will take a stand for God because America's moral and spiritual walls have crumbled. Walls are for keeping evil out, but the moral gates of the nation are broken down. Godless secularism has slowly crept in and taken over. This grieves the heart of God. The church has sat on the sidelines and watched as our country has descended into ever-thickening moral darkness. Immorality is flagrant. The family unit is in shambles. Sin is celebrated. Violence is a plague. Greed and idolatry are rampant.

Educators, big business, politicians, and, sad to say, many of our churches are more concerned about profits and political correctness than they are about God's truth and His righteousness. My father once said, "The great flaw in the American economic system has finally been revealed: an unrealistic faith in the power of prosperity rather than in the ultimate power and benevolence of God."

The progressives have infiltrated our schools, our government, and our nation. Progressivism is nothing more than godless secularism, and it has stormed through the gates of America's bulwark.

This was the topic that chief political anchor Bret Baier of the Fox

News Channel raised in a special he hosted, *The 2016 Election and Evangelical Christian Voters*. He caught up with me on our fourth stop in Concord, New Hampshire, and asked me why I was going to all fifty states. I answered, "I think that faith voters are taken for granted. The Republican establishment just assumes that the faith voters are going to vote for them. It's the wrong assumption. This is why I have taken on the effort of this fifty-state tour. I want to get evangelical Christians to vote. I am not going to tell them who to vote for. Politicians will tell you anything. They'll say, 'Oh yes, I'm a Christian, I love God,' and as soon as they get into office, so many of them live a different life and vote differently than what they promised. So I say to them, 'Don't take our vote for granted. It's not coming your way; you have to earn it.'"[3]

The temperature in New Hampshire was bitter, but the outpouring of people's support and resolve that day warmed my heart. I expected a small crowd, but God showed up through His people. They knew their rights as declared in their state constitution: "Every individual has a natural and unalienable right to worship God . . . and no subject . . . shall be restrained . . ."[4] God's presence in our nation is woven into the fabric that has wrapped the USA in His care from its humble beginnings. We must not be passive. We cannot be silent.

Only by standing on biblical truth can we overturn the wickedness that has opened the floodgates to the heart of the nation in protest of God. Make no mistake; many politicians and judges are openly hostile to Christianity. Christians are on the verge of losing this country.

It is time to quit backing up. We better wake up and stand up with a firm resolve. Our nation is at a crossroads, and it is time to make a decision to follow Jesus Christ and obey His Word. The Bible says, "Stand at the crossroads and look . . . ask where the good way is, and walk in it, and you will find rest for your souls" (Jeremiah 6:16 NIV).

There is still time for our nation to turn back to almighty God for a renewal of our God-given foundation. Sometimes standing up for

God and His truth offends people, and that's okay, for we speak the truth by conviction and by the love of God.

Personalities or Platforms

Examining where candidates stand on critical issues that face our troubled nation is vital. After all, *we the people* empower our leaders by our vote. Will they continue to lead us down the road of irresponsible socialism where the biblical injunction for hard, honest work is ignored? Or will we embrace a resurgence of vigorous entrepreneurship and industry that have been hallmarks of our nation since its founding?

These were among the questions I posed to those who would carefully consider the answers. I did not tell anyone who to vote for; but as people struggled with the candidates' personalities and flaws—and we all have them—I challenged everyone to look at the party platforms and vote biblical principles.

The message was not gladly received by all. Some protestors carried signs that said, "Billy Graham spoke about love." Yes, he did. And as he also said many times, "The most loving thing a preacher can do is speak God's truth." He penned his thoughts about America throughout his ministry and wrote: "Our nation grew strong in an era when moral standards were emphasized, and it will grow weak when we condone that which we once condemned.[5] The nation's image has become more like a chameleon—accepting whatever trend marketers concoct. Gone are the days of reverencing a holy God in the church or within ourselves."[6]

There were some Christians who thought I was engaging in politics. Others criticized me by pointing out that my father stayed out of politics. Really? One of the many definitions of politics is: "The activities associated with the governance of a country . . . especially the debate or conflict among individuals or parties having or hoping to achieve power."[7]

I did not hesitate to remind people that the government of the United States is "of the people, for the people, and by the people," and we are part of that distinctive assembly. So how can we remain silent? We elect government leaders to represent us; how can they do that without hearing from the people—their constituents? No, my father was never a passive or apathetic citizen.

"What would your father say about this if he was still preaching today?" This was a repetitive question many people asked. "If he were able to speak out today," I answered, "I believe he would be doing exactly what we are doing right now—encouraging people to pray for our nation and make a difference for Christ at every level." The question was designed to put me on the defensive, but my father's words are weighty.

In 1952, the year I was born, he said, "I think it is the duty of every individual Christian at election time to study the issues and candidates and then go to the polls and vote. If I were a pastor, I would explain to my people where each candidate stood morally, spiritually, and in relationship to the church. I feel that we're going to have to meet our political obligations as Christians and make our voice known if America is to be preserved with a type of Christian heritage that has given us the liberties that we now enjoy. Unless America turns back to God, repents of its sin, and experiences a spiritual revival, we will fail as a nation."

And he didn't finish there. "I believe God honors leaders in high places who honor him. Today we need political leaders, men and women, who are willing to stand for God and His principles. America is being stripped of its biblical heritage and God-inspired foundations." Sixty-four years later his message rings just as true.

In 1976, as another election approached, my father encouraged believers to "get involved in the political process." He said, "I would like to challenge every deeply committed American who is qualified, to consider running for political office. I don't believe that we as Christians should withdraw."

"But Franklin," you may ask, "how about separation of church and state?"

How about it? We are Christians, and we are Americans, and we have every right to let our voices be heard. Elections are not only to choose a president every four years. We have elections at some level every year. If we were more aware and involved in local and state elections, perhaps the presidential elections would not be so traumatic.

Imagine the difference if Christians were mayors, county commissioners, and school board members. We need Christians at every level of government. These are prime positions that give voice to godly influence. As my father has said, "Christians can make the impact of Christ felt in every phase of life—religious, social, economic, and political—but we must not do it in our strength. We must not do it in our own wisdom. We can do it only as we surrender ourselves completely to God, allowing Him to work through us."

Text Me

Our *Decision America Tour* received overwhelming response. Of the 235,000 people in attendance, collectively in fifty states, and those watching the events that were streaming live, more than 9,000 people confirmed that they had received Jesus Christ as their Lord and Savior.[8]

Because we were on capitol grounds with limited time and no way to distribute materials, we established a texting program that would allow individuals to respond right then. I would hold my phone up and say, "If you want to receive God's forgiveness for sin and invite Jesus Christ into your hearts, text me at 21777, and type in the word *decision*. Before you leave here today, you will receive materials that will help you grow in your new life with Christ." With people still standing at the rally, the BGEA was able to record their decisions and follow up with them, just as we had always done in our crusades.

Those in attendance at the rallies, and those watching via the Internet, were also given the opportunity to sign a pledge, using the same texting method. Nearly 115,000 signed the pledge to honor God at home and in public. "Pray, Vote, and Engage" was our slogan, and listeners responded, pledging to *pray* faithfully for the United States of America; to *vote* in federal, state, and local elections for candidates who will uphold biblical values; and to *engage* in their communities. I also asked people to pray about seeking public office and making their Christian voices heard. Will you do the same?

The prayer rallies were not just one-time events held at *high noon* one cold or blistering hot day in 2016. Believers returned home and began prayer groups—and yes, many got involved immediately in their spheres of life.

While on the capitol grounds, not only did we pray for our nation, but I also led us in prayer for the states' governors, lieutenant governors, attorney generals—many times by name—and legislators and employees. We also prayed for our military and our law enforcement, our men and women in blue who are being attacked all across the country. We must pray for those who risk their lives daily to keep us safe.

God gave us government not to rule our faith but to protect it. Scripture instructs us to pray for governing authorities at every level, that they will fulfill their divinely appointed rule of rewarding good and punishing evil, exhibiting godly character and wisdom publicly and privately (1 Peter 2:14). We must pray for people of character to run for office and be elected, for they represent the people who defend God's most precious institution—the sanctity of marriage between one man and one woman. Government officials are the very people we elect to write the laws with the intent to protect the family unit and society in general.

The Bible tells us that all authority in heaven and on earth has been given to Jesus Christ and that His plans can never be frustrated by earthly powers.

Fake News and Political Correctness

The minute-by-minute details crowding headlines during the 2016 election left the country weary and exhausted. Lives of candidates and campaign staffs were scrutinized; motives were questioned, and skeptics ridiculed. Fake news was exalted, and political correctness was attacked. The national media hammered politicians, and outsiders put the press in the hot seat.

In the aftermath of such a tumultuous election year, people were anxious about the ultimate outcome. I believe we did see the hand of God move in a dramatic way. In the end, the polling data was deemed ineffective, and the candidate favored by the media to win conceded the race late into the night.

This impassioned election came down to two very different people. More important, it was about two very different visions. Many have told me that they believe God used our *Decision America Tour* to ignite a fire among Americans who had resigned themselves to a country that was destined to slide further into a place of godless, socialistic secularism of no return.

Two Visions: Two Americas

To help people sort through the election dialogue, BGEA's September 2016 issue of *Decision Magazine* summarized the party platforms that distinguished the two very different agendas.

One agenda exalted abortion, same-sex marriage, pluralism, and decreased military spending. The other agenda had provisions to protect life, support marriage between a man and a woman, protect faith values, and strengthen our national defense. Had the election tipped left, the corrupt progressivism that has frayed the moral fabric of our nation would have reigned supreme, and religious freedom would have been trampled underfoot in lightning speed.

We give thanks to God for empowering His people to show up at the polls and cast votes for the party that, at least, promises to right the wrongs and put America back on the right track. Friends, we can't stop speaking out for truth, and we can't stop praying.

I believe that the prayers of God's people moved President Trump to appoint capable men and women to his cabinet to serve this country and send it in a new direction. Let's acknowledge God's sovereignty by thanking Him for giving the citizens of the United States an opportunity to turn this battered ship around.

Trump Says "Thank You"

In the days following the election, Donald Trump did something no other president-elect had done—he went on a thank-you tour to eight key states that had made a significant impact on his victory. He wanted to personally thank his supporters for standing together to *Make America Great Again.*

It was a brilliant move and a strong finish to the high-strung year. His last stop was in Mobile, Alabama, on December 17, 2016. I was surprised and humbled when the president-elect invited me to be with him at Ladd-Peebles Stadium to lead the crowd in prayer. People turned out by the tens of thousands to see the soon-to-be new president say thank you. The mood was electrifying.[9]

While I did not campaign or endorse him or any other candidate, as an American citizen I thank God that Donald Trump won the election. I appreciated the vision he cast for America to be "one people under one God saluting one American flag."[10] Oh that our nation would experience such blessing again.

Shortly after that rally, I was asked to participate in President Trump's 2017 inauguration. My connection to inaugurations dates back to 1965. My father prayed at more inauguration ceremonies than any other person in history, including the inaugurations of presidents

Lyndon Johnson, Richard Nixon, Ronald Reagan, George H. W. Bush, and Bill Clinton.

He was invited to pray at President Bill Clinton's second inauguration in 1997. Almost eighty at the time and growing weaker, my father had difficulty getting up from a chair. Up to that point he had been helped by his longtime team member T. W. Wilson, a childhood friend. However, T. W. was growing older, too, and not in good health. My father did not want one old man helping another, so he asked, "Franklin, would you go with me to the inauguration, and when it is time for me to pray, you can help me without making a scene."

I told him it would be an honor to be by his side, so we went together. While my father was somewhat feeble in body, his mind was strong, and his interaction with people was as good as it had always been. What an opportunity it was for me to observe him shaking hands with people and so graciously speaking with the most powerful and prestigious dignitaries in government. No matter the setting, he was a strong and consistent voice for the Lord Jesus Christ. While some did not share his faith, their respect for him was obvious.

I stood back and watched, never imagining that four years later I would stand in the same place as my father to deliver the invocation at the first swearing-in of George W. Bush as the forty-third president of the United States.

And did it ever create a firestorm! Doing something he had done his entire life was no longer acceptable—to pray in the name of Jesus. Billy Graham was never accused of offending anyone when He prayed in Jesus' name. This was not an issue with Americans or people from the Western world. How times had changed and so quickly.

Praying in the name of Jesus at the first inauguration of President George W. Bush in 2001 triggered the modern-day prayer wars, and the media loved it. To say it got me in trouble is an understatement. Just days following the ceremony, famed attorney Alan Dershowitz wrote a *Los Angeles Times* opinion commentary saying that my prayer had "excluded the tens of millions of Americans who are Muslims, Jews, Buddhists, Shintoists, Unitarians, agnostics and atheists."[11]

My prayer even caused the new president some headache when noted atheist Michael Newdow (who once sued to remove the words "under God" from the Pledge of Allegiance[12]) filed a lawsuit against the government for allowing the prayer and against George W. Bush for inviting me.[13] The storm passed when Newdow lost the suit. But the rains of controversy baptized inaugural prayers, and the angst comes to the surface every four years.

It was no different sixteen years later when I was asked to participate in the inauguration of the forty-fifth president of the United States.

Rain Is a Sign of God's Blessing

In Trump fashion, President-elect Donald Trump rebuffed political correctness when he was called on to disinvite me to participate in the ceremony by ignoring the dustup.

On January 20, 2017, America—and the world—watched the profound and peaceful transfer of power from one administration to another, reflecting the time-honored protocol of our forefathers. On Inauguration Day patriotism rules; at least, that is our hope every four years.

While there was a sense of excitement for the day's events, the weather forecast was daunting—some felt it dampened the anticipation. News coverage seemed to focus on a prediction by meteorologists: the skies would rain on Trump's parade. Media and others hostile to the incoming president murmured that rain signaled doom.

For security reasons, umbrellas were not allowed to accompany the swelling masses of people who filled the National Mall that faces the US Capitol. While some talking heads debate the crowd's size, it was the largest audience in history to watch an inauguration via television and live streaming via the Internet. But as citizens stood faithfully to witness the swearing-in of Donald J. Trump at high noon by Supreme Court Justice John Roberts, the rain began to fall. The new president paid no attention. As former presidents seated on the platform covered up in plastic or swept the moisture from their brows, Trump delivered his inaugural address undeterred by the showers.

It occurred to me how easy it is to exalt the negative while ignoring the positive. When President Trump concluded his inaugural speech to the American people, Rabbi Marvin Hier, Bishop Wayne T. Jackson, and I stepped to the podium. It was my privilege to address the new commander in chief and read from God's Word.

Mr. President, in the Bible, rain is a sign of God's blessing, and it started to rain, Mr. President, when you came to the platform. And it is my prayer that God will bless you, your family, your administration, and may He bless America. The passage of Scripture comes from First Timothy. . . .

"I urge, then, first of all, that petitions, prayers, intercession and thanksgiving be made for all people—for kings and all those in authority, that we may live peaceful and quiet lives in all godliness and holiness. This is good, and pleases God our Savior, who wants all people to be saved and to come to a knowledge of the truth. For there is one God and one mediator between God and mankind, the man Christ Jesus, who gave himself as a ransom for all people.

"Now to the King eternal, immortal, invisible, the only God, be honor and glory for ever and ever," in Jesus' name. Amen. (1 Timothy 2:1–6; 1:17 NIV)[14]

When I concluded and stepped away from the podium, the president thanked me with a strong handshake. As we stood side by side for the brief moment of final prayers, I prayed silently for this man who had just inherited a colossal mess. He took the helm of a nation that had grown increasingly hostile and intolerant of the very foundation and principles upon which it was so nobly founded—the Christian faith and biblical values.

My prayer is that President Trump will come to know the Lord Jesus Christ in a very personal way and realize that without the strength of almighty God leading the way, our nation will continue in peril. The key to ruling with strength and wisdom is found only by calling on the powerful name of God who rules the universe. That is the master key to having liberty, freedom, and justice for all.

Others, however, took to social media, suggesting that I had misused Scripture about rain being a blessing. But the Word of God speaks truth: "The Lord will open to you His good treasure, the heavens, to give the rain to your land in its season, and to bless all the work of your hand" (Deuteronomy 28:12).

But the ominous clouds hanging over our nation and threatening destruction—clouds of terrorism, uncertainty, immorality, and disobedience—may clear if our government leaders will look to God for direction. We may be praying for sunshine when God wants to send showers of blessing that come through repentance. We may be excusing sinful behavior while God's Spirit is bringing conviction. We sometimes get overanxious for results while God waits patiently to forgive people who will stand before Him and acknowledge their sins, repent, and receive Jesus Christ as Lord and Savior of their lives. Let's be ever mindful to exalt His way and silence our own selfish purposes.

My prayer for all people, and especially those who seek to lead others, is to make God the ultimate authority and follow Him, for one day all people of the nations of the world will bow before the Lord Jesus Christ and worship Him as King of kings.

This was a foundational belief when our nation was birthed. The first citizens bestowed upon America's future this testimony and instilled a godly heritage to honor the Lord, lift up Jesus Christ, and serve one another so that our hope in Him will guide our children, grandchildren, and generations to come.

It is high noon in America. It is time to make a decision to turn from pagan ways and inaugurate a new way of life by living for Jesus Christ. This is certainly my vision, and I hope it is yours also: to preserve our nation's heritage and show the world that America's legacy remains "In God We Trust."

13

Legacy

You have given me the heritage of those who fear Your name.

—PSALM 61:5

The legacy we leave is not just in our possessions,
but in the quality of our lives.

BILLY GRAHAM

Everyone wants to leave a legacy: philanthropists, inventors, politicians, celebrities, activists, and families. The word has a certain charm, bursting at the seams to tell a story.

Businesses are emerging that tout "Discover Your Legacy," "Create Your Own Legacy," and even "Contest Your Legacy." And people actually do.

What is your legacy? Few people consider the word while in their prime. Most people begin talking about legacy as they approach the end of life.

While the Bible does not speak of people leaving legacies, it talks a great deal about heritage—a way of life passed down from one generation to another that speaks of values: character, reputation, and integrity.

My father wrote on the subject of integrity in his book *The Journey: How to Live by Faith in an Uncertain World*. "Integrity means that if our private life was suddenly exposed, we'd have no reason to be ashamed or embarrassed. Integrity means our outward life is consistent with our inner convictions. A person of integrity is like Daniel of old, whose enemies diligently searched for his weaknesses, but in the end 'could find no corruption in him' (Daniel 6:4 [NIV])."[1] This is a worthwhile legacy.

In one sense, a legacy is the tangible side of heritage—what is handed down to the next generation—depicted in the form of monetary value or heirlooms, meaningful treasures passed down from one generation to another. Often their value lies in sentimental remembrances of a loved one who perhaps held on to an old diary, a military uniform or rifle, a long-ago-written letter, or perhaps the family Bible—something that has become nearly extinct.

The word *legacy* has evolved to mean how an individual will be remembered after death. Other words we use to speak of legacy are *birthright, inheritance, memories,* and *family traditions*.

My Father's Legacy

Through cover stories and documentaries, media outlets around the world have pondered the legacy of Billy Graham. They have asked, and tried to answer, how will he be remembered? What did he leave behind?

My father would want to be remembered for two things. That he lived a life obedient to the Lord Jesus Christ and that he faithfully preached God's Gospel.

As his son and namesake, I would add to that legacy what he passed on to his family: integrity and compassion. Billy Graham was a loving father who taught his children values found in the Word of God and lived those values both privately and publicly. My parents left us children a tangible legacy, but more valuable was the heritage they left in how they lived their lives.

Our national legacies are contained in museums, most notably "America's Museum," the Smithsonian Institute, in Washington, DC. It is the largest procurer in preserving our heritage and has been described as a mirror of the nation.[2] This is where you will find Morse's telegraph, Bell's telephone, Ford's Model T, Farnsworth's television dissector tube, and many other national treasures.

The Henry Ford Museum at Greenfield Village in Dearborn, Michigan, showcases the development of Americana—cobblestone streets lined with Edison's Menlo Park laboratory and the Wright brothers' home and bicycle shop.[3] We love our history of bright ideas and ingenuity, but we generally don't like to showcase our failures.

Preacher Fathers, Pilot Sons

When I was preaching a crusade in Ohio years ago, I visited the aeronautical museum at Wright-Patterson Field, named for the Wright brothers. I love seeing the progression of technology and, on occasion, attending a trade show where the latest aircraft are displayed.

On this occasion the airplane was the Embraer Legacy 600, made in Brazil. This design has come a long way from the Wright brothers' 1903 Flyer that made its brief maiden voyage from Kitty Hawk, North Carolina.[4]

My aunt Rosa's husband, Uncle Don Montgomery, was a pilot. I remember him flying a small plane from their home in New Mexico to North Carolina to see the family. I loved all of his stories and would dream of flying myself someday.

My father had friends who owned airplanes, and I grew up longing to fly. I was fascinated to hear how the late R. G. LeTourneau converted a World War II B-24 bomber into a corporate plane. I will never forget the first ride I took in a private jet in the late sixties. A friend of my father's had a small Lear jet, and he took us up for a ride. Not only did it look like a bullet, but it felt like one as we roared through the sky. Years later, my father agreed to pay for flying lessons while I was a student at LeTourneau College. I had no idea what was required to get a pilot's license, much less keep the license current.

Learning to fly was just the beginning. Then came the multiengine ratings, instrument ratings, commercial ratings, Airline Transport Pilot (ATP) ratings, and numerous type ratings to fly aircraft over 12,500 pounds. I soon discovered that ongoing education is required for pilots.

My father found his release from tension on the golf course. I found mine climbing into the clouds. So I have a special appreciation for the innovation of Wilbur and Orville Wright, also sons of a preacher— Milton Wright, a circuit-riding preacher in the late 1800s. Like my own father, he was away from home much of the time. The "preacher's kids" regarded their father's long absences not as a detriment to their development but rather as an enhancement, gleaning important lessons by living life through their father's eyes.

I am not a historian. But as a pilot—and most of all an evangelist— the story of the preacher's boys fascinates me. They were the first to sustain free flight in a manned aircraft that came to be known at that time as the "aeroplane."

The Wright brothers never lost sight of their humble beginnings. Their father instilled in them a faith greater than the faith he had in their aeronautical invention. It wasn't until 1910, when he was eighty-two, that he soared with his legendary offspring. The brothers were uncertain as to how their father would respond to the experience. But on that day they enjoyed watching their father's thrill. As the engines roared to life and the wind buffeted their faces in the open-air cockpit, the parson leaned up to his son and with pastoral projection shouted, "Higher, Orville, higher."[5]

I laughed when I read the account, remembering the first time my father climbed on board with me at the controls. He was apprehensive for sure, but after a smooth liftoff, his posture relaxed—sort of. As he watched the wingtips puncture the clouds, he flinched. When we safely landed, he said with a sigh of relief, "Franklin, you're a good pilot. I think I felt safe all the way." Coming from my father, who was always apprehensive of flying, it was a memorable sound bite.

The Wright brothers were just as surprised by their father's delight as the world of technology was with the accomplishments of the preacher's boys. Folks seemed baffled because the brothers did not fit the criteria for greatness, according to society. Neither boy had earned a high school diploma. They had no special training in science and engineering. They were not wealthy, nor did they have friends in high places.

What they did have was a rich heritage that taught them the importance of a strong and creative work ethic. Milton and Susan Wright instilled in their children love and respect for one another. Wilbur and Orville learned the art of working together while relying on one's strength to make up for the other's weakness. They did not compete with each other; they complemented each other.

Their parents taught them by example to live according to a standard of high moral character. For boys who learned the art of free flight, they were grounded in foundational beliefs that would sustain them in times of disappointment, while carrying them to celebrated heights.

My father was much like Parson Wright. In order to effectively minister, he had to be away from his family months at a time. But my father's travel on airplanes had a big influence on my desire to fly.

I remember the times my mother would take us children to the train station to welcome him home. I was especially excited when we could go to the Asheville airport to watch his plane come in for landing. To stand behind the gate and watch a Piedmont Airlines DC-3 touchdown was a thrill. The engine growled and billowed smoke and oil from the exhaust. It was a boy's dream. To this day I recall the smell of raw avgas and thick blue smoke.

Impatiently, I waited to hear the rear door pop open. When my father stepped out of the plane and walked down the tarmac, we jumped and called out to him, hungry for his attention.

In those days, international travel was expensive and required him to be gone for long periods of time. Once he was in Australia for six months. My mother always made his homecoming a big event.

Though I was gone plenty when I began my ministry, air travel opened horizons for me that fifty years before would not have been possible. While I don't fly a Legacy 600, I have been fortunate to pilot an aircraft that enables me to preach in Toronto in the evening and sleep in my own bed late that night, or to tour the aftermath of a hurricane in south Texas in the morning and begin meetings in Honduras a few hours later.

The Wright brothers left behind something valuable to the world, but their testimony of love and respect for family speaks of their greater treasure.

Museums of the Heart

Our country was built on families like the Wrights. While most do not have buildings in which to store their memorabilia, they often pack their possessions in boxes or cedar chests.

The history of the cedar chest goes back to the time of the Egyptian pharaohs, who used these chests to preserve ancient treasures of gold and writings on papyrus. Some speculate that its origin evolved from the ark of the covenant (or testimony) that went before the children of Israel, in times of battle like at Jericho. In it they carried tangible evidence of God's miracles.

With the passing of time, the chest evolved into a safe, a trunk, and then a sea chest, when the Pilgrims selected the more practical container to accompany them on their voyage to the New World.

Only one furnishing had the capacity to sum up a family's possessions: a hickory trunk lined with red cedar. The fragrant wood repelled insects and mildew and warded off the musty odor from humidity engulfing the hull of the ship.

I can recall my mother's cedar chests. She had more than one—all crammed to the top. In today's throwaway world, preserving memories is an antiquated idea. But there is still a remnant that thrives from the "yesterworld." Treasures that come from these chests are testimonials to their owners.

The human heart is a type of cedar chest, storing valuable lessons, special memories, and the important pieces of one's life that live on throughout generations.

Mankind shares a legacy: sin that has been passed down from the beginning of time. But forgiven sinners inherit the promise of heaven.

Are we building reserves of faith, hope, and love? Or do we just accumulate "stuff" that mildews in the heat of despair? Are we amassing eternal treasure that will live forever in the hope chest of the heart? Or do we harbor debris from broken dreams?

My father once said, "We are not cisterns made for hoarding; we are channels made for sharing. God has given us two hands, one to receive with and the other to give with."

Do we live our lives for the purpose of leaving a lasting legacy behind as a testimony of what Christ has done in us?

Wishing and Hoping

The word *hope* is often interchanged with the word *wish*. But a wish is only a fleeting thought—a whim with no anchor.

My mother was a curator of hundreds of antique books, some made in China—others first-edition prints. My father never understood her fascination with them. She shopped for them, collected them, traded them, and often gave them as gifts. Inside the cover of an old antique diary she gave a friend of mine was this definition of *hope*: "To look forward to something with expectation of its fulfillment."

The Bible says, "Now faith is the substance of things hoped for, the evidence of things not seen" (Hebrews 11:1). This wonderful verse is the preamble to the great faith chapter that recounts the patriarchs—the biblical examples of trusting God with hopeful expectation.

My father was the patriarch of our family, and his absence is deeply felt. But I am thankful for the rich testimony of his faith in Christ. "Your testimonies I have taken as a heritage forever" (Psalm 119:111).

A Testimony That Lives On

This all came to mind when we opened the Billy Graham Library. People began to ask me what my father's legacy would be. I would much rather tell you about the testimony that lives on. His testimony is not buried. He spent his life preaching the Gospel around the world—and his messages live on. They are still being heard through the miracle of modern technology.

My father was not particularly fond of the idea of building a library. He was certainly familiar with presidential libraries designed to preserve the accomplishments of men who had served their country at the highest level, but a library for a preacher? My father was reluctant, to say the least.

The board of directors for BGEA presented the idea of preserving what God had done as a testimony to generations that would follow. They asked my father to review a proposal and preliminary plans.

"Daddy," I assured him, "the library will document what God has done through you—the work of an evangelist. This is God's testimony to a world still searching for peace with God. The Lord has used you, your team, and all who have supported the ministry to herald His Gospel. One day you'll be in heaven, but the ministry God gave you will go on. People will continue to come to Christ by what they see and hear at the library. It will be an ongoing crusade. If we move ahead with the library, it will not be a memorial to a man or a monument to good deeds but rather a testimony for the Lord Jesus Christ."

Eyes that had been set in unmovable resolve softened. *A testimony about what God had done?* My father sat in silence, eyes traveling through a time tunnel. With a raspy and weak voice he said, "Let's give some time to prayer and see how the Lord might lead."

It was not a green light—more like a yellow light. Proceed with caution, and pray, pray, and pray some more.

From North to South

So we did. The Lord moved in my father's heart as each phase of a master plan unfolded. The BGEA had already relocated from Minneapolis, Minnesota, to Charlotte, North Carolina. That was a miracle in itself. Here was an organization that had enjoyed a hospitable home in the north. To cut the cord after fifty wonderful years was emotional for many of the long-term employees who had served the Lord so faithfully. But God worked in their hearts, and many moved their families south. My son Roy, who works with BGEA, was a tremendous help to me in this transition.

The first hurdle in that process had been to find the right location in North Carolina's "Queen City." I turned to Charlotte-based board member Graeme Keith for counsel. He had been a lifelong friend to my father and had served many years on the BGEA board of directors. I will never forget sitting in my office one evening talking with Graeme by phone about the right location in Charlotte.

Charlotte had successfully developed its downtown grid into a corporate financial hub. What once was a "big little city" had become something quite uptown. In fact, that is exactly how it is referred to today. The downtown area became known as Uptown Charlotte, its beautiful skyline displaying a pristine silhouette against the Carolina sky.

As we bantered about "location, location, location," we seemed to run into the limitations of a downtown area. Then we talked about the South Park area, which sprawled its way along major arteries.

A friend of mine was sitting in the office, listening to the conversation, and scribbled something on a pad of paper and held it in front of my face: "The Billy Graham Parkway."

I thought, *Not a chance! The cost of land along one of the busiest stretches of highway linking two major interstates and leading to Douglas International Airport would be prohibitive.*

But as we talked through the options, I cautiously said, "Graeme, what about the Billy Graham Parkway? Think about it. Daddy has traveled the world. The city of Charlotte, in a sense, always felt it shared my father with the world. Travelers fly in and out of Charlotte Douglas International Airport and have to get on the Billy Graham Parkway to enter and exit the airport. It's an ideal location."

Graeme thought I was off the wall at first. He said, "There's no land available along that stretch!"

I said, "How can the BGEA come to Charlotte and locate on any other road but the Billy Graham Parkway?"

Graeme said, "Let me do some checking and I'll get back to you, but we're really reaching out there."

When the call ended I thought, *That's exactly how God works. He reaches beyond the boundaries of men and often does something so remarkable that no other explanation is acceptable other than* "That they may know that this is Your hand—that You, Lord, have done it!" (Psalm 109:27).

Some years before, Charlotte had built a parkway leading to the airport that linked Interstate 85 and Interstate 77. A Piedmont Airlines ticket agent, the late David Rich, contacted state and city officials petitioning that the road be named Billy Graham Parkway. The proposal was received with great enthusiasm, and the City of Charlotte, along with then North Carolina governor Jim Hunt, honored my father at a ribbon-cutting ceremony in 1983.

God worked in the hearts of the city's elite, paving the way for us to secure property along this very stretch of road. Week after week, month after month, the Lord's hand methodically moved in the hearts of those who had the power to shut us out or welcome us in.

God grew our faith, stretching it all the way from downtown Minneapolis to the heart of the South—the Queen City's parkway named for my father. With tremendous cooperation and enthusiasm from city officials, an unlikely vision became reality.

In 2002, at the groundbreaking ceremony, my father and I were humbled to stand with the then Charlotte mayor Patrick McCrory, who later became North Carolina's governor, and the then governor Mike Easley and turn the red clay soil a few hundred feet from the parkway. God had graciously entrusted to us this miraculous tract of land smothered in southern pine.

Charlotte with all of its warmth and excitement welcomed Billy Graham—its favorite son—back home. Within two years after organizational restructuring and settling into the facilities God provided, we broke ground once more, just yards away, in the spot that would cradle the Billy Graham Library.

At the Foot of the Cross

There was a lot of skepticism as the library began to take shape. I wouldn't be speaking the truth if I claimed there was unity in the camp over the structure of the building. Some wanted a brick building, while others wanted a limestone and glass building more conducive to Charlotte's motif.

My father and I are country boys at heart. There isn't an urban bone in our bodies. I asked the designers for several concepts that would embrace a country setting, specifically one drawing of a structure similar to a barn, much like what had once stood on the old Graham dairy farm. When I showed it to my father, he said, "Franklin, that's where my roots are. I like that idea."

His answer did not surprise me. My father treasured his heritage.

But there were those who were not convinced a rustic barn structure was the way to go. As I wrestled with opposing views, a trusted friend of mine listened quietly, and then calmly recited these words:

> On a hill far away stood an old rugged cross,
> The emblem of suff'ring and shame;
> And I love that old cross where the dearest and best
> For a world of lost sinners was slain.
> So I'll cherish the old rugged cross,
> Till my trophies at last I lay down;
> I will cling to the old rugged cross,
> And exchange it someday for a crown.[6]

I contemplated the meaning of this powerful message. It did not take me long to sharpen my resolve.

When I met with the architects, I suggested that we put some glass in the front of the barn-shaped building to allow light inside. After all, this is precisely what happens when people surrender to Jesus. He illuminates our souls with His everlasting light.

The designer and I began sketching what it might look like. "Would something like this be doable?" I asked as I slid the paper across the table—a rough drawing of a cross at the front of the barn. The designer said, "Absolutely. We can do that."

After some modifications, I presented the various designs to my father and the board of directors along with the drawing of the barn and glass entrance in the shape of a cross. "If we were to proceed with this structure," I said, "everyone visiting the library would enter at the foot of the cross. This reflects the work of the BGEA, pointing people to the cross, the symbol of Christ's love for mankind. This is where sin is forgiven and lives are changed, and that is the purpose of the library."

When questions were satisfied and discussions ended, my father, along with the board of directors, chose the barnlike structure. Within weeks the walls were raised.

None of this could have been accomplished without Bill Pauls, a member of the BGEA board who also served as the chairman of our building committee. Bill, a land developer from Denver, Colorado, brought enormous expertise to this project, having developed large properties across the United States and around the world. He whole-heartedly supported the design and stated that it represented my father's humble beginnings.

"Too Much Billy Graham"

There was a lot of excitement in Charlotte, but a few criticized "the barn." In the early stages of the project, the *Washington Post* ran a negative article quoting others who likened it to a theme park.[7] But Charlotte's television and radio stations were fair in their reviews, and the *Charlotte Observer* ran positive articles conveying that the library would reflect my father's testimony to what God had accomplished through his ministry.

Still, when he saw the first video presentation of the plans for the exhibits and galleries, he was solemn. When the screen went black and the lights came on, Bill Pauls looked at my father and asked, "What do you think, Mr. Graham?"

"Too much Billy Graham," was his only response. I got on the phone and called a colleague. "Daddy doesn't want all this 'Billy Graham' in the library. Can we reconfigure the four galleries to depict more ministry?"

The answer was an enthusiastic yes. With in-depth research and leaning heavily on Scripture, the content of the four galleries was rewritten and redesigned to highlight the Gospel message, emphasizing the heart of my father—the glorious Gospel. As one reporter stated, "Although the library is about the man, the man is about God."

The theme was now in place: one man's journey testifying of the Man, His message, His ministry, and His mission.

- It would glorify not the man Billy Graham but the Man Jesus Christ.

- It would spread not man's message but God's message.

- It would emphasize not the BGEA but the ministry of Jesus Christ.

- It would spotlight not humanitarian work but the Great Commission.

This became the treasured content of the library, a sort of walk-in hope chest, because its message speaks of hope in Jesus Christ.

Men leave legacies behind. God's children deposit testimonies that never die. The Bible says, "What you heard from me, keep as the pattern of sound teaching, with faith and love in Christ Jesus. Guard the good deposit that was entrusted to you—guard it with the help of the Holy Spirit who lives in us" (2 Timothy 1:13–14 NIV).

My father's testimony that lives beyond his earthly life was built upon the heritage of what was done two thousand years ago. While his voice is now silent and though he will never again step to the pulpit to preach the Word, the testimony he left behind is underscored in the library with these inscriptions—just as the Bible says . . .

For the Son of Man is come to seek and to save.
For Christ (sent) me to preach the Gospel.
Let's devote ourselves to the ministry of prayer.
Go into all the world and preach the Good News.

The Bible has a lot to say about inheritance. "In [Christ] also we have obtained an inheritance . . . having believed, [we] were sealed with the Holy Spirit of promise, who is the guarantee of our inheritance" (Ephesians 1:11, 13–14).

If Walls Could Talk

We've all heard the expression, *If walls could talk* . . . Well, they do talk at the Billy Graham Library.

My father's testimony hangs from banners that speak of an unchangeable heritage in Jesus Christ, as stated on one banner:

When my decision for Christ was made . . . the direction of my life changed because of what Christ did. During all my years as an evangelist, my message was the Gospel of Christ. People did not come to hear what I had to say. They wanted to know what God had to say. Nowhere in Mark 16:15—nor in any other similar passage—did Christ command us to go only into the Western or capitalist world. "For God so loved the world" is what I hope people will remember when they think of me. And may it sink into their souls.

The Savior of the world whom we serve, whom Billy Graham spent his life preaching about—Jesus Christ—is the Man proclaimed throughout the library.

Jesus Christ left His glorious splendor. He left the adoration of His heavenly creation. He left the fellowship and love of His Father—to come to us. Jesus came in the helpless form of a baby, born in obscurity, born to a humble mother in a stable—a barn, so to speak—with animals that no doubt bowed their heads that wonderful Christmas night and worshipped the Christ Child in the manger.

The legacy my father leaves behind encompasses his service to the King of kings as he walked through this world, in His steps.

Lorna Dueck, a popular television host and a writer for Canada's largest national newspaper, the *Globe and Mail*, visited the Billy Graham Library before the official opening. She had found some of the controversy disturbing: Questions like, if this is a library, where are all the books? Where are the transcripts and sermons?

When she finished the tour, her eyes snapped with excitement and determination to answer the critics. "Franklin," she said, "I have heard God's Word in the songs piped through the speakers. I have observed the many worn Bibles in glass cases, and my ears have welcomed hearing your father's voice come across the mural-size screen saying, 'For those watching by television.' I have walked through the library and counted the Bible verses on the beams, in the galleries, on the video clips, in the display cases, and in the bookstore. This is a library with only one Book—the Word of God."

I appreciated her comments because they accurately described the foundation upon which the library was built—the Bible.

My hope is to continue building upon this testimony to the Lord. The seed of the Gospel is planted in the human heart, and the harvest is placed in the hollow of the Savior's hand.

A Glassy Vision

As the library took shape, I went to Charlotte several times a month. The first time I drove onto the construction site and saw the forty-foot glass cross glistening in the Carolina sun, it signified that Christ is the centerpiece of the library.

The years of praying, planning, and preparing culminated on May 31, 2007, when the Billy Graham Library was dedicated in the presence of a thousand guests: supporters, city officials, family, and staff. With former president Jimmy Carter, former president George H. W. Bush and former first lady Barbara Bush, and former president Bill Clinton in attendance, my father addressed the distinguished guests. He turned to behold the cross in the background of the platform and said:

> Many have asked me, why do I preach about the cross? My answer is because the cross is the symbol of Christianity. The cross is the focal point in the life and ministry of Jesus Christ. It represents God's sacrifice through the shed blood of His beloved Son for the sins of mankind. It represents His loving forgiveness and redemption, which we cannot ourselves earn.

The library was now framed in for the glory of God and for a heavenly purpose. My hope and my prayer is that the Billy Graham Library will always be a witness to what God has wrought.

Since the doors have been open to the public, we have seen visitors from all over the world. Letters and testimonies have poured into our offices, telling how the message throughout the ninety-minute self-guided tour speaks of Christ. Guests have been moved to tears to hear the gospel music piped through outdoor speakers as they approach the foot of the cross.

Our prayers have been answered. Lives have been changed. Hearts have been touched.

The Towering Silo

The Bible puts a great deal of emphasis on farming and harvest. Life is completely dependent upon the fundamentals of planting, sowing seed, reaping, and harvesting—the sustenance of physical life. Our Lord often used parables and metaphors to speak of spiritual seeds that reap eternal life. The importance of sowing the Gospel seed should not be minimized.

A silo is a storehouse for harvested crops and feed. Before Joseph rose to second in command under Pharaoh, he had predicted a great famine. When he was put in charge of the land, he set in motion a seven-year stockpile of food and grain to carry the kingdom through seven years of famine.

To emphasize God's provision, a towering silo was placed near the library. It represents the great harvest of souls from the fields and highways along life's rocky road. My father has traveled through those fields and along the roads scattering spiritual seed. What takes root in the spiritual soil of one's heart only God knows. In eternity He will separate the wheat from the tares and will gather an abundant harvest around Him. The silo stands tall as a testimony of what God has done.

Gratitude is expressed to all those who make the ongoing ministry possible. And because of the faithfulness of God's people, His Word is going forth, reaching into hearts today and into the future, preparing for a generation not yet born. Heavenly riches are being stockpiled in God's great storehouse.

The library is designed to carry on Billy Graham's ministry in the name of the Lord Jesus Christ and multiply the evangelistic seed that has been scattered near and far by testifying of His sacrifice and love for mankind. The Scriptures promise that if we are faithful, to live according to His teaching and true in testifying of Him, He will bring a great harvest of souls.

Is your heart a storehouse for eternal treasures? Is your mind filled with the testimony of what God has done in you? The Bible says that "future generations will be told about the Lord. They will proclaim his righteousness to a people yet unborn—for he has done it" (Psalm 22:30–31 NIV).

Legacy of Faith

When my father realized that the library could be a beacon of light, it pleased him to know that many would come and hear what God had done through His people.

"Man's chief end is to glorify God," my father proclaimed, "and to enjoy Him forever. In heaven God—not man—will be at the center of everything. And His glory will be dominant."

This is the centerpiece of the Billy Graham Library.

In the first six months of the library's opening, more than one hundred thousand visitors, from every state in America and numerous countries, walked through its entrance at the foot of the cross. Many have said, "No one can walk through the library and miss the message." Our staff has witnessed this as they have prayed with children and adults. Hearts are moved as the Holy Spirit speaks to those listening to God's message of loving forgiveness.

As followers of Jesus Christ we are given a legacy—a rich heritage at the foot of the old rugged cross. Our testimonies speak of what we have done with that heritage. Do we peer into our hope chest—the Bible—and breathe in the heavenly fragrance from its pages?

You know paper is derived from wood. Just as the red cedar preserves man's precious treasures, so are the truths and promises preserved in the pages of Scripture. Our minds, hearts, and souls are the possessions of the Father and Son, preserved by the Holy Spirit.

The word *testimony* means evidence, witness, or demonstration of a claim. This testimony is embodied in our Savior and is the testimony that all must carry who follow in His steps. Do our testimonies reflect His footsteps? Do our hearts mirror His image? Have our hearts engulfed the great treasures of His promises, His love, of the ever-lasting heritage that He has left behind?

The Holy Spirit of God moves in our hearts, and God the Son stands with hand extended to lost souls. We don't need a telegraph or telephone to reach Him. God the Father has preserved the work of the cross to assure our eternal heritage.

Wood, Hay, or Legacy?

Are the keys to the hope chests of our hearts rusty? When the lids are opened, what do we find? Prosperity that coerces, possessions that corrode, power that corrupts, prestige that collapses?

Or are the treasure chests of our hearts abundantly filled with prayers that grant power, purpose that brings promise, position that brings perspective, peace that brings profit? Are we prideful or purged, permissive or purified, passive or passionate, paupers or pearls?

When we open our hearts to others, does joy overflow with a sweet aroma that tells all who cross our paths, "Christ lives here"?

Everything else pales in His glory.

When God opens the book of life—the heavenly treasure chest—He will not find pictures of our blackened hearts. He will not find evidence of our failures, our sorrows, or our defeats. He will peer into the deep chest and find it filled with souls redeemed by His blood—and He will smile.

What is your spiritual legacy? My generation has been given an immeasurable gift of technology, opportunity, and knowledge. What will we do with it? We are given the chance to build on a foundation of faithful men and women who have struggled tilling the ground, forging new frontiers, and pointing future generations to Christ.

Are we treasuring our heritage so that Christ will be exalted in generations to come? My father said, "God gives us a message of hope for the present and future."

My Father's Home

Billy Graham had many opportunities to invest in business ventures, but he knew they would be used only to distract him from his calling in life.

When my father said goodbye to this world, his body was returned to Charlotte, as he had instructed, and buried near his home in the shadow of the cross.

The Graham home that had once stood a few miles away on Park Road has been relocated to the library, thanks to my cousin Mel Graham. As a young man, my father would never have imagined that in death he would return to his roots and be buried in the Carolina soil behind his childhood home at the foot of a cross.

When Jesus was on earth, the Bible says that He had no place to lay His head, yet He met the needs of all those who crossed His path.

Many make the long trek to the Holy Land to feel closer to Jesus. But you will not visit museum displays of the old rugged cross. There are no display cases exhibiting the nails that pierced His hands and feet or His seamless robe won by the spin of the dice. There is no thorny crown. But one day we will touch the nail prints in His hands, and we will behold Him robed in glory with many crowns of jewels upon His thorn-scarred brow.

Christ came and left His legacy—the heritage of Himself. He bestowed on us a gift He willingly gives to those who trust in Him—eternity in heaven. We lay ourselves aside and become His treasured possessions. The Bible tells us to guard that inheritance, to hold it in our hearts, and to proclaim to the lost world that their inheritance is waiting to be claimed (1 Timothy 6:20).

"In My Father's house are many mansions; if it were not so, I would have told you. I go to prepare a place for you. And if I go and prepare a place for you, I will come again and receive you to Myself; that where I am, there you may be also" (John 14:2–3).

I am grateful for the legacy I inherited from my parents, but I treasure more their testimonies that have beckoned many to the foot of the cross, giving millions the rich heritage of salvation in Jesus Christ. I want to tell the next generation about what Christ has done for all. "One generation shall praise Your works to another" (Psalm 145:4).

Someday I will leave this world and join my father in heaven. I won't get on board a Legacy 600 aircraft to get there. Christ will lead the way on the clouds of glory. Until then, I will be about my Father's business.

Postscript

If you do not know Jesus Christ as your personal Lord and Savior, I pray that you will settle this in your heart before you close this book. Ask the Lord to forgive you of your sin. Accept His forgiveness. Turn from your old ways and invite Him to dwell within you and make you a new creation. He is waiting for you to reach out to Him. You're not coming to me for salvation. Only Jesus Christ can make you whole. The Bible says we must do more than admit our sin. We must confess it—and He waits.

Pray this prayer:

Dear God:

I am a sinner. Please forgive me. Help me to turn from my sins. I believe that Jesus is the Son of God, who died for me and rose again. I invite Him to come into my life and take control and be the Lord and Master of my life. In Jesus' name.

Amen.

If you have made this decision for Christ, just write to me at the address below and let me know that Jesus Christ has made you new.

Billy Graham Evangelistic Association (BGEA)
1 Billy Graham Parkway
Charlotte, NC 28201

On our websites
bgea.org *and* billygraham.com

And on Facebook at
Franklin Graham

Afterword
Beyond the End

My father once said, "Someday I hope to write a book titled *Beyond the End*." He never penned that work, but when he died on February 21, 2018, his soul was set into motion, and what followed his death is enough to fill such a book. His work here is now complete and the final chapter written. He has traveled *beyond the end* and has been welcomed into eternity with Jesus Christ. The afterlife that my father died to see is heaven.

I was in Dallas, Texas, when the phone call came. My father had just passed away. I thought I was prepared for this. In January I had met with my team who had been assisting me with my father's funeral plan. We had worked on it for twenty years, making adjustments and changes as he continued to outlive his team and circle of friends.

But that life-changing call jolted my memory. I had been with my father three days before, on Sunday afternoon. He was quiet, and his mind seemed preoccupied as he sat in his chair. His body was there, but I believe his mind was on heaven, and the oil lamp of his soul was still burning, trimmed and ready, just as the Bible describes in the Gospel of Matthew. But never could I have imagined that three days later that flame would be snuffed out from his earthly body to be called home to live in the everlasting light of the Son of God.

My father often talked about how he still missed his father, who had been in heaven fifty years. Now I see through his eyes what he meant. I will miss him until the day I die: his counsel, his wisdom, his instruction, and, more importantly, the example he set for his family and, yes, even the world.

The winter's day my father's body arrived at the Billy Graham Training Center at The Cove in Asheville, North Carolina, was not cold and dreary; the air was crisp and the sky clear. Springtime had come to my father's soul. The birds chirped, and the breeze softly whispered as though to speak peace and joy.

The family gathered around his casket as we welcomed his long-time friends and colleagues. It brought us great comfort to see my father's wonderful and faithful staff put their hands on his casket to say their last goodbyes. The nursing staff had become like family to us. My siblings and I knew that our father never would have lived this long had it not been for their constant gentle and loving care. As my father's body was placed in the hearse, bells began to ring and these precious caregivers spontaneously started singing "This Little Light of Mine." It brought tears as my father's last journey from western North Carolina began.

The North Carolina State Highway Patrol had organized a motor-cade to travel through Swannanoa and Black Mountain, the towns surrounding Montreat. Streets were lined with hundreds, at times thousands, of people who cared enough to pay their respects and catch a glimpse of the procession as they waved goodbye to their neighbor and fellow North Carolinian.

We kept rolling past intersections jammed with people raising banners in paint-stroked messages, holding Bibles and scriptures, and bearing signs of appreciation, "Thank you, Preacher Graham." Along the roadsides some knelt in prayer. Traveling the one hundred and thirty-mile trek, our family was amazed to see enormous gatherings of well-wishers and hear the mesmerizing drone of a bagpiper off in the distance.

People stood shoulder to shoulder as we veered onto I-40, a route my father had traveled countless times. But when we turned southeast to merge onto Highway 321, we were astounded to see that the traffic moving northwest was at a standstill for miles. All the way to Charlotte, every overpass that spanned the divided highway was crowded with firetrucks hoisting American flags as police officers saluted and people bowing in reverence with hands over their hearts. Others captured pictures and videos in order to remember.

My father had always said, "When I die, I want to be buried near my parents and ancestors; I want to go home to Charlotte." I made a promise to Daddy and kept it. As the ten-car motorcade left the state highway, it carried us through downtown Charlotte along Trade Street, the epicenter of the Queen City. It wasn't the skyscrapers that housed some of the largest corporations in the state that took our breath away—it was the crowds of thousands who had come out to see "North Carolina's favorite son" pass through his hometown just one more time. Church bells echoed, and they comforted us.

After the four-hour commute, we turned onto the Billy Graham Parkway just miles from where my father was born, and there on the property his casket rested in his boyhood home.

Many years ago in our country when loved ones died, their bodies were placed in the living room of the family home, where others would come to pay respects and comfort one another. We thought it was fitting for my father to be at rest in his childhood home, where he had once sat with his parents and siblings, studying school lessons, reading comic books, learning about life, and listening to Mother Graham read Scripture.

It was here that former president George W. Bush, former first lady Laura Bush, and former president Bill Clinton came to say their last goodbyes to my father. They honored our family by giving their time and sharing their remembrances of a man that had prayed for them and spent time with them.

Never to be forgotten are the multiple thousands of people that made their way to this spot, placing flowers and notes at the gates. Buses lined up, bringing supporters from across the Carolinas and many others from various states and nations. I was so proud of my son Roy, who stood near his grandfather's casket to greet and thank nearly everyone who had clicked the pause button of their lives to come and offer condolences. My wife, Jane Austin, joined our son for many long hours, hoping to convey our deepest gratitude for the outpouring of love.

In the meantime, I had received calls from President Trump and Vice President Pence. They not only had called me upon hearing the news of my father's death, but President Trump told me that he was working with Congress to solidify a formal invitation to my family for our father to lie in honor at the Capitol Rotunda in Washington, DC. When Speaker of the House Ryan and Senate Majority Leader McConnell made the invitation official, our family was overwhelmed at such a gesture and believed that the Gospel of the Lord Jesus Christ my father had proclaimed for a lifetime would be lifted up in our nation and around the world—and it was.

Before sunrise on February 28, the family boarded a Samaritan's Purse cargo plane that ordinarily carries relief supplies around the world. That morning it carried our family and my father's body to the nation's capital. The hearse that carried my father displayed two early-twentieth-century Christian flags that represented the tenets of the Christian faith—the red represented the shed blood of Jesus on the cross, the blue stood for the rebirth of the soul, and the white represented the purity of Christ.

We were escorted to the Capitol steps and watched as a full military honor guard, serving as pallbearers, carried my father's casket up the grand steps onto the portico and through the curved seventeen-foot bronze doors depicting America's rich history.

The procession halted at the interior door, and the reverent silence was broken by the procedural knock that still echoes in my mind. When the door opened, we were ushered into the very seat of power of the greatest nation on earth. Every branch of government was standing to receive my father's body, which was placed under the majestic Capitol dome. There to greet us were president Donald J. Trump and first lady Melania Trump, vice president Mike Pence and second lady Karen Pence, members of the Cabinet, the US Supreme Court, and Congress, leadership of both the House and Senate, Democrats and Republicans all representing the great citizens of America.

As the president stood near the casket, he said, "Here in this room, we are reminded that America is a nation sustained by prayer." It was moving, surreal, and unforgettable to think that a Gospel preacher would be in such a rare number, only the fourth private citizen to be honored in this special way.

Some may have thought they were honoring just the man Billy Graham, but what was lifted up was the very message he preached—the man Jesus Christ, who came to seek and to save a lost and dying world. What a historical moment for America, what a time for the spreading of the Gospel. I marveled to think about our nation honoring a Gospel preacher. Then the great hall of faith chapter came to mind: "He being dead still speaks" (Hebrews 11:4 NKJV). Yes, the voice of my father is silenced in death, but the technological age has made possible the continuation of his preaching ministry—Christ is alive, and God will keep speaking to this sin-sick world through my father and others who are obedient to Him.

We were graciously received that evening at the White House by President and Mrs. Trump, where our family had been invited to have a relaxed dinner with them, joined by Vice President and Mrs. Pence.

When they said good night, we knew we would welcome them two days later in Charlotte for my father's funeral.

President Trump had issued a proclamation directing all flags to be lowered to half-staff on the day Billy Graham was laid to rest on March 2, 2018. That morning, however, the nor'easter winter storm Riley whipped up seventy-mile-per-hour gusts throughout the eastern states. Federal buildings were shut down in DC, and the US Air Force told the president that they would not be able to fly to Charlotte. He told them, "I have to go!"

They managed to move Air Force One and Air Force Two to Dulles Airport, where the president and vice president and their wives boarded the planes and flew to Charlotte. I personally appreciated the great effort they made to attend. It is doubtful almost any other past president would have gone that extra mile.

How gracious of the most powerful men in the world to come and join the family, the North Carolina government delegation, church leadership from around the world, and my father's faithful supporters who stood with him in his ministry. My father was no longer with us, but in the aftermath of his death, his home going culminated under a great canvas cathedral, a flashback to his 1949 Los Angeles tent meeting. His ministry had come full circle—you might say that his own funeral was his last crusade. Two thousand invited guests attended the televised funeral, with more than five hundred members of the media carefully documenting this momentous day. We were reminded of Revelation 14:13: "Blessed are the dead who die in the Lord . . . that they may rest from their labors, and their works follow them." His desire was that, perhaps, even in death God's message would draw people to the foot of the cross.

My father's only remaining sibling, Jean Ford; my sisters, Gigi, Anne, and Ruth; and my brother Ned stood before this congregation of longtime friends and expressed their remembrances. In turn, our family was comforted by colleagues in ministry who brought words of comfort and reinforced my father's message. The cutting winds chilled people to the bone, but God's Word warmed hearts.

"Mr. Graham loved the Bible, and it governed how he lived and governed how he died," my father's South African–born pastor, Dr. Don Wilton, recalled.

The great statesman from Korea, Dr. Billy Kim, brought greetings on behalf of a million international Christians around the world and expressed thanks to Daddy for bringing the message of salvation to the greater part of Asia.

My close friend Rev. Sami Dagher, a powerful preacher from Beirut, Lebanon, gave a tribute: "Dr. Graham has used the best methods of teaching. He's never used a computer or Facebook or a blackboard, but he taught by example. He has made a great effect in the Middle East for all believers. [To the] American people, I thank you in the name of Jesus for standing [with] this great man to fulfill the mission which was given to him by God."

As I prepared to take my place at the podium that my father had preached from perhaps thousands of times, our precious friend Rev. Robert Cunville from India led a prayer of thanksgiving. His words spoke peace to me before delivering the Gospel message one more time before my father was laid to rest: "May this day, O God, be the dawn of a new era in the proclamation of the Gospel of Jesus Christ," he prayed.

Stepping to the microphone, I drew attention to the platform's backdrop—the Billy Graham Library. This place tells us about the *journey of faith* that my father traveled his entire life. With a lump in my throat, my heart was moved by the looming cross reflecting the sunshine. It reminded me of how many souls are still footsteps away from realizing the life-changing impact the cross of Christ can make in the lives of people who are searching for answers and longing for peace.

Pointing people to Jesus was my father's passion. He preached on heaven, told millions how to find heaven, wrote a book about heaven, and today is in heaven. He preached repentance of sin, receiving the grace of God, and following Jesus. And a few days ago my father followed Jesus all the way to heaven. Last week he embarked on a journey he had been looking forward to all of his life and was escorted by God's angels to the throne of God.

When I watched my father's grandsons gather as pallbearers around his casket later that day, the finality began to sink in that this was the last goodbye here on earth. Our family followed along, down the steps to the prayer garden, where he would now rest beside his beloved wife, and our blessed mother, at the foot of the bricked crosswalk. He had finished his journey and was finally home.

My father's image will remain etched in my mind, and his voice will ring in my ears. The lessons I have learned through my father's eyes have anchored me and made me realize that what he taught me was what he also learned through his Father's eyes from heaven, truth that compels us to keep in step with the Savior.

Because He lives, I know I will see my father again. But, *above all*, we wait with expectation for the coming of Jesus Christ, when He gathers the family of God to be united forever, and then Christ's followers will see life eternal *through our Father's eyes. To God be the glory!* But *until then* we will be faithful in our service of proclaiming God's living Word that draws people to the cross and prepares us for life *beyond the end.*

Notes

Foreword

1. Billy Graham, *World Aflame* (New York: Doubleday, 1965), xvi.
2. Billy Graham, *Storm Warning* (Nashville: Thomas Nelson, 2010), 46.
3. Billy Graham, *Hope for the Troubled Heart* (Dallas: Word, 1991), 207.
4. Graham, *World Aflame*, 89.
5. Billy Graham, *The Journey* (Nashville: Thomas Nelson, 2006), 3, 4, 9.
6. Billy Graham, *Storm Warning* (Dallas: Word, 1992), 18.
7. Graham, *Storm Warning* (1992), 19.
8. Graham, *World Aflame*, 218.
9. Graham, *Storm Warning* (1992), 19.
10. Graham, *World Aflame*, xvii.
11. Billy Graham, *Facing Death—And the Life After* (Minneapolis: Grason, 1987), 11.
12. Billy Graham, *How to Be Born Again* (Dallas: Word, 1977), 22.
13. Billy Graham, *The Jesus Generation* (Grand Rapids: Zondervan, 1971), 31.
14. Billy Graham, *The Secret of Happiness* (Minneapolis: Grason, 1955), 19.
15. Graham, *Storm Warning* (1992), 22–23.
16. *The Journey*, packaging copy.
17. Billy Graham, *Answers to Life's Problems* (Waco, TX: Word, 1960), 236.
18. Graham, *The Secret of Happiness*, 22.
19. Graham, *How to Be Born Again*, 10.
20. Billy Graham, *The Holy Spirit* (Nashville: Thomas Nelson, 1978), xi.

21. Graham, *Storm Warning* (1992), 80.

22. Ibid., 24.

23. Graham, *World Aflame*, xvi.

24. Billy Graham, *Unto the Hills* (Dallas: Word, 1986), 289.

25. Graham, *The Jesus Generation*, 136–37.

26. Graham, *World Aflame*, 152, 156.

27. Billy Graham, *Calling Youth to Christ* (Grand Rapids: Zondervan, 1947), 120, 117, 127–28.

28. Graham, *The Journey*, viii.

29. Billy Graham, *The Heaven Answer Book* (Nashville: Thomas Nelson, 2012), 157.

30. Graham, *Answers to Life's Problems*, 9–10.

31. Billy Graham, *Approaching Hoofbeats* (Waco, TX: Word, 1983), 19.

32. Billy Graham, *Just as I Am* (New York: HarperCollins, 1997), xiii.

33. Graham, *Calling Youth to Christ*, 21.

34. Billy Graham, *The Reason for My Hope* (Nashville: W Publishing Group, 2013), 172, 178.

35. Billy Graham, *Nearing Home* (Nashville: W Publishing Group, 2011), 177.

36. Graham, *World Aflame*, 257.

37. Billy Graham, recalling a similar statement by nineteenth century American evangelist Dwight L. Moody, from Russ Busby, *Billy Graham: God's Ambassador* (Alexandria, VA: Time-Life Books, 1999), back matter page.

38. Graham, *The Secret of Happiness*; Billy Graham, *Till Armageddon* (Waco, TX: Word, 1981); Graham, *Just as I Am*.

Preface

1. Billy Graham (speech, British Embassy, Washington, DC, December 6, 2001), Billy Graham's personal papers.

2. Billy Graham, *Just as I Am* (New York: HarperCollins, 1997), 727.

Introduction

1. *Merriam-Webster's Collegiate Dictionary*, 10th ed., s.v. "shadow."

2. Billy Graham, *Just as I Am* (New York: HarperCollins, 1997), 160.

3. Morrow Coffey Graham, *They Call Me Mother Graham* (New York: Revell, 1977), 21–22.

4. Edward E. Ham, *When Billy Graham Found Christ* (Murfreesboro, TN: Sword of the Lord, 1955), 15.

5. Billy Graham, *Billy Graham Talks to Teen-Agers* (n.p.: Miracle Books, 1958), 10–11.

Chapter 1: My Father in Heaven

1. Billy Graham, *Hope for the Troubled Heart* (Dallas: Word, 1991), 207.

2. "Through It All" by Andraé Crouch, © 1971. Renewed 1999 by Manna Music, Inc. 35225 Brooten Road., Pacific City, OR 97135. All rights reserved. Used by permission. (ASCAP).

3. John MacArthur. Used with permission, November 21, 2008.

4. Jon Meacham, "Pilgrim's Progress," *Newsweek*, August 14, 2006, http://www.newsweek.com/pilgrims-progress-109171.

5. Tom Flannery, "Billy Graham's Apostasy," WND, August 10, 2006, http://www.wnd.com/2006/08/37410/.

6. Billy Graham, *Facing Death—And the Life After* (Minneapolis: Grason, 1987), 216–17, 219–20.

7. Graham, *Hope for the Troubled Heart*, 198.

8. Roy Gustafson, *What Is the Gospel?* booklet (Minneapolis: BGEA, 1960).

9. Graham, *Facing Death*, 221.

10. Ibid., 267.

11. Herbert Lockyer, *The Life Beyond* (Grand Rapids: Fleming H. Revell, 1995), 110.

Chapter 2: Made in China

1. Ruth Bell Graham, *Sitting by My Laughing Fire* (Waco, TX: Word, 1977), 238. Used by permission.

2. "Pearl History in China," Shecy Pearls, https://www.shecypearljewelry.com/pearl-guide/china-pearls.html.

3. Richard Bewes, *In Celebration of the Life of Ruth Bell Graham* (Charlotte, NC: BGEA, 2007), DVD.

4. Ruth Bell Graham, "Prayer for the Murderer," *Prodigals and Those Who Love Them* (Colorado Springs: Focus on the Family, 1991), 143.

5. Mark Twain, quoted in Milton Meltzer, *Mark Twain Himself: A Pictorial Biography* (Columbia, MO: University of Missouri Press, 1960), 22.

Chapter 3: The Bible Says . . .

1. Lewis Drummond, *The Evangelist* (Nashville: W Publishing Group, 2001), 110.

2. "Encore Presentation: Billy Graham, America's Pastor," *CNN Presents*, September 10, 2006, http://transcripts.cnn.com/transcripts/0609/10/cp.01.html.

3. *Merriam-Webster's Collegiate Dictionary*, 10th ed., s.v. "Bible."

4. Billy Graham, *Just as I Am* (New York: HarperCollins, 1997), 139.

5. Billy Graham, interview by Woody Allen, *The Woody Allen Special*, September 21, 1969, CBS, http://www.youtube.com/watch?v=K_poGsbBgpE.

6. Author unknown.

7. "The Religious Affiliation of Influential Philosopher Voltaire," Adherents .com, last modified July 12, 2005, http://www.adherents.com/people/pv /Voltaire.html.

8. *Merriam-Webster's Collegiate Dictionary*, 10th ed., s.v. "in."

9. Voltaire, quoted in "Sharing the Truth of God's Word: II Thessalonians 3:1," Don Robinson's Sermon Archive, http://www.brandonweb.com/sermons /sermonpages/2thessalonians1.htm.

10. "Sharing the Truth of God's Word," Don Robinson's Sermon Archive.

11. Robert Ingersoll, quoted in "Bible Quotes," Tentmaker, http://www .tentmaker.org/Quotes/biblequotes.htm.

12. "All-Time Bestselling Books and Authors," Internet Public Library, accessed January 28, 2008, http://www.ipl.org/div/farq/bestsellerFARQ.html.

Chapter 4: For Those Watching by Television

1. Tim Goodman, "Milton Berle 1908–2002: 'Mr. Television' Dies at 93," SFGate, March 28, 2002, http://www.sfgate.com/news/article/MILTON -BERLE-1908-2002-Mr-Television-dies-at-2861231.php.

2. "Big Dream, Small Screen," *The American Experience*, PBS, transcript, February 10, 1997.

3. Mary Bellis, "Learn When the First TV Was Invented," ThoughtCo., updated August 7, 2017, https://www.thoughtco.com/the-invention-of-television-1992531.

4. "Average Home Has More TVs Than People," *USA Today*, September 21, 2006, http://www.usatoday.com/life/television/news/2006-09-21-homes-tv_x.htm.

5. Billy Graham, *Just as I Am* (New York: HarperCollins, 1997), 318.

6. Daniel Stashower, *The Boy Genius and the Mogul* (New York: Broadway Books, 2002), 44.

7. Graham, *Just as I Am*, 322.

8. Donald Wilhite, personal interview with author, November 13, 2007. Used by permission.

9. Billy Graham, *The Secret of Happiness* (Minneapolis: Grason, 1955), 64.

10. Philo T. Farnsworth and Kent Farnswoth, quoted (Philo) and interviewed (Kent) in "Big Dream, Small Screen," *The American Experience*.

11. "TV Curses Up a Blue Streak," September 24, 2003, Emmys, http://www.emmys.com/news/tv-curses-blue-streak-0.

12. Billy Graham, *Hope for the Troubled Heart* (Dallas: Word, 1991), 9.

13. *Time*, http://content.time.com/time/magazine/0,9263,7601900507,00.html; "Filth Decade," *Time*, May 7, 1990, 92. Also see Donald P. Myers, "Dirty Words Washing Over Everything," *Newsday*, Life & Leisure section, May 30, 1993, 61.

14. Focus on the Family poll, October 1, 2003, cited in "Statistics on Pornography, Sexual Addiction, and Online Perpetrators," TechMission, www.safefamilies.org/sfStats.php.

15. Billy Graham, *The Jesus Generation* (Grand Rapids: Zondervan, 1971), 169.

16. "Statistics on Pornography," TechMission.

17. *Webster's New World College Dictionary*, 4th ed., s.v. "pornography."

18. "William Wilson Quinn, Lieutenant General, United States Army," Arlington National Cemetery Website, last modified November 26, 2005, www.arlingtoncemetery.net/wwquinn.htm.

19. Henry Stansbury, "A Collector's Story," Henry Stansbury Decoys, September/October 2003, https://www.asionline.com/decoys/Quinn%20Article%2010-03.htm.

20. James Warren, "Nixon, Billy Graham Make Derogatory Comments About Jews on Tapes," *Chicago Tribune*, February 28, 2002, www.fpp.co.uk/online/02/02/Graham_Nixon.html.

21. Ibid.

22. Lewis Drummond, interview by Alan Keyes, MSNBC host, "Alan Keyes Is Making Sense," March 26, 2002, 2nd half of broadcast, transcript, https://web.archive.org/web/20031222201216/http://www.renewamerica.us:80/show/transcripts/02_03_26akims.htm.

23. "Jewish Population Dips in NYC," CNN, June 17, 2003, http://www.cnn.com/2003/US/Northeast/06/17/ny.pop/.

Chapter 5: Pray, Pray, Pray

1. Billy Graham, *The Secret of Happiness* (Minneapolis: Grason, 1955), 36.

2. Billy Graham, *Unto the Hills* (Dallas: Word, 1986), 6.

3. Hudson Taylor, *The Life and Ministry of Hudson Taylor* (self-published).

4. Martin Luther, sermon on Matthew 8:1–13, quoted in "Intercessory Prayer," Sprithome.com, http://www.spirithome.com/intercessory-prayer.html.

5. Douglas MacArthur, "MacArthur's Prayer for His Son," in Jerry Shackle, "Where Is Arthur MacArthur?," Canadian Senior Years, 2003, http://archive.is/bZaD4.

6. *General Douglas MacArthur: Wisdom and Visions*, compiled by Edward T. Imparato, Col. USAF (Ret.) (Nashville: Turner Publishing Company, 2001), 81.

7. Walter A. Mueller, quoted in "Quotations About Prayer," The Quote Garden, http://www.quotegarden.com/prayer.html.

8. Charles Spurgeon, "Intercessory Prayer" (sermon 404), August 11, 1861, The Spurgeon Archive, http://archive.spurgeon.org/sermons/0404.php.

9. Ruth Bell Graham, *Legacy of a Pack Rat* (Nashville: Oliver Nelson, 1989), 203.

10. Billy Graham, *Hope for the Troubled Heart* (Dallas: Word, 1991), 148.

11. *Merriam-Webster's Collegiate Dictionary*, 10th ed., s.v. "pray" (emphasis added).

12. Lewis Drummond, *The Evangelist* (Nashville: Word, 2001), 132–33.

Chapter 6: Preach the Word

1. Billy Graham, *The Holy Spirit* (Nashville: Thomas Nelson, 1978), 182–83.

2. Morrow Coffey Graham, *They Call Me Mother Graham* (New York: Revell, 1977), 45.

3. Ibid., 35.

4. Roy Gustafson, *What Is the Gospel?* booklet (Minneapolis: BGEA, 1960).

5. Morrow Coffey Graham, *They Call Me Mother Graham*, 54.

6. Rev. J. Wilbur Chapman, D.D., *The Life and Work of Dwight Lyman Moody* (1900), chap. 20, BibleBelievers.com, http://www.biblebelievers.com/moody/20.html.

7. Ibid.

8. Ibid.

9. Billy Graham, *Hope for the Troubled Heart* (Dallas: Word, 1991), 36.

10. Bill Fitzgerrel, "Readers Write," *Christianity Today*, August 2007, 10.

11. L. Nelson Bell, *While Men Slept* (New York: Doubleday, 1966), vii–viii, x–xi, 2, 3.

12. Billy Graham, *How to Be Born Again* (Dallas: Word, 1977), 88.

13. Ibid., 58–64.

14. "Preach the Word," lyrics by Jim E. Davis, © R2M. Used by permission.

Chapter 7: Just Write to Me ... That's All the Address You Need

1. Kathryn Burke, "Letter Writing in America," National Postal Museum, Spring 2005, http://www.postalmuseum.si.edu/LetterWriting/index.html.

2. "Fascinating Facts," Library of Congress, accessed September 25, 2007, http://www.loc.gov/about/facts.html.

3. United States Postal Service, accessed January 30, 2018, https://about.usps.com/who-we-are/postal-facts/size-scope.htm.

4. Erin Roach, "Graham's Bonds with Presidents Examined," Baptist Press, August 9, 2007, http://www.bpnews.net/26215/grahams-bonds-with-presidents-examined.

5. Lindsay Terry, "Ronald Reagan, a Man of Kindness," Crossway, July 1, 2004, www.crossway.org/product/663575729419.

6. Nancy Gibbs and Michael Duffy, *The Preacher and the Presidents* (Nashville: Center Street, 2007), 331.

7. Billy Graham, *The Journey* (Nashville: W Publishing Group, 2006), 112.

8. Billy Graham, recalling a similar statement by nineteenth century American evangelist Dwight L. Moody, in Russ Busby, *Billy Graham: God's Ambassador* (Alexandria, VA: Time-Life Books, 1999), back matter page.

Chapter 8: About My Father's Business

1. "Letter from President Thomas Jefferson," Montana Rojomo, http://rojomoexpedition.com/lewis-and-clark/jeffersons-letter/.

2. Billy Graham, *Hope for the Troubled Heart* (Dallas: Word, 1991), 139.

3. Charles Stanley. Used by permission.

4. *60 Minutes*, CBS, November 11, 2007.

5. Billy Graham, *Storm Warning* (Dallas: Word, 1992), 18–19.

6. Graham, *Hope for the Troubled Heart*, 177.

Chapter 9: You're Not Coming to Me ...

1. "What Hath God Wrought?," Today in History: May 24, American Memory U.S. Historical Collections, Library of Congress, http://memory.loc.gov/ammem/today/may24.html.

2. Lewis Coe, *The Telegraph—A History of Morse's Invention and Its Predecessors in the United States* (New York: McFarland, 1993), 26–27.

3. Ibid., 14, 27.

4. Kenneth W. Dobyns, *The Patent Office Pony: A History of the Early Patent Office* (1994), chap. 19, MyOutBox.net, http://www.myoutbox.net/popch19.htm.

5. Ibid.

6. Samuel Morse, quoted in *The Cincinnatus*, vol. 3, ed. F. G. Cary (College Hill, OH: Farmer's College, 1858), 417.

7. "'Mr. Watson, Come Here,'" The LOC.gov Wise Guide, http://www.loc.gov /wiseguide/mar04/bell.html.

8. "Bell System Advertisements," The Porticus Centre, http://www.beatriceco .com/bti/porticus/bell/bellsystem_ads-1.html.

9. Billy Graham, *The Jesus Generation* (Grand Rapids: Zondervan, 1971), 117.

10. Billy Graham, *The Journey* (Nashville: W Publishing Group, 2006), 285–86.

11. "The Way to the Cross," lyrics by Darrell K. Toney and Mike Hix. © 2004 Billy Graham Evangelistic Association. Used by permission.

12. "Just as I Am," lyrics by Charlotte Elliott (1789–1871).

13. Billy Graham, *World Aflame* (New York: Doubleday, 1965), 96.

Chapter 10: In His Steps

1. Johann Wolfgang von Goethe, quoted in "Challenges," Proverbia, http:// en.proverbia.net/citastema.asp?tematica=172.

2. Richard Proenneke, *One Man's Wilderness* (Portland, OR: Graphics Arts Center, 1973).

3. Daniel Nelson, "DNA Is Called the Blueprint of Life: Here's Why," October 26, 2017, https://sciencetrends.com/dna-called-blueprint-life-heres/.

4. William Janz, "Son Retraces Father's Steps on Deadly Iwo Jima," *Milwaukee Journal*, April 7, 1995.

5. Ibid.

6. Billy Graham, *Hope for the Troubled Heart* (Dallas: Word, 1991), 187.

7. John Foxe, *Foxe's Book of Martyrs* (Grand Rapids: Zondervan, 1978).

Chapter 11: From Stepping-Stones to Milestones

1. C. H. Spurgeon, "A Memorable Milestone," Metropolitan Tabernacle Pulpit, http://www.spurgeongems.org/vols49-51/chs2916.pdf.

2. Billy Graham, *The Reason for My Hope: Salvation* (Nashville: Thomas Nelson, 2013).

3. *"My Hope America" with Billy Graham*, Fox News, http://video.foxnews.com
/v/2817785481001/?#sp=watch-live.

4. Donna Lee Toney, "Billy Graham's Thoughts on the Promise of Heaven,"
Decision Magazine, September 28, 2015, Billy Graham Evangelistic Association.

5. Ibid.

6. Billy Graham, *Where I Am* (Nashville: Thomas Nelson, 2015).

Chapter 12: High Noon: The Hour of Decision for America

1. Billy Graham quotes in this chapter are taken from transcripts and video archives
of the Billy Graham Evangelistic Association unless from personal conversations
with the author or otherwise noted.

2. All quoted material in this chapter from the *Decision America Tour 2016* is taken
from transcripts and video archives of the Billy Graham Evangelistic Association.

3. "Franklin Graham: The 2016 Election and Evangelical Christian Voters," Fox News,
February 12, 2016, 2:50:00, https://www.youtube.com/watch?v=k7MjmwJUxZg.

4. New Hampshire Bill of Rights, Article V, Natural Law, Natural Rights, and
American Constitutionalism, http://www.nlnrac.org/american/founding-era
-constitution-making/documents/new-hampshire-bill.

5. Billy Graham, *Answers to Life's Problems* (Waco, TX: Word, 1960), 26.

6. Billy Graham, *Storm Warning* (Nashville: Thomas Nelson, 2010), 173.

7. Google "politics definition."

8. All numbers associated with the *Decision America Tour 2016* are taken from
the *Billy Graham Evangelistic Association 2016 Annual Report*.

9. "President-Elect Donald Trump LAST Thank You Rally," CDN, https://www
.conservativedailynews.com/2016/12/live-stream-president-elect-donald-trump
-last-thank-you-rally-mobile-al-121716-3pm-ct/.

10. "Trump Holds Final Rally in Grand Rapids," updated November 8, 2016, WoodTV,
http://woodtv.com/2016/11/07/donald-trump-at-devos-place-in-grand-rapids/.

11. Alan M. Dershowitz, "Bush Starts Off by Defying the Constitution," *Los Angeles
Times*, January 24, 2001, http://articles.latimes.com/2001/jan/24/local/me-16180.

12. Jessica Reaves, "Person of the Week: Michael Newdow," *Time*, June 28, 2002,
http://content.time.com/time/nation/article/0,8599,266658,00.html.

13. Associated Press, "Warren's Inauguration Prayer Could Draw Ire," NBCNews
.com, updated December 30, 2008, www.nbcnews.com/id/28439786/ns/ . . .
/warrens-inauguration-prayer-could-draw-ire/.

14. "Franklin Graham Reads Scripture at 2017 Presidential Inauguration," Billy Graham Evangelistic Association, January 20, 2017, https://billygraham.org/video/franklin-graham-reads-scripture-2017-presidential-inauguration/.

Chapter 13: Legacy

1. Billy Graham, *The Journey* (Nashville: W Publishing Group, 2006), 189.

2. Steven Lubar and Kathleen M. Kendrick, *Legacies: Collecting America's History at the Smithsonian* (Washington, DC: Smithsonian Institution Scholarly Press, 2001).

3. "Greenfield Village & Henry Ford Museum," National Park Service: Detroit, http://www.nps.gov/nr/travel/detroit/d37.htm.

4. "The Wright Brothers—First Flight, 1903," EyeWitness to History, accessed January 30, 2018, http://www.eyewitnesstohistory.com/wright.htm.

5. Tom D. Crouch, *The Bishop's Boys: A Life of Wilbur and Orville Wright* (New York: W. W. Norton & Company, 203), 12.

6. "The Old Rugged Cross," lyrics by George Bennard.

7. Laura Sessions Stepp, "Graham: Wife to Be Buried in Charlotte," June 14, 2007, *Washington Post*, http://www.washingtonpost.com/wp-dyn/content/article/2007/06/13/AR2007061301447.html.

FRANKLIN GRAHAM, president and CEO of Samaritan's Purse, is also president and CEO of the Billy Graham Evangelistic Association. The fourth of Billy and Ruth Bell Graham's five children, Franklin is the author of several books, including the bestselling autobiography *Rebel with a Cause* and the 2013 release of *Operation Christmas Child: A Story of Simple Gifts*. He and his wife, Jane Austin, live in Boone, North Carolina, and have four children and twelve grandchildren.

———————

DONNA LEE TONEY, a colleague of Franklin Graham for more than thirty-seven years, has been involved in the ministries of Samaritan's Purse and the Billy Graham Evangelistic Association and has been in literary collaboration with them since 1982, most recently on the release of the *New York Times* bestseller *Where I Am* and the bestselling *The Reason for My Hope: Salvation* with Billy Graham.

———————

JOHN HOWARD SANDEN is an American artist who has painted hundreds of distinguished personalities around the world, including the official White House portraits of president George W. Bush and first lady Laura Bush. He also painted the portrait of Billy Graham used for the cover of *Through My Father's Eyes*.

STEPS TO PEACE WITH GOD

1. RECOGNIZE GOD'S PLAN—PEACE AND LIFE

The message in this book stresses that God loves you and wants you to experience His peace and life.

The BIBLE says, "For God so loved the world that He gave His only begotten Son, that whoever believes in Him should not perish but have everlasting life." *John 3:16, NKJV*

2. REALIZE OUR PROBLEM—SEPARATION FROM GOD

People choose to disobey God and go their own way. This results in separation from God.

The BIBLE says, "For all have sinned and fall short of the glory of God." *Romans 3:23, NKJV*

3. RESPOND TO GOD'S REMEDY—THE CROSS OF CHRIST

God sent His Son to bridge the gap. Christ did this by paying the penalty of our sins when He died on the cross and rose from the grave.

The BIBLE says, "But God shows his love for us in that while we were still sinners, Christ died for us." *Romans 5:8, ESV*

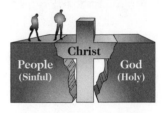

4. RECEIVE GOD'S SON—LORD AND SAVIOR

You cross the bridge into God's family when you ask Christ to come into your life.

The BIBLE says, "But to all who did receive him, who believed in his name, he gave the right to become children of God." *John 1:12, ESV*

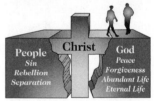

THE INVITATION IS TO:

REPENT (turn from your sins), ASK for God's forgiveness, and by faith RECEIVE Jesus Christ into your heart and life and follow Him in obedience as your Lord and Savior.

PRAYER OF COMMITMENT

"Dear God, I know that I am a sinner. I want to turn from my sins, and I ask for Your forgiveness. I believe that Jesus Christ is Your Son. I believe He died for my sins and that You raised Him to life. I want Him to come into my heart and to take control of my life. I want to trust Jesus as my Savior and follow Him as my Lord from this day forward. In Jesus' Name, amen."

If you are committing your life to Christ, please let us know!

Billy Graham Evangelistic Association

BillyGraham.org	BillyGraham.ca	BillyGraham.org.au
Toll-free: 1-877-247-2426	Toll-free: 1-888-393-0003	Toll-free: +61 2 9241 1692